EXE MEN

EXE MEN

THE EXTRAORDINARY RISE OF
EXETER CHIEFS

ROBERT KITSON

POLARIS
PUBLISHING

First published in 2020 by

POLARIS PUBLISHING LTD
c/o Aberdein Considine
2nd Floor, Elder House
Multrees Walk
Edinburgh
EH1 3DX

www.polarispublishing.com

Distributed by

ARENA SPORT
An imprint of Birlinn Limited

Text copyright © Robert Kitson, 2020

ISBN: 978-1-913538-01-9
eBook ISBN: 978-1-913538-02-6

3

British Library Cataloguing-in-Publication Data
A catalogue record for this book is available on request from the British Library.

Designed and typeset by Polaris Publishing, Edinburgh

Printed and bound in Great Britain by Clays Ltd, Elcograf S.p.A.

CONTENTS

For Fiona, Alex, Louisa and Greg.

And for Dad, who would have loved the Chiefs.

'The roots run deep, in this rocky red ground
And I could feel that pull, every road I went down'

'Growing Up Around Here', Will Hoge

'I begin to think there is something in the air of Devonshire
that grows clever fellows. I could name four or five, superior
to the product of any other county of England.'

Thomas Gainsborough, 1727–1788

PROLOGUE

PROLOGUE

The thwack of deflated rubber on damp tarmac is unmistakable. Oh no. Not now. Not tonight. At least there is space to pull over on a steep terraced street in Bristol but the bigger picture is a concern. Barring a laptop malfunction on deadline – imagine Edvard Munch's *The Scream* with a set of posts in the background – being late for an important game is every sportswriter's recurring dread.

What to do? Hidden in the recesses of the boot is one of those strange-looking space-saver tyres. There should be time later to replace the punctured original with this temporary, slim-fit alternative. Right now, though, the only option is to run the final mile and a half to the Memorial Ground, as people of a certain vintage still call it. Shouldering my heavy laptop bag, I set off down the hill, alternating between a stiff jog and a hobble. It's a glamorous life, working in the media, until the ticking of the clock drowns out all else.

Luckily there is one seat left for a sweat-soaked, dishevelled latecomer in the tightly packed press box. Immediately to my right are some unfamiliar faces. A second glance suggests they are the visiting side's coaching staff. This is no time, though, for idle chat. If Exeter Chiefs can defeat Bristol in this Championship play-off final second leg – they already hold a 9–6 lead from the first leg – and win promotion to English rugby's top tier it will be the greatest achievement in the club's 139-year history.

It also means that, by accident, the *Telegraph*'s Rob Wildman – otherwise known as 'Borneo' – and this correspondent have the best seats in the house. Thrashing away at my keyboard, praying for a readable first-edition piece to emerge, it strikes me how unnaturally calm the Exeter contingent seem. For the most part there is no great shouting or arm-waving. It is almost as if everything on the field is pre-programmed. When the head coach speaks – which is seldom – he is composed, precise and appears at least three phases ahead of the play. Out on the field his team look similarly well drilled. Where are the supposed nerve-riddled underdogs? With the weather worsening there is only one winner long before Simon Alcott's last-minute try caps a 29–10 victory on the night. The Chiefs are going up.

On-the-whistle filing, sadly, allows scant time for leisurely reflection. There is the aggregate scoreline to get right, for a start, plus the small print – the teams, scorers, attendance etc. – and the headline facts. If *Guardian* readers want poetry they will have to find another newspaper. With a flurry of breathless adjectives safely sent, the next job is to squeeze out of the press box in the main stand and scuttle around the clubhouse to the distant media Portakabin where the post-match press conferences will be happening. If ever there was a night for gushing 'We're over the moon, Brian' quotes, this is surely it.

Except they never come. The same tall, strong-jawed head coach who has largely kept his counsel during the game – aside from the occasional clench-fisted celebration towards the end – now speaks at length, without a trace of hyperbole, about his belief that this is just the start. 'This hasn't just happened overnight,' he tells the anorak of reporters clustered around him. 'We've been planning this for years.' After he leaves, his audience are briefly silent. 'Blimey,' says someone eventually, 'that Rob Baxter's impressive, isn't he?'

The slow crawl home offers an opportunity to mull over a few more things. The Kitson household has always looked west with affection. My father was raised in the Quantock Hills outside Taunton, his father lived and farmed on Dartmoor and there are strong Devon links on both sides of the family. Dad's job as a land agent took him away to rural Hampshire but almost every family holiday involved a pilgrimage back down the A303 or A30. His timeless local sporting heroes – Harold Gimblett, Arthur Wellard and Bertie Buse – were similarly embedded in our consciousness, the County Ground in Taunton a spiritual home from home.

We did once buy Dad a Plymouth Argyle mug for Christmas but, otherwise, Exeter's promotion was the biggest sporting success story in the West Country since the Somerset team of the late 1970s and 1980s started making Lord's one-day finals. A generation of Wessex country boys imagined they could see something of themselves in apple-cheeked local heroes like Peter 'Dasher' Denning from Chewton Mendip, Frome's Colin Dredge and Vic Marks from Middle Chinnock. Pride in those who make it big from small rural communities, on the rare occasions they leapfrog the city slickers, is among sport's deepest and most genuinely heartfelt emotions.

Some of us felt similar romantic stirrings whenever Cornwall came good in rugby's County Championship. The days of major touring teams being turned over down in Redruth's Hellfire Corner, though, were long gone even before professionalism's arrival. Despite the non-existence of elite-level football, Premiership rugby had never been sighted further west than

Bristol. Good players – and there had always been plenty of those – with ambition had little option but to go and play elsewhere. No wonder Exeter's elevation to the big league felt as refreshing as a cold cider on a warm day. By coincidence we were also due to be moving house to the Somerset/Devon border the following month, back down to the steep-sided country lanes and evocative red fields my fondly remembered dad loved so much. Someone, somewhere was smiling down benignly on us.

Good timing indeed. The seed sown that evening – Wednesday 26 May 2010 – has since become one of the best upwardly mobile stories in modern British team sport. Perhaps only Wimbledon's 'Crazy Gang', Brian Clough's European Cup-winning Nottingham Forest and Sir Alex Ferguson's Aberdeen have risen as steeply from such humble beginnings. None of that round-ball triumvirate, though, sustained their success in the way Exeter are looking to do as they approach the club's 150th anniversary year. Already the Chiefs have rewritten the accepted map of English club rugby and transformed how their region feels about itself. An everyday tale of county folk? Not remotely. The individuals who made it happen are an extraordinarily eclectic bunch: misfits, rejects, fishermen, farm boys, local lads, exiled Zimbabweans, Aussies and Celts, cider drinkers and cake lovers. This is their story, not mine.

ONE

ONCE UPON A TIME IN THE WEST

Tucked into the low-slung, metal cattle shed otherwise known as the East Stand, it feels deceptively mild for the last weekend in December. Streaks of pale-blue sky are discernible and up on the horizon, above the corner flag diagonally across the pitch, is the hulking outline of Haldon Hill. Wintry, asset-stripped trees with grey, swaying halos peer over the top of the South Stand. To the right, beyond the David Lloyd fitness centre, is the Baker Bridge over the dual carriageway, named in memory of a long-serving council employee. It becomes an unofficial amusement park on match days, swaying and wobbling beneath the feet of the approaching patrons. For unwary newcomers it is a disconcerting welcome. It is an early sign that not everything at Sandy Park, the Chiefs' hilltop lair, is entirely as it seems.

The distant far bottom corner of the north-east terrace is another educational vantage point. Among other things it offers a chance to appreciate fully the vast acreage of English rugby's biggest in-goal areas. Not only could they accommodate a fair-sized flock of sheep but they lull first-timers into a false sense of security. Plenty of room down there, think the visiting playmakers – only to find a strengthening wind has mysteriously propelled the ball dead. Scrum back, Chiefs' ball, have some more of that, my lovers. Entire chapters could be written on the vagaries of 'Windy Park': the swirls and hair-raising gusts, the deceitful calm spots. The Chiefs have lost the odd game on a ball's capricious bounce but, over the years, local knowledge has won them loads more.

Today the mood is particularly thoughtful. Technically it is a 3 p.m. kick-off but there is a high-noon feel. Exeter v Saracens is that kind of fixture nowadays. The embattled gunslingers from the Big Smoke, heading out west to dish out some summary justice to the country boys; the narrow-eyed Chiefs on their porch fronts, silently watching them trot into town. Wayne Barnes is the referee but John Wayne would have been right at home. Every ticket was sold weeks ago. As Exeter take their usual deliberate jog in front of the East Stand 'Library' regulars before heading back down the tunnel, you can almost see tumbleweed blowing across the West Stand.

Victory over Saracens would settle a few scores, real and imagined. There is the Premiership salary cap saga, last season's heartbreaking Cup final defeat, assorted personal rivalries and, last but not least, good old-fashioned bragging rights. The two clubs are not bosom buddies. The customary pre-match crunch of body on tackle pad has an extra urgency, the warm-up less about loosening muscles than preparing for a title bout. The director of rugby, Rob Baxter, stands on his own a few metres back, watching intently, as if auditioning to be the world's sternest exam invigilator. Motivation is not going to be a problem today.

Because this date had been circled in Devon diaries for months, even before Saracens' defrocking. Baxter stitches together a music-backed highlights package of every Chiefs victory to show his players prior to their next fixture but this week motivational speeches are superfluous. 'I made a conscious effort not to say very much. Very early in the week, players were in meetings talking very emotively about the game. I was concerned about us mentally playing the game too early. I just talked very matter-of-factly. It was one of those games when I was at my most confident we'd be very good. The way the lads were talking, the things they said, their ambitions for the game. You could just feel it.'

Saracens, in festive red and featuring seven players involved in the World Cup final the previous month, also understand their champions' aura is not as iron-clad as it once was. Their pre-match tally of -13 points and rock-bottom status in the table means they are now perceived differently, not least around here. Worse still, they have turned up on a day when local pride is practically dripping from the stands. Out of the tunnel emerge the familiar figures of Jack Nowell and Luke Cowan-Dickie, each celebrating his 100th appearance for the Chiefs. What an image it is: two rock-hard sons of Cornish trawlermen, blood brothers since the age of five, now among England's finest. The stadium announcer, James Chubb, reckons the atmosphere is as charged as any he can recall in eight seasons of doing his job. Nowell is carrying his young daughter, Nori, in one of his ink-decorated arms. As the bloke next to me observes, she's done well to have played a century of first-team games at her age.

Nowell, though, is determined to mark a special personal landmark for himself and his growing family. 'Times like that don't come around often. If I'm honest, during the warm-up, I was thinking about that moment more than the game. It'll probably never happen again and I wanted to enjoy it for what it was. A packed-out Sandy Park, Nori in my arms and my best mate beside me. Running out to play for a club we signed for when we were 17. What made it even more special was the way the crowd reacted – and how the boys reacted as well. Nori enjoyed it until I gave her back to one of our conditioners.

She took one look, thought, "I don't know you," and started crying. But when I show it to her in 12 years' time she'll say, "That's cool."'

By now the collective anticipation swirling around the record attendance of 13,593 is seriously intense. In many respects this unflashy place already has a different vibe to other grounds. Never, for instance, has the humble pasty been elevated to such lofty gastronomic heights. Not to be clutching one feels as culturally insensitive as walking into the Ritz and ordering a packet of pork scratchings. On an average match day here they sell almost 3,500 pasties and pour 35,000 pints; the all-time single day record for bar takings is £187,400. 'My wife said that was just my bar bill,' jokes Tony Rowe, the club chairman. There is also a hog-roast roll so vast and popular there was uproar when it (temporarily) disappeared from the media menu last season. No army marches on its stomachs quite like the ever-ravenous – and thirsty – press pack.

On top of everything else – and that is where he prefers it – is Derek the Otter. For a long time no home game was complete without a large furry otter chasing members of the public around the pitch at half-time accompanied by a Benny Hill soundtrack. Until recently, the man in the suit was an undercover officer with the National Crime Agency who spent the rest of his week busting drug dealers. Hurtling around in defiance of all health and safety directives and flattening patrons who just had to have it, 'Derek' soon became a cult figure. There were occasions, though, when even he came off second best, not least the day his previous occupant, Patrick McCaig, whose family run Otter Brewery, was tackled by a member of the Military Wives choir. Everyone laughed at the time – 'My back's never been the same since I was sat on by a Military Wife' is a line rarely heard at Twickenham – but, eight years on, McCaig was still in sufficient pain to require an operation to fuse two of his vertebrae together.

Today's first half is almost as punishing. Chiefs seize on a loose ball to register a kick-and-chase score for Nic White, as reassuringly irritating at scrum-half as ever, but make too many errors themselves. It allows Sarries some respite but Owen Farrell, unfortunately for him, is not privy to the secret of mastering the local wind conditions. Twice the England captain takes aim with kickable penalties and twice the ball fades stubbornly right when, theoretically, its flight should have been straight. Seven-nil at half-time does not sound much but, with the diminutive Joe Simmonds having held up the heftier Jamie George over the try-line just before the break, it feels like more from a psychological perspective.

Beneath dappled, darkening skies the third quarter is clearly going to be crucial. The last time Saracens were rendered scoreless turns out to have been 2010. There is no way they are going to drive home without firing a solitary shot. A gentle Otter-fuelled hum ripples around the ground, with some wondering aloud if Sarries have been on the Christmas sauce. Probably just the cranberry but they are looking distinctly mortal.

Local sympathy is not in plentiful supply. Exeter, in fact, are actively looking to wind their opponents up: Jonny Hill ruffles Will Skelton's hair after Barnes spots a knock-on which prevents the big Australian lock from making some rare yardage. There is also a terrier's snap to the home side's tackling which Billy Vunipola is not appreciating. A skein of 17 geese fly high and purposefully over the West Stand, heading towards the Exe Estuary. Their formation is significantly tighter and more impressive than anything Sarries have yet managed.

Once the relentless South African flanker Jacques Vermeulen touches down beneath a pile of bodies to register Exeter's second try, crisply converted again by the dead-eyed Simmonds, the visitors know there is no way back. Elliot Daly's chip ahead rolls too far and Mako Vunipola needs lengthy treatment. The strains of the Tomahawk Chop, the hosts' familiar battle cry, echo more loudly around the ground, reinforcing the slightly ghoulish feel. Appropriately, with darkness falling, on comes Ben Moon, one of the 'Originals' who have been around for every yard of the incredible journey from the Championship to the summit of the English game.

The lights are fast going out on Sarries: their quarterback Farrell is sacked behind the gain line, their forwards are being driven backwards. When White and Duncan Taylor tangle near the touchline, players from both sides rush in and a mass fracas takes place next to the advertising hoardings. The substituted Harry Williams, previously sin-binned, gets involved and is shown a red card from Barnes for his trouble.

Later, a different narrative emerges. The confrontation was significantly inflamed, according to the home players, by a comment directed at White by Billy Vunipola. In the view of England's No. 8, Sarries had hoisted the silverware when it really mattered and this result changed little. Baxter still argues that the visitors were out of order: 'When you see how disappointed our players have been and the things they've not had to celebrate and you then hear a Saracens player telling Nic White: "Unlucky, you haven't got a Premiership winners' medal," that sticks in the craw. That's what some of their lads were saying. They were rubbing in the fact they were quite happy to cheat to win titles. If people had experienced that, they would really understand what it has been like.'

Among Exeter's players the widespread view is that Saracens have 'a reputation of saying narky things when they lose'. Don Armand, the Chiefs' outstanding Zimbabwean back-row forward, believes they have shown insufficient respect at times to him and his teammates. 'It's not necessarily their players' fault but when they've won all those titles and been as gloaty as some of them have been . . . if you've been caught cheating and you know you've done it the wrong way and that cheating has helped you get those titles, surely you should have a bit of humility?'

On this midwinter occasion there is absolutely no argument about the better team. Saracens secure a consolation penalty try but, at 14–7 down, then kick the ball away rather than try and steal a last-gasp draw. Baxter is in no mood to spend the entire evening talking about Saracens but, eventually, delivers a blunt assessment to BBC Radio 5 Live: 'There are supporters of rugby clubs who have watched coaches getting sacked and players leave and all different kinds of things. Part of that has been because of Saracens cheating.

'You can't run away from it. Sometimes the people who have pointed out that Saracens have cheated almost get painted as the bad guys. Well, the people who have made comment on it aren't the cheats. And that is the bit some rugby supporters have felt frustrated about.' Rowe, who has presided over Exeter's ascent since taking over in 1998, has also been outspoken in his public criticism of Saracens. Baxter cannot understand why some have disapproved of him doing so. 'I've seen some of the criticism of Tony and I don't get it. What people don't understand is that he feels for the players. That's what really hurts him and that's what really bothers me. When you live day to day with the players and see what they have been prepared to put in . . . I can see how some guys would use that as a really big motivation.'

That is precisely how Armand feels. He firmly believes the whole sorry saga will have the effect of propelling Exeter to greater heights. Even with Saracens removed from the frame, he also suspects the Chiefs' agonising defeat in the 2019 final will, ultimately, prove a blessing in disguise. 'In the next two to three years you'll see the benefit. There are things that don't need to be spoken about but will go forward as part of our psyche and our culture.

'If we'd have won we wouldn't have learned as much and wouldn't have done as much to Saracens' momentum as I think we did. Even though they won, it was one of those games when you know the opposition has really come at you physically and that the next time you play them it's going to be tough.' Hence the home side's confidence on this last Sunday of the year. 'Some of their players you just didn't notice – and some of them were guys they'd normally rely on. I think it was a subconscious carry-over.'

Back outside in the evening gloaming, Cowan-Dickie, Nowell and full-back Stuart Hogg, swiftly settled into his new surroundings having swapped his native Scottish Borders for the small town of Ottery St Mary, embrace their loved ones and pose for selfies. Cowan-Dickie and Nowell have already had some photos taken in the dressing room, proudly standing with their fellow local hero, Gareth Steenson, who has just clocked up his 300th appearance in an Exeter jersey. As one Chiefs fan, Dave Church, tweets: 'When they make the M5 embankment under the East Terrace into a Mount Rushmore-style sculpture, I'd imagine this is what three of the faces will look like.' It is not the worst proposal for the side wall of the proposed new Sandy Park stadium hotel, the next part of the masterplan to secure Exeter's finances for the long term.

Walking back to Digby & Sowton station car park – £4 in the charity bucket, beware the waist-high bollard halfway down the dimly lit lane – another thought occurs. At certain venues around the country it is possible to walk away from a club ground and wonder whether enough people truly care. Not at Sandy Park, not when Saracens have just been sent packing. If you yearn for old-school sporting fulfilment – and a decent pint – there are worse places to look for it.

* * * * *

It is another grey afternoon, almost 10 months later. Otherwise, much has changed. Normally 27,000 noisy supporters would be jammed inside Ashton Gate. Not any more, with fears of a second wave of Covid-19 infections on the way. The biggest occasion in the European club-rugby calendar, the Heineken Champions Cup final, is going ahead behind closed doors. It feels like a high-society wedding without any guests.

The tension, even so, is unbearable in every West Country living room. Just over an hour ago all was fine. Exeter had taken a 14–0 lead over France's Racing 92 inside the first quarter, making the inconceivable look almost routine. Two close-range drives had produced a brace of converted tries for Luke Cowan-Dickie and Sam Simmonds and a disjointed Racing, beaten in two previous European finals, looked odds-on for a hat-trick. The Chiefs, having never previously advanced past the quarter-finals, were bossing the game.

Now the scoreboard reads 28–27 with just over five minutes left. Exeter have also been reduced to 14 men, their replacement prop Tomas Francis yellow-carded for what the referee Nigel Owens has been advised is a deliberate knock-on. It is only a reflex finger-tip graze of the ball but these days that merits 10 minutes in the sin-bin. 'I don't make the laws,' says Owens, apologetically, as he explains his decision. No matter, Francis's match is over.

In his absence, the Chiefs are under siege. They have already weathered 18 brutal phases close to their own line but how much more punishment can their bodies and minds withstand? Which is exactly what Antonie Claassen, whose father Wynand captained South Africa in the early 1980s, is thinking as he takes a flat pass from his scrum-half Maxime Machenaud five metres out and charges for the line. One slightly mistimed or weary tackle and the No. 8 will be over, destined to be feted in his adopted city of Paris for years to come.

Standing in harm's way is Sam Skinner, another Exeter replacement facing the most pressurised moments of his sporting life. Now or never. The 25-year-old goes low and somehow stops his rampaging opponent six inches short. Just behind him the red-haired Jannes Kirsten, who like Claassen used to play for the Blue Bulls in Pretoria, dives in bravely and twists the Racing man's upper body skywards as he drives for the line. With Claassen on his back, the ball is momentarily exposed. Sam Hidalgo-Clyne, Chiefs' replacement scrum-half, spots the opportunity and clamps his body straight over the top. For the defending side, the peep of Owens's whistle is the sweetest-possible sound. Penalty to Exeter, disaster averted.

At last the clock is the Chiefs' friend. Another penalty following a line-out allows Henry Slade, scorer of his side's vital fourth try, to swing a cultured left leg and punt his forwards even further up the touchline. Exeter can now attempt to dictate proceedings. A few close-quarter phases eat up further precious seconds but, as ever, a tiny miscalculation could still wreck everything. Entering the final minute Racing's desire to force a turnover spills over and Owens spots another ruck offence 45 metres from the French line. Surely this must be it?

Instead, chaos ensues. Exeter seem uncertain whether or not to go for goal and Owens decides they are delaying too long. The referee orders an extra five seconds to be factored into the equation but when he asks for the clock to be restarted nothing happens. Ignoring the confusion, Exeter's impressive young captain Joe Simmonds kicks the long-range penalty to widen his side's advantage to 31–27. No one on the pitch seems entirely certain if the 80 minutes is officially up or whether the game should restart.

The world momentarily seems to have frozen like some mad H. M. Bateman cartoon. Is it possible that homely Exeter, just 10 years on from their Championship promotion in this same city, are about to become the champions of Europe? Can a team who were playing Havant, Aspatria, Walsall and Redruth in Courage League Division Four when the Heineken Cup was launched in 1995/96 really have conquered the ultimate club peak? Or is it all a cruel illusion, about to be shattered in one of the more extraordinary late twists of the modern era?

Owens, who has had an excellent game, is still frowning and talking. Gradually it seems a consensus is being reached. In theory the ball bisected the posts three seconds before the clock turned red. Because of the delay in re-setting it, however, the timekeeper instructs Owens that the game is officially over. Cue a lilac-and-purple haze of delirium. Devon is suddenly home to the best club team in Europe, the first side since the introduction of the English leagues to have hoisted every trophy from the fourth-division title upwards. The steepest ascent in British club history is complete.

In their moment of euphoria it is almost forgotten that the Chiefs still have a Premiership final to play the next Saturday. Even the absence of a crowd briefly ceases to matter, at least until players start pulling out mobile phones and making emotional calls to their families and loved ones at home. Up soars the trophy into the Bristol evening sky as Racing's beaten players and coaches, gracious in defeat, stare on blankly. They are not the first to discover that the country boys of Exeter have hidden depths. As Butch Cassidy and the Sundance Kid used to mutter, while gazing down at the mysterious posse continually on their trail . . . 'Who are those guys?'

TWO

GET ON, EXE!

Across the River Exe from the northern fringes of Devon's cathedral city, it would be easy to miss the unpretentious farmhouse tucked away in a quiet valley off a narrow winding lane. The sun is making a timely reappearance after months of incessant rain and shafts of golden spring light flood in through the windows. It is bright enough for Bobbi Baxter to offer to draw the curtains to ensure her beloved husband, John, is not completely dazzled as he settles into his chair in the front room.

The enchanting Devon sunshine is what brought the Baxter family south from Lancashire in the first place. Even now John vividly recalls the day his life turned upside down. It was the late 1950s and the Baxters were looking to move from the village of Upholland, just outside Wigan, where the family had been well established for years. His father, Ted, had heard there was a small farm in the Lake District that might be worth a look. On the day the family visited, though, all they saw was rain. Gallons and gallons of it, cascading down from slate-grey, depressing northern skies. It was not the kind of weather to make the heart soar, let alone yearn for a fresh start in the saturated locality.

Sixty years on, every detail of what happened next remains sharp. The following week Baxter senior received details of another property, 250 miles away in Devon. When the family headed south to check it out it was as if Walt Disney himself had choreographed the backdrop. The sky was cornflower blue, the birds were singing, the hedgerows were alive with wild flowers and the Lake District felt like a different universe. It would have taken a heart of granite to resist so much bucolic charm and the Baxters were instantly bowled over.

What if it had rained instead? There is every chance the whole extraordinary Chiefs story might not have unfolded. Even at the time it cannot have been a straightforward decision. The family roots in Upholland ran particularly deep. Locals still refer to Baxter's Pit, once a prominent mine in the West Lancashire coalfield, while other members of the extended Baxter clan ran the local grocery store and butcher's shop. In 1929 the *Wigan Observer*'s report on the golden wedding of a Mr & Mrs Baxter of Brooklands House offered some insight into the extended family genes. 'They were married at St Peter's Swinton on Oct 29, 1879 and have had ten sons and three daughters . . . all ten sons were over 6ft in height, the tallest being about 6ft 4¼ in.'

Ted Baxter and his wife, Annie, were never going to rear shy, retiring kids. John's brother, Paul, was named Alexander Paul Baxter after Alexander the Great. For John they chose the first name William, after William the Conqueror. Young W J Baxter, however, was less interested in great historical characters than rugby league. Wigan were the mightiest force in the land and his absolute favourite was Billy Boston. One day, walking across the car park towards the boys' enclosure at Central Park, he spotted Boston ahead of him. Unable to contain himself, he rushed up and tapped the latter on the shoulder. Far from being irritated,

Billy turned around and rewarded his besotted young fan with a smile wider than the Pennines. John knew in that split second what he wanted to do in life: to emulate his hero and play for Wigan himself.

Instead, aged 15, he was uprooted to a place where rugby league was an entirely alien concept. At school in Crediton it was union all the way. It was also swiftly apparent that the newcomer with the northern accent was a more than useful player. At the local town club the senior players took him under their wing and dropped him back home to the family farm after games. Playing-wise, he went on a couple of tours to the Midlands, rubbing shoulders with English internationals who, to his eyes, were nothing special. Back home, people started to whisper in his ear. 'John, come and join us . . . you'll get your county and international cap if you come to Exeter.'

It was unquestionably a club with proud traditions. Founded in 1871, the same year as the Rugby Football Union, Exeter had been around longer than allegedly more distinguished sides like Gloucester, Bristol, Leicester and Northampton. Another attraction for the abrasive young forward was the chance to play with Dick Manley, one of the rare breed of Exeter players to have caught the eyes of the faraway England selectors. It said it all, though, that even the well-regarded Manley, a cabinet maker, was a month short of his 31st birthday when he was finally capped at flanker against Wales at a straw-strewn Cardiff Arms Park in the long, freezing winter of 1963. Exeter was seen as a distant backwater and the club struggled to gain fixtures with the top London sides, with travel not easy in the years before the M5 opened fully in 1977. Baxter senior remembers the interminable coach trips well. 'To get to anywhere in the early 1960s was very difficult. We used to kick off every season with Moseley away. Trying to get up there for a 3 p.m. kick-off around the holiday period, before the M5, was impossible. We were as good as anybody; it was just geography. Us, Bristol, Bath, Gloucester . . . we were all on a par.'

As well as good, hard local players, there was also a ready supply of talented student teachers from St Luke's College. Among them were distinguished future England players and coaches such as Don Rutherford and Mike Davis, both of whom helped to raise standards. Importantly, too, there was Bob Staddon, originally from Ilfracombe in north Devon, who would become one of Exeter's most loyal servants.

A talented all-round sportsman – he also opened the batting for Devon – Staddon had been quietly thrilled to arrive at St Luke's to discover his personal tutor was Martin Underwood, who won five caps on the wing for England in the early 1960s. One Friday night in October 1964, Underwood had been due to play against Bristol at the Memorial Ground but was forced to cry off. The inexperienced Staddon was taken aback to receive a phone call inviting him to make his first-team debut. He was even more surprised to be asked to play at centre, a position he had never previously occupied. The opposition were more than handy – the erstwhile England captain Richard Sharp was at fly-half with Roger Hosen at full-back – and Staddon's first taste of senior rugby involved having his hand trodden on by Bristol's Jimmy Glover, whose daughter Helen Glover would strike Olympic rowing gold half a century later. Exeter, despite everything, lost only 19–16 and the youthful Staddon was warmly welcomed into the fold. More than half a century of selfless service later, he is the club's president.

When it came to no-nonsense forward play, Exeter could also be relied upon to supply a certain – how to phrase this – physical vigour. Baxter could always be found in the vanguard. 'It was physical in a different way. The scrum was totally different. It was a genuine competition. Front rows would not go down because they knew if they did they'd get the hell kicked out of them.' Staddon recalls some particularly lively exchanges with

Plymouth Albion, and not just on the field. 'We played one game there in the early 1970s when the referee stopped the game and asked for the club secretary to come out of the stand and have old man Baxter removed from the ground. The secretary was too afraid to do it.'

Nor was John Baxter the kind of opponent with whom to take liberties. 'John was the enforcer in our team. He had a reputation and it was richly deserved. There was a famous Cup final in Torquay when there was an incident involving me. I wasn't the bravest of rugby players but John took exception. In front of the referee he came up to the prop in question, who was a chef, and gave him a haymaker. We thought he'd be sent off but the ref just said, "Don't do that again." John was a hard, physical player and a very good one.'

He was also not renowned for communicating in flowery rhyming couplets. Staddon's former teammate, great friend and Shaldon neighbour, John Lockyer, had moved up to play for Exeter from his local club Teignmouth in 1969/70 when it was just becoming de rigueur for hookers to throw in. Lockyer, who also captained Exeter and remains a passionate summariser on BBC Radio Devon – 'I think we've got 'em now, Nigel!' – was understandably keen to keep his line-out jumpers happy.

'How do you want it, John? Quick and flat?'

'Just chuck the fucking thing in. I'll catch it.'

It was not unknown, either, for the occasional unidentified clenched fist to emerge from the second row if a member of the opposition took too many liberties, although Exeter's front-rowers argued they accidentally copped the majority of them. There were plenty of other characters in the squad, not least Paul Baxter who, when it came to team photographs, liked to roll his sleeves up to emphasise how big his forearms were. It was also the latter who, as captain in the club's centenary season of 1972/73, decided it was time for Exeter to abandon the amateur tradition of the team being picked by committee men in smoke-filled rooms. 'Right,' he said, looking around the room at the old boys all puffing on their pipes. 'From now on, as captain, I'm going to be chairman of selectors.'

Other pivotal figures included Andy Cole, a Cullompton farmer who narrowly missed out on a Cambridge blue. He could play prop as well as back row and captained the club for four years. His teammates reckoned he was the hardest, fairest player around, not to mention the strongest. Witnesses still talk about the day he arrived to help Staddon move house and picked up the chest freezer all by himself. Cole also had the whitest boot laces of anyone in the West Country, courtesy of his mother who boiled them clean after every match.

Even before you laced up a pair of boots, playing rugby for Exeter also required serious commitment from a geographical point of view. Staddon, for instance, soon grew familiar with every twist and turn of the A35 on his way from Bridport, where he was teaching, to attend training on Tuesday and Thursday nights and play at the weekends. Away fixtures were an even bigger undertaking in those pre-motorway days. When playing, say, Bridgend in South Wales, Exeter would leave home at 6 a.m. and travel up to Gloucester before winding their way slowly back down through the valleys. Clubs like Leicester would head on tour to Devon at Easter but not every leading club fancied getting dragged into the mire at the reliably wet, clay-based County Ground. As Staddon put it: 'Teams didn't like to come to the County Ground. It was invariably a very difficult place to play rugby.'

Even touring Springbok sides found life awkward in the Devonshire mud, while Exeter's rising profile was increasingly reflected in the make-up of the Devon side which was prospering in the County Championship. Perennial high-fliers Gloucestershire were beaten at Torquay, with eight Devon players selected in a combined Devon and Cornwall XV to face the All Blacks at Redruth in January 1973. Lockyer featured at hooker alongside the renowned Cornish stalwart Stack Stevens and John's brother Paul Baxter with the 18-year-old John Scott at lock, although local rugby politics – and a partisan local printing firm – meant only the Cornish-based players had their full biographies printed in the match programme.

Circumstances, though, frustrated John Baxter's ambitions to win a full Test cap. He was picked to play in an England trial but the timing was unfortunate. 'I hadn't played for six weeks beforehand because I'd twisted my knee. "Sod it," I thought, "at least I'll get a decent meal."' He finished on the losing side but the invitation was a vindication of sorts. He was 'carded' for an England summer tour but, as with Manley a few years earlier, felt obliged to decline the invitation. 'I couldn't go because I couldn't bloody afford it. That was the end of it.'

He also had to stop turning out for Exeter in 1973, aged just 27. 'I'd suffered some hearing problems and I was going deaf. Money was tight and I just couldn't afford to carry on playing. I had too many other responsibilities. You try milking cows on a frosty morning when you're injured. Trying to put the cups on with freezing fingers when you've just played a big game the previous day. It wasn't Mickey Mouse rugby, it was proper stuff. If I couldn't get into the club I'd train on the farm in the evenings, carrying a sack of potatoes around. I used to keep weights in the barn. Whether I was ever fit I don't know but I always thought I was pretty strong. Rugby was a release, a pleasure; a chance to get away from it all and let off steam. I like to think I gave as good as I got.'

By now, John was also a family man. One fateful evening he and a mate had driven up from Morchard Road to Barnstaple to attend a dance at the Wrey Arms. From her vantage point across the room, Bobbi instantly decided she liked the look of the tall, muscular stranger. Coincidentally she had also moved down from the north-west as a young girl and settled with her parents in Braunton. The shared connection was immediate and, before too long, they were married. Four children – two girls and two boys – followed as the family moved between various farms. Joanne arrived first, followed by her brother Robert, who was born in Tavistock Maternity Hospital on 10 March 1971.

Both he and the couple's third child, Richard, were chips off the solid old Baxter block. Soon enough the two young boys were running around behind the posts at the County Ground, collecting balls and helping out with the ground's old-fashioned scoreboard on match days. They did their best but, all too often, a vital number or a crucial supporting pin would be missing. Spectators had little option but to fill in the blanks mentally until the next score materialised.

No one seemed to mind too much, not least because the team were winning regularly. Throughout the mid-1970s they enjoyed consistent success, particularly when they beat the mighty Bristol and, to their rivals' consternation, qualified ahead of them for the national John Player Cup. In January 1978 they were drawn at home to Bath, with England's John Horton at fly-half, in the first round of the Cup and won, convincingly, by 20–6.

In rugby, though, success is tough to sustain. By the early 1980s, many of Exeter's stalwarts were growing older and the lack of a formal recruitment strategy was starting to tell. Results began to nosedive: between 1983 and 1985 Exeter were beaten by, among others, Crediton, Sidmouth, Devon and Cornwall Police and Tiverton. To make matters worse, their old rivals Plymouth were growing stronger. All concerned could feel the balance of power shifting. 'We got a bit arrogant,' acknowledges Staddon. 'You could almost hear other clubs muttering, "That'll teach you, Exeter." People were not exactly broken-hearted.'

* * * * *

Illustrious Devon sportspeople were also a lesser-spotted breed. A case could arguably be made for the Tavistock-born Sir Francis Drake, although details are hazy as to whether he actually did continue playing bowls on Plymouth Hoe as the Spanish Armada approached in 1588. Alternatively, step forward Sir Walter Raleigh, born in East Budleigh, who sailed similarly far and wide and introduced multiple generations of British athletes to the concept of the relieving pre-match fag.

Twentieth-century contenders in team ball games are even harder to find. Perhaps the outstanding individual was the Exeter-born Dick Pym, Bolton's flat-capped goalkeeper in three victorious FA Cup finals in the 1920s, during which he conceded not a single goal. Pym was very much his own man, famously deciding to return with a parrot from an Exeter club tour to Brazil. When the parrot died it was buried beneath one of the goalmouths, only to be exhumed after supporters started to fret about the Grecians' lack of goals at that end. Within days of the old bird being dug up, the goals began to flow again. Pym, who won three caps for England, hailed from a fishing family and, after retiring from football, returned to spend his latter days catching fish on the Exe Estuary at his native Topsham.

The Plymouth-born Trevor Francis also represented his country but never played first-team football for the Argyle. Neither Plymouth nor Exeter City have ever featured in the top tier of league football despite being founded in, respectively, 1886 and 1904. Otherwise, apart from Sir Francis Chichester (the son of a north Devon clergyman and the first yachtsman to circumnavigate the world single-handed), Tom Daley, Sharron Davies, Jo Pavey and Sue Barker, the ranks of non-equine world-beating performers from England's third-biggest county have been relatively few.

It is a curious phenomenon given that Devon – with its plentiful fresh air and wide open spaces – has all the makings of a sporting hotspot. There are surfers and sailors everywhere and – viruses permitting – the granite uplands of Dartmoor are covered in teenagers competing in the annual Ten Tors hiking challenge. Cyclists, jump jockeys, golfers, cricketers and open water swimmers jostle for recognition as well.

First among equals, though, remains rugby, as synonymous with the south-west peninsula of England as the cream tea. It has ever been thus. They were playing a version of the game at Blundell's School in Tiverton in 1868, Exeter played their first official match in October 1873 and, following the reorganisation of the English County Championship in 1896, Devon emerged as one of the country's strongest teams. They won the title in 1899, finished runners-up in 1900 and then either won or shared the title in five of the next 12 years.

The most frequently recited story from that time, however, involved a defeat so big some simply could not believe it. Within a week of Dave Gallaher's 1905 All Blacks arriving in Plymouth by boat, they faced Devon at the County Ground in Exeter on 16 September. When the final score was phoned through to a London agency it read 'Devon 4 New Zealand 55'. Convinced it must be a mistake, a sceptical sub-editor reversed the result to read 'Devon 55 New Zealand 4'. A long-running debate also rumbles as to how, exactly, the first recorded reference to the 'All Blacks' appeared in the paper. While the touring team's kit was black, some claimed it was actually a spelling error and referred to the ease with which every visiting player ran and passed the ball. As one breathless newspaper correspondent wrote, they were 'all backs'.

In an effort to establish the truth, the respected Kiwi sportswriter, Ron Palenski, dug his way back into the archives and came across the following post-match reference in the local *Express & Echo*: 'The All Blacks, as they are styled by reason of their sable and unrelieved costume, were under the guidance of their captain

(Mr Gallaher) and their fine physiques favourably impressed the spectators.' What no one disputed was that Devon's finest came a distant second, prompting Lord Baden-Powell, of subsequent boy scout fame, to suggest England's youth were in decline and comprised 'thousands of young men, pale, narrow-chested, hunched-up, miserable specimens smoking endless cigarettes'.

For the next century and more the south-west generated few national sporting headlines. Yeovil's sloping pitch did briefly capture the public imagination following a 1949 FA Cup giant-killing win over Sunderland, while Argyle memorably reached the FA Cup semi-final at Villa Park in 1984. The sight of Trelawny's Army pouring up to Twickenham in 1991 to watch Cornwall win the County Championship final and claim their first title since 1908 was similarly evocative. To more youthful observers, though, there was an analogue feel to much of it. Celebrating the Wurzels, Jethro and the Beast of Bodmin Moor is all very well but, eventually, you need something more in your locker. If ever there was a sporting region desperately seeking a fresh hero or two it was the slow-paced, success-starved south-west.

THREE

TAKE ME HOME, COUNTRY ROADS

A new era, of sorts, was starting to dawn in English rugby. The game was still officially amateur, of course, but on the field Bath were setting fresh standards under the canny Jack Rowell. Jeremy Guscott, Stuart Barnes, Richard Hill, Jon Hall, Gareth Chilcott and Graham Dawe were a collective cut above: there was only one champion team in the West Country and it wasn't Exeter. In 1982/83, to underline the point, the latter endured their worst season playing-wise since 1957/58, losing to Sidmouth, Barnstaple, High Wycombe, Tiverton, Camborne and Devon & Cornwall Police. When they ventured up to the Rec it was not even a contest, Bath setting a new points record in a painfully one-sided 74–3 victory.

It was hardly a surprise, then, when the first official merit tables were drawn up and Exeter did not feature among the country's top 24 sides. Only in the following 1985/86 season were they included in the imaginatively named Merit Table C alongside Nuneaton, Roundhay, Morley and Metropolitan Police. They were fortunate still to be involved in the third tier when the

Courage National Leagues – consisting of three divisions of 12 with sides playing each other only once – were finally launched in 1987/88. Even faithful club servants like John Lockyer could not ignore reality. 'Had the leagues been formed a year earlier we might have gone. We were that poor.'

Exeter duly won just three of their 11 fixtures in that inaugural league season and finished below Vale of Lune, Fylde and Maidstone. They also trailed in a lowly ninth the following season while Plymouth finished up unbeaten on top of the table and earned promotion. Local rivalry was fierce, so much so that, after one particularly one-sided game, an exultant Plymouth supporter could not resist winding up John Baxter. 'You're finished now,' he informed him gleefully. Baxter's retort was instantaneous. 'Don't you worry. Exeter will soon be on the way back.'

It was very much Baxter's view that such chastening experiences would fuel Exeter's desire even more. Having taken over as club chairman in 1986, he also knew that some decent young players were emerging. Richard Gibbins and Andy Maunder had appeared from Blundell's School along with Harry Langley from Sidmouth and Andy Green from South Molton. Graham Bess, uncle of the current Somerset and England off-spinner Dom Bess, and Patrick Chenery had also turned up to bolster the pack. Chenery, a bear of a man, went on to captain Montpellier in the days before the French side decided to prioritise the signing of cash-hungry Springboks.

Maunder and Green were to become one of the most illustrious half-back pairings in south-west history. Maunder, whose family had been prominent local butchers since 1898, ended up playing 13 seasons and over 300 games for Exeter, captained the club and sat on the bench for the South West in the old Divisional Championship behind the Bath and England scrum-half Richard Hill for four years without taking the field.

He also captained Exeter for seven seasons before handing over the job to Rob Baxter but singles out Staddon as the primary catalyst for the club's on-field turnaround. 'Bob would say, "No, you can't go out and get pissed on a Friday night. And if you don't train on these particular days you won't be selected." He slowly cajoled people round from doing what they wanted to, in a nice way, doing what he wanted.'

Improving Exeter's image as a welcoming place to play was another priority. In the mid-1980s even Maunder, from just past Cullompton, was not considered a true local. 'Exeter's reputation was very cliquey. If you weren't from Exeter you weren't welcome. The only reason I was let through the door was that Richard Gibbins was from Stoke Canon and they knew who he was.' The arrival of Green also helped, as did Staddon's strategy of playing (and beating) as many local clubs as possible and being charming company in the bar afterwards. If the best local young players subsequently fancied joining a prestigious, friendly, upwardly mobile club just up the road, so much the better. As Maunder puts it: 'People didn't like Exeter but gradually they started to say, "They're not that bad."'

Brave, tactically sharp and reliably good at exploiting a blind-side gap, Maunder scored 49 tries in 149 league games and complemented his half-back partner Green perfectly. The latter sold veterinary drugs for a living and had a freewheeling approach to rugby which his scrum-half still remembers fondly: 'The predictable thing about Andy was that he was completely unpredictable. I don't think he ever really knew what he was going to do, so no one in the opposition did either. He also had incredible speed off the mark, which made him difficult to play against. If you gave him a bit of space, he'd find the gap and get through it. He would win games on his own purely by spotting something. Occasionally we'd look silly but he always played with a smile on his face.'

Even the hard-nosed John Baxter rated Green highly. 'Andy Green had the best sidestep and turn of pace over 10 to 15 yards you'd ever want to see. He was the epitome of a Welsh fly-half.' In addition he was a fine goal-kicker with a highly unusual defensive technique. As Maunder recalls, he also enjoyed a challenge: 'He was incredibly brave and would mountain-climb up the biggest players, put his foot on their knee, slide up round on to their shoulders and then slide down the back. It was almost like he'd put crampons on. It was quite an art really.'

The planets were also aligning in other ways. One of the great coaches of the era, Chalkie White, had been appointed by the Rugby Football Union as the South West division's technical administrator, based in Taunton and living in Wellington, after 14 years of consistent success as coach of Leicester. Many felt he was the best coach England never had. Now here he was, in his mid-sixties, putting Exeter's young colts through their paces at 9 p.m. on Tuesday night. Among those whom Chalkie had helped transform how they saw the game was none other than Clive Woodward, England's 2003 World Cup-winning head coach. Woodward never forgot White's mantra that the first piece of ball a team received in a game might be the best bit of possession it enjoyed all afternoon. 'Chalkie wanted to play from the opening minute, from anywhere on the field. We all benefited from that kind of philosophy and we went out to play in a way we enjoyed. One of the biggest shames of that era was that Chalkie didn't become national coach.'

Fate, though, can intervene in curious ways. Among the fresh-faced wannabes in Exeter's colts' team was a young Robert Baxter, thirsty for knowledge and keen to improve. His primary school teacher in Newton St Cyres had initially encouraged him to play at nearby Crediton but, in his mid-teens, he switched to Exeter Saracens, who had an excellent youth set-up at the time. With his game progressing nicely, the next step was to take his A-levels at Exeter College before going on to university.

Along with his younger brother Richard, though, he had inherited the family's passion for farming. Midway through his final year at college, he felt his priorities beginning to shift. 'I talked to my dad and decided to come back on to the farm. I was already with (his now-wife) Jo and university didn't feel like what I wanted to do. It wasn't the biggest thing for me at 17 or 18.' When his A-level grades eventually came through they were nothing much to write home about but, on the farm, the bales were perfectly stacked. A warm, sunny summer soon massaged away any twinges of academic regret.

* * * * *

When the Romans first settled in Exeter around AD 200 they swiftly decided on a suitable name. The Latin word *Isca* translates as 'Watertown' and there has always been plenty of it around. The River Exe rises near Simonsbath on Exmoor and flows for almost 60 miles before reaching the sea at Exmouth. It has been a familiar presence for millennia but, in other respects, the cathedral city has been transformed. Nowadays it has over 130,000 inhabitants – still far fewer than, say, Leicester's population of around 350,000 – and is home to the Met Office among other prominent employers.

Significant rainfall was certainly a regular feature down at the mud-spattered old County Ground. For big-boned local lads such as the Baxter boys, however, it was sacred ground. Even the Grand Slam-winning 1984 Wallabies, still remembered as one of the great touring sides, could only manage a 12–12 draw against the South and South West in Exeter. Among those wedged into the stadium on that Saturday afternoon in October was a 13-year-old Rob Baxter and running out for his first senior game felt like a similarly momentous occasion. 'When I made my senior debut for Exeter I was really proud. The County Ground, as run-down as it was getting, was still the focal point for many of the big games held in the south-west. We built some history there – and we also built some ambitions. With my family connections, it was a big thing when I made the team.'

The 1987/88 season during which Baxter made his league debut at Nuneaton in mid-October – Exeter lost 27–14 – also happened to be the first year of the Courage Leagues in England. The 12-strong list of top-division sides makes interesting reading now, with Coventry, Moseley, Nottingham, Orrell and Waterloo all members of the original elite. At the end of the campaign, Coventry and Sale were relegated with Rosslyn Park and Liverpool St Helens promoted. Exeter, by contrast, were still playing parochial local derbies which, in the view of Baxter and others, were every bit as intense as their league fixtures. 'Some of our biggest games were Devon Cup games. They felt huge. I remember some real humdingers against Barnstaple, Brixham and Okehampton.' Having graduated from his duties as ballboy and scoreboard operator, he was also helping out as a groundsman, mowing and marking the pitch. 'Being on the farm there was some flexibility about being able to get down there. When I look out at the pitch at Sandy Park and watch it being mown and marked I think, "I could go out and do that now." It's not an alien thing to run a line down the side of it. In hindsight, it's part of what now makes it all feel so nice.'

The process was not necessarily cutting edge in all respects. The first mow of pre-season was particularly hard work. 'It would take a long, long time. We'd borrow a mower off Radmore & Tucker who were a sponsor but I'd spend as much time walking to the local petrol station for refills of petrol. We had a ride-on mower but it was a small one that collected the grass. At the start of the season you'd do one stripe and it would already be full. You look back now and think, "Really?"' Painting the pitch lines straight on to the oozing mud was no easy job either. 'Some days to get a line it would literally be a case of going along with the powder, a pint mug and a bucket to sprinkle the lines in. You couldn't run the rollers over the mud. It just wouldn't lay a line down.'

Early mornings on the family's 300-acre farm at Exwick had at least instilled a relentless work ethic. In the summers most of the work had to be done by hand and haymaking kept everyone fit and strong. 'Once the fields were mown and baled, every square bale had to be picked up by hand. Then there were the cattle and sheep to feed and check and hedges to mend.' In his twenties, in an attempt to broaden his skills further, Rob decided to teach himself how to shear sheep. 'I was entirely self-taught. We went and bought the equipment ourselves. That was always an interesting few days.'

Only if the brothers had worked hard enough would they be allowed to nip away early to club training. Pre-season was always the trickiest juggling period. 'If you have fields of hay down and your training sessions are at 6 p.m., you've got to go pretty hard. If there was a lot that needed doing and the hay was dry, we'd be up very early. Often, though, you'd work late. If it was a nice evening you'd carry on. It definitely breeds a work ethic.' Thirty years on John Baxter gazes out into the sunlit yard – his sons both still live a few yards away in adjoining homes attached to the main property – and his eyes soften. 'They both knuckled down. There was a lot of sheep, hay and straw but they always got their work done. We never, ever had to force them out of bed. Bobbi and I couldn't have wished for two better sons.'

Even a home-loving Baxter could sense, however, that there might be life beyond the farm gate. There was also a growing sense of camaraderie within the Exeter dressing room, a product of having to fight to be the best in Devon, never mind the rest of the country. Andy Maunder still singles out a feisty Devon Cup final at Plymouth's Beacon Park in 1991/92 as a pivotal moment in the club's modern history. At the time it was Albion who generally held sway and Maunder had the scars to prove it. 'We used to get an absolute hammering. And get beaten up. They were just nasty. There was never a game that didn't have four or five fights in it. No player would ever go from Plymouth to Exeter or vice versa.'

On this occasion the tables ended up being turned on Albion. Exeter had to employ all their subs and employ a reserve scrum-half on the flank but simply would not lie down. As Maunder and his players hoisted the trophy aloft, it felt like a truly significant achievement. 'The psychological difference from that moment was massive. That was when Exeter became the top team in the region. I look back on that game as being monumental. They had their full team out, it was an evening game in front of a packed Plymouth crowd and the pitch was muddy and shitty. To hold the trophy aloft in their ground . . . I remember thinking, "This is quite something."'

It proved a decent springboard for the 1992/93 season when Exeter enjoyed an excellent campaign, reaching the quarter-finals of the Pilkington Cup where they were rewarded with an away tie against Leicester at Welford Road. It was both a notable achievement and a serious reality check: despite slotting only four of their 13 conversion attempts, the Tigers still won 76–0. Having again missed out on promotion, the 21-year-old Rob Baxter was now faced with a dilemma. Exeter's motto, bestowed on the city by King Charles II in 1660 after its inhabitants supported him during the English Civil War, is *semper fidelis*: always loyal. No one could ever accuse the Baxter family of not abiding by the local maxim. Then again, if Rob had ambitions to play with the big boys more regularly, here was a potential opportunity to discover if the grass really was greener elsewhere.

Eventually a move to Gloucester was arranged late in the season – too late, it transpired, to make him eligible to play league games because of the six-month stand-down period that, quaintly, was compulsory at the time. It began to dawn on Baxter that he might have miscalculated. 'I just really wanted to see if I was going to play first division rugby but I wasn't allowed to play in a league fixture at Gloucester until after Christmas.' He'd had a couple of decent non-league games but, at the crucial moment, it all went pear-shaped. 'I've only got myself to blame. Probably the worst couple of games I played for Gloucester were just before I became eligible. Gloucester were struggling a bit, dropped Dave Sims back to No. 8, won a couple of games and I never really got beyond being a bench player. It was before the game was professional, I was travelling up the M5 three times a week and there were a lot of travel expenses. I was a squad player at best and they said to me, "I don't think this is going to work." I came back to Exeter and got on with things.'

The deflating experience, though, was not entirely wasted. 'I learned a massive amount. It changed me as a player and showed what you could achieve. I saw guys come in from local Gloucester club sides and stand and fight together and win games they shouldn't necessarily have won. It's important to go and experience that. You realise that everyone is human. Give guys the environment and the opportunity and the game is what develops them. I don't think I'd have been as successful as a player or, subsequently, a captain if I hadn't done it.'

FOUR

THE SPEED MERCHANT

When people talk nostalgically about the cultural transformation in Britain in the late 1950s and early 1960s, they forget the unglamorous reality for working-class families in cities like Portsmouth. The residents of the council houses on Grove Road were less bothered about Beatlemania than with making ends meet. Times were tough and money was tight. Only a couple of households possessed a car or a television and the Rowe family was not among them. The absence of parked vehicles in the street theoretically made it easier to kick a football around but not every local kid was blessed with nimble footwork or dreamed of playing up for Pompey.

The Rowes' only son, Tony, was not a massive football lover. He did not much fancy school, either. His mum, Matilda, was a cleaner and his stepfather, Reginald Rowe – originally from Ivybridge – was a crane driver. Both would head out for work at around 7 a.m., leaving young Tony to make the short walk up the road to Grove Park School. It was barely five minutes away but it wasn't long before he stopped going completely. 'I'd leave it until 8.55 a.m. and then think, "Bugger it." I just stayed at home.' His sister, also Matilda, was 15 months older and owned a Dansette record player which she firmly refused to let him touch. When he was home alone, though, Tony could relax and play all her favourite 45s. On would go Johnny Kidd and the Pirates – 'Shakin' All Over' – and the various other cherished singles in her collection.

To try and cover his tracks school-wise, Tony also took to writing his own sick letters to explain his absences. Only in later years, having belatedly been diagnosed with dyslexia, did it occur to him the school must have known all along his mum wasn't writing them. Either way, no one seemed to care greatly when he left school at 14. For entertainment he preferred to hang out with his mate Albert. Albert's elder brother had a Ford Popular, which they liked to imagine was Gosport's answer to Al Capone's bulletproof Cadillac. Sometimes they would go scrumping for apples, leaving the car with its doors wide open and engine running as they loaded up with illicit cargo before jumping back in and roaring away with a satisfying screech of rubber.

Had he remained in Portsmouth there is a good chance such opportunist raids would have progressed well beyond apples. Two of his best friends ended up on the wrong side of the law and Rowe might have been diverted – 'I'd probably have got in trouble, yeah' – down a similar path. The void left by his absent 'real' father was another niggling issue. He knew precious few details, other than that his mother had split from him when he was barely one. Not until years later did he discover the true identity of the mysterious figure about whom he had so often wondered. Chris Christian turned out to have been a well-known circus performer who worked as a lion tamer, among other things, before going on to become a ringmaster with Billy Smart's Circus. He appeared in the 1960 film *Circus of Horrors* starring Anton Diffring, Erika Remberg, Yvonne Monlaur and

Donald 'Blofeld' Pleasence and introduced stars such as Dorothy Squires (who sang in a big cage alongside a group of tigers) and Jayne Mansfield at Variety Club gala performances.

Armed with these exotic biographical details, his sister Matilda finally obtained an address in Essex and decided, after some deliberation, to approach him. Tony agreed to accompany her. 'We went knocking on this farmhouse door to try and meet him but he wouldn't answer.' It emerged that Christian had also fathered four children with his second wife, Wendy, a former Billy Smart's dancer and trapeze artiste/aerialist. His first wife, Marjorie, was a hairdresser he had met in Plymouth during another Smart's show. One day Tony was informed by an aunt that his natural father had passed away in 2010, at the age of 87. Any burning desire to understand more about his imaginary alter ego Tony Christian – 'Maybe I'm related to that bloke off *Mutiny on the Bounty*?' – was abruptly extinguished.

* * * * *

School or no school, the 15-year-old Rowe had his own furrow to plough. Even at that age he sensed there might be life beyond Portsmouth and he did not wish to be a burden upon his hard-working parents. 'In a way I suppose they were glad when I left home. I was ready to leave. I was bored and just wanted to get out there and do something.' And so, in 1964, he left to join the Royal Marines band on the advice of a history teacher who told him he had some ability as a drummer. As a trainee drum bugler, life instantly became more varied. It also gave him a chance to rekindle the interest in rugby that had briefly flared at secondary school. Based in J Wing in Deal barracks, he enjoyed playing hooker despite a recurring inability to throw the ball in straight. At other bases there was a lack of accommodation for the bandsmen recruits, requiring some of them to be paid to live in civilian quarters, which is how the 18-year-old Rowe unexpectedly came to find himself living in a luxury flat, doing part-time jobs on the side such as delivering cars and playing in a pop group in the evenings.

The furthest he travelled during his time on attachment with the Royal Navy was Gibraltar, on an old battlecruiser named HMS *Tiger*. Otherwise he would often start work at 8 a.m., finish by midday and only put on his uniform to collect his pay packet once a fortnight. Being posted to Lympstone in Devon also had its compensations, such as learning to waterski on the Exe Estuary. Soon enough, though, it was decision time. The armed forces were making cutbacks and, at the age of 22, he had two choices: stay in or try something else. 'My boss offered me a promotion to corporal, which I was quite keen about, but I was still young and wanted to do more outside the forces. By that time I'd also got into waterskiing and I liked the idea of messing around on the water. They told me that if I applied for redundancy I would receive £500.'

In the early 1970s that was a lot of money and Rowe, not for the first or last time, took a calculated punt. It was partly swayed by his changing domestic circumstances. 'I had every intention of going back to Portsmouth but I'd met my first wife, stupidly got married too young and stayed in Exmouth.' Linda gave birth to two children, a daughter called Emma and a son named Lee, but the marriage was not destined to last. 'It was too early and only lasted a couple of years. I was always ambitious and wanted to get on and get things done. If you look at a lot of successful people in business who have worked really hard to get where they are, very few of them have been able to hold their relationships together.' By the time her eldest child was seven, Linda had opted to refuse to allow their father access. The echoes of his non-relationship with his own father were deafening. Not for the first time, Rowe was left to ponder what might have been.

Before leaving the Marines, fortunately, he had already retrained as a marine engineer specialising in outboard motors with two-stroke engines. He fancied starting a business but could find no one who was prepared to lend him any money. He spent six months as a lorry driver before finding a lock-up garage in Exmouth and persuading his sister to lend him another £500. Exe Marina Services was born and, before long, it was going well enough to allow Tony to turn his attention from waterskiing to driving powerboats.

Catamarans swiftly became his passion but he had to be fit to race them. His business was based in Victoria Way in Exmouth; next door was a car repair garage run by Mervyn Richards, who played rugby for Withycombe RFC. Mervyn invited Tony to come up and train with them; on occasions he also turned out for the club's third team. Increasingly, though, powerboats were overtaking all else. Now weighing barely 11 stone dripping wet, Rowe was both fast and, it seemed, blessed. He raced catamarans for five or six years and, despite flipping them over at least once a year, escaped with nothing worse than a sore finger. In early June 1976 he won the British Championships, emerging as the fastest of 22 competitors in the Formula 3 class in Bristol docks with an enthusiastic Murray Walker in the commentary box.

That success led to him being invited up to Lake Windermere to make an attempt on the British circuit powerboating speed record. It was October and absolutely freezing when he and Mervyn set off in a Volkswagen camper bound for the Lake District. Finding an affordable hotel was out of the question so the pair slept in their van which had no heating. When they awoke the next morning, a mist hung over the lake and the water resembled a sheet of glass. When you are racing catamarans this is not good news: ideally a little bit of a rippled surface helps you fly further and faster. Stiff and weary from his night in the van, Rowe had no great expectations. He was amazed, therefore, to return to shore to discover he had broken the record. It still stood in 1994 when they discontinued that specific class. Subsequently he was also part of the only all-English team to win the Rouen 24-hour race, the powerboating equivalent of Le Mans. Life in the fast lane seemed to suit him.

After a while, though, Rowe could feel himself falling out of love with powerboats. 'Any money we won was going on wine, women and booze. I said to the racing mechanic, "I can't keep on doing this. I need to get a proper job."' In 1982, just in the nick of time, fate intervened. Margaret Thatcher's government announced its intention to privatise the telecommunications industry and Rowe could sense a potential opportunity. All he needed was some help. Reaching for the phone he called up his mate, Brian, who helped repair his boats.

'Brian, we need you. How about it?'

'Tony, I'm a boat builder, I can't even wire a fucking electrical socket.'

'Don't worry, we'll get you on the courses.'

It proved a life-changing call for both men. Brian Lodge would go on to become managing director of Rowe's company South West Communications, which would one day employ around 150 staff and have a turnover of approximately £25 million. Not that it was entirely plain sailing. For a while Rowe had two independent computer shops which proved successful, until the bigger high-street stores started to undercut him. Unable to compete, both his shops went bust. A chastened Rowe decided the time had come to sell his boat business and concentrate on bolstering his fledgling telephone company. At no time did he imagine he was destined to end up centre stage, like his real father, in a totally different arena.

* * * * *

Early in 1993, two men sat in The Globe pub in Topsham, drinking lager. They enjoyed each other's company and were regular drinking companions. Mostly they discussed wine, women and song. By this time Rowe had another failed marriage behind him – his second wife, like the first, was called Linda – and a third child, a daughter named Kim. Sadly, the relationship faltered when Kim was only four years old, with domestic bliss once again proving elusive. Hence the frequent visits to The Globe where the conversation would sometimes drift around to rugby. John Coxwell had played in the second row for Exeter in the 1980s and was now on the club's committee. On this particular day, he decided the time was right to have a quiet word with his mate Tony.

'Tony, the club's in a hell of a bloody mess. Would you consider sponsoring us?'

'Why do I want to sponsor a rugby club?'

'It would be great if you could help.'

'Really?'

'Just come along and meet our chairman. Then you can make your mind up.'

'Okay, okay. I'll meet him.'

By this stage Rowe had been running SW Comms for 10 years but had only attended a few Exeter games without being bowled over by his surroundings. The County Ground had barely changed since he had first experienced it as a teenager, wedged into the back of the old grandstand one evening to watch speedway or, more specifically, the great Ivan Mauger. The New Zealand world champion subsequently signed for Exeter in April 1973, with 10,500 fans turning up to watch his debut against Poole. He was a significantly bigger draw than the local rugby side and, in those days, speedway still caught plenty of imaginations. Exeter's track was narrow and the big steep fence surrounding it was notoriously unforgiving. 'It used to frighten the hell out of a lot of riders,' Mauger later confided to the *Express & Echo*. 'If there was a crash in front of you there was no escape.'

Considerably fewer regular punters attended the rugby, while the speedway riders also shared their home with the greyhounds. Rowe, on his first visit, could not believe the basic state of the facilities. 'The ladies' toilets were an old Second World War air-raid shelter. Concrete, with a bit of brick. It was diabolical. Then just through the gates on the left was something we called the Millennium Club. It was a ramshackle building which the greyhound owners used to use. It was awful. I can still remember the curly sandwiches. I asked them where the toilet was and they said, "It's over there." I went over to the corner and . . . well, let's just say you wouldn't let your dog go there.'

Things were basic on the field, too. If a player went down injured he could expect the arrival of a trusty club retainer called Les, armed with a bucket and a sponge. If a player was knocked out, there might be smelling salts. If he was covered in blood, a smear of grease usually did the job. When Rowe turned up for his meeting, the perilous nature of Exeter's finances became instantly apparent. The club were halfway through putting an extension on the clubhouse but were struggling to find the money to finish it off. Everyone was feeling the pinch, not least Andy Maunder as club captain. 'The club was pretty much bankrupt. We hardly toured, we had one shirt a year, the wives did the teas and we still paid subs. It was all needed because they had no money. In that period, from the mid-1980s to the mid-1990s, the club could have disappeared if they hadn't gone into the National Leagues.'

There was not even sufficient cash to pay for a playing strip for the following season but Rowe swiftly discovered John Baxter did not do defeatism. 'Why don't I buy the club?' he asked the incumbent chairman one day. The latter's response was short and not particularly sweet. 'It's not for sale,' growled Baxter. 'It'll never be for sale.'

The latter was determined not to be railroaded into selling the club down the Exe but, equally, he could see the potential value of Rowe's business acumen. It required a second meeting but, eventually, a modest deal was struck. Rowe agreed to become a sponsor and offered to put in £4,000 to put the club on a slightly more stable footing. He also proposed tidying up the facilities and making a few minor improvements. 'The first thing I persuaded them to do was to turn a storeroom into a shop. All they had before was a cupboard on the end of the same building as the ladies' toilet. The wife of one of our props, Phil Sluman, used to go in on match day and sell the occasional shirt out of the window. It was like a broom cupboard.'

Such amateur traditions, however, were under growing strain and everyone at Exeter could sense it. As Maunder recalls: 'It was a tense time. Even smaller clubs were paying quite healthy boot money and Exeter weren't. They couldn't afford it.' As captain, he had to fight to secure even a modest rise in the players' expenses. The noble tenets of respect and loyalty were all very well but they did not pay the bills. 'The club played for a very long time on the honour of playing for Exeter, the heritage and the region. They were fortunate they had a number of local people playing who had jobs which meant they could spare the time.'

The question was whether Exeter actively wanted to jump aboard this onrushing new wave and try and ride it like the skilful, athletic board surfers of Croyde and Newquay. Rowe remembers having a conversation with John Baxter in 1995 when the rumour mill was rife with talk of the sport potentially going professional. Baxter Snr would eventually change his mind but instinctively he was a traditionalist. 'Oh, I don't really think that's good for the game.' There was also a terse exchange with Maunder after Exeter had been beaten disappointingly at home one Saturday. 'We'd just lost and I was waiting for my first pint of ale for rehydration purposes. I remember Tony coming up to me at the bar and saying: "That really wasn't good enough. I'm putting a lot of money into this club."'

Maunder is a charming, patient man, but even he has a breaking point. Did Rowe not appreciate all the players were still paying subs and the club still had a tea rota in operation? 'You're not paying me,' replied the captain evenly. 'And this isn't the time.' The collision of old and new was unfolding on an increasingly frequent basis.

FIVE

WAITING FOR THE GREAT LEAP FORWARD

The portents for the future were less than auspicious at the end of the 1994/95 season. Exeter won just three of their 18 league games in Courage National Division Three and were duly relegated while the Yorkshire trio of Morley, Otley and Harrogate, among others, stayed up. With the now-returned Rob Baxter installed as skipper, however, the club bounced straight back in 1995/96 by scooping the Division Four title. The following year they continued their forward momentum by winning their last 14 league games on the trot to pip Fylde and Leeds to the Division Three title and reach the second tier of the English leagues for the first time. The timing of their promotion was critical: the top end of the English club game had now turned professional and Staddon, for one, reckoned it was a decisive outcome. 'If we'd not gone up, I really don't think we'd be where we are today.' Rob Baxter does not disagree. 'Looking back, if we'd have lost any one of our last 14 games we wouldn't have got promoted. Would it have happened eventually? I don't know. Maybe, but we never got dented into thinking, "We'll just settle into this league." That's probably been the most important factor about everything.'

Even now people still talk about the final game, away at Reading in mid-May, which had to be won to complete Exeter's rise to the next level. With Leeds' players looking on, Baxter remembers the hard-fought 13–3 victory as fondly as any. 'Reading were a decent side at the time but we had the feeling we were going to dog it out. It was a hot day and we just went flat out.' It was also the day John Baxter fully realised how much the club meant to his son. 'On the way home we stopped off at a big pub in Taunton. The players were absolutely shattered, exhausted. Robert was sitting in this chair across from me and he just collapsed. He'd not been drinking, he'd just given everything he had.' When John finally got home, he told Bobbi their son had done them all proud. 'I said to her, "I never knew it meant so much to Robert." That was the first time it really struck me. He couldn't have put more in as a player.'

The patient, happily, made a swift recovery, although sophisticated nutrition techniques did not play much of a part. 'Once our physio, Polly Evennett, had force-fed me a couple of Mars bars I felt absolutely fine. It was probably heat exhaustion as much as anything else. Nowadays you get told how to eat and hydrate properly. Back then, you didn't really want to go into a game with a bellyful of food. I'd have had beans on toast at 8 a.m., got on the bus at 9 a.m. and eaten nothing else.'

In the cold light of day there was also a genuine sense of achievement. Allied Dunbar 2 – or the 'Allied Crowbar' as it was known in Exeter – might not have been the Premiership but it was a higher level of league rugby than the club had ever experienced before. It was also an opportunity, as far as John Baxter was concerned, to remind Plymouth Albion of the new order of things. 'I was determined not to see Plymouth get above us. I remember one occasion at an Exeter end-of-season dinner.

We were struggling a little at the time and the Devon chairman was the guest of honour. He also happened to be chairman of Plymouth Albion. During my introduction I said it was our intention to become a Championship side. He got up and the first words out of his mouth were "We're already a Championship side." When he finished his speech I couldn't resist. I stood up and said, "There's no way I'm going to let anyone from Plymouth Albion have the last word at an Exeter dinner." There was such a huge roar. I remember thinking, "There's not much wrong with this rugby club."'

Life in 'Allied Crowbar 2', though, was far from straightforward. Exeter trailed in a lowly 11th in 1997/98 and would have been relegated had it not been for a timely reorganisation of the league structure. Along with bottom-placed Fylde, they stayed up only because the division was being expanded to 14 clubs for the 1998/99 season. Defeats in six of their final seven league games, even so, had concentrated everyone's minds. Rowe's view was that the time for prevarication was over. Either Exeter properly embraced the modern world and found ways to increase their income or they would slip back down into the lower divisions, probably forever. One day Rowe took a walk around the ground with John Baxter and asked about the pitch-side advertising boards.

'Are you getting the money for all these signs?'

'Some of them haven't paid for a couple of years.'

'Paint them out.'

'What?'

'We need to get more commercial.'

The men's and women's toilets also received a belated, if modest, overhaul. The dogs and their owners were given their marching orders to make room for some basic corporate facilities. Rowe removed the old benches from the grandstand and launched the Gold Card club, setting aside the best 50 seats in the house for those who signed up. The next step was to discuss precisely how high the club wanted to aim. John Baxter invited Rowe to share his thoughts.

'What do you think we should do, Tony?'

'Well, you've got a choice. Either you embrace professionalism and have a real go at it, which means putting some proper money in. Or you don't.'

'Would you be interested in working with us?'

'Yeah, okay. But the only way you're going to survive is by looking after your assets. You'll need to form a limited company.'

It made obvious business sense and Rowe, by now a director, was immediately invited to take over the reins. John Baxter, however, was adamant about one thing. Exeter would remain a members' club. Those in charge would never spend beyond their means. 'I was determined I was not going to bankrupt the club. I could see that coming as plain as day if the players were going to be paid.' It had been the same in his playing days, when Exeter would go over to Wales and see opposition players tucking brown envelopes into their kit bags. 'There had always been sham amateurism but at Exeter we'd never been part of that. I was well looked after as an Exeter player . . . we stayed in the best places, kit was provided and if we needed medical attention we got it. But no one was putting money into our pockets. We were concerned that we did things properly. We weren't going to take any shortcuts.'

Baxter could also see, however, that the club needed someone like Rowe. 'He was the right man at the right time. No two ways about it. He was hard-headed in his approach and absolutely clear about what he wanted. It was a case of "This is where we're going to go, back me or sack me." I backed him to the hilt. We needed to form a board of directors and get on a serious business footing. At the same time, I always saw it as the marriage of rugby and business. I never thought of one having a stranglehold over the other. It was a joint venture which has made us what we are today. I still believe that.'

Not everyone on the committee was instinctively keen but they were persuaded by Baxter that, ultimately, it was the best way forward. 'There were always arguments about one thing or another but once you'd made your decision and had sufficient backing, that's the way you'd go. You can never please all the people all of the time; you'll always have your critics. But there were some hard decisions to make and we made them. The people who mattered stuck with me through the thick of it and we are where we are now. They'd say, "Do what you think is best for it, John." There was a degree of trust that, at such an uncertain time, was really quite astonishing. It was an interesting time because you were dealing with the RFU as well. They were dyed-in-the-wool amateurs. They never wanted the game to go professional. People were in denial. We decided we'd do it but only within our means.'

Rowe's first priority was simple enough: to survive in the new dog-eat-dog world the club needed a decent coach. In conjunction with John Baxter and the club's then-chairman Steve Byrne, a shortlist was drawn up. The final candidates were invited down to the SW Comms offices at Marsh Barton for polite interrogation. Rowe remembers the day well. 'The last person we had to interview was this Irishman called Ian Bremner. We'd allowed three-quarters of an hour but two hours later he was still interviewing us.'

* * * * *

Bremner had something different about him, no question. He was a character and unapologetically old-school on occasions. He was also still slightly bruised from his experience at London Irish where the money had abruptly run out two months into the 1996/97 season following the club's promotion back to the Premiership under Clive Woodward. Bremner had been the man charged with renegotiating the contracts of good friends such as Conor O'Shea and Jeremy Davidson and was pondering his next move in Clonakilty – 'The home of the world's best black pudding' – when he popped into the newsagents to buy a paper. The shop had sold out of the *Irish Times* so he picked up a *Daily Telegraph* instead. Idly browsing through the jobs section, he came across an advert Exeter had placed in their search for a coach. At his interview, he made it clear the 'shambles' at London Irish had crystallised his views on professional rugby. 'Maybe that's why I came across so forcefully. I said to them, "If you say you're going to do something, do it. Don't piss around."'

His evident passion struck a chord and, in the spring of 1998, he was offered the job. Having watched them concede 50 points to Rotherham – 'They were absolutely dreadful' – in their final fixture of the season just before he took charge, he was instantly aware of the challenge awaiting him when pre-season training began in June. 'It was pretty shambolic. You couldn't train on the pitch for dog crap, so we trained on a couple of council pitches at Barton Fields. It was an open park so we would often run into similar problems. Things were at a pretty low ebb, no question.

'I remember the first training session. There had been no medical checks or off-season programmes set. At first about 35 players were there but after a while I noticed we were down to around 15. I walked in and there were 20 of them sitting outside the physio room. They were used to walking off the pitch if they got a bit tired or sore. They were all buggered.'

It also quickly transpired the coaching group had fallen out and, in some cases, weren't talking. There was plenty of scope, too, for conditioning and medical improvement under Dave MacLellan, a Scot who had previously worked at Leicester Tigers and had just returned from an educational spell in New Zealand. The way the Kiwis operated was more advanced than most English rugby clubs and, within six weeks of relocating to Exeter in 1997 with the vague notion of playing the odd game, MacLellan had been invited to become the club's physio. He was particularly keen to do something about the tiny medical room beside the dog track. 'There was a little pop window with mesh over it. Every time the speedway bikes went past, grit and stones would fly in. It was filthy. Every time you walked into the medical room you picked up handfuls of the stuff.'

It was not the only potential health hazard. One of the match-day duty doctors had a reputation for enjoying a liquid lunch and was not always easy to find when the time came to stitch up injured players. The weight training 'facilities' were located in the greyhound kennels. The good news, from MacLellan's perspective, was that the people were good fun. 'It was just a proper, earthy rugby club. There were no airs and graces at all.'

From the moment Bremner arrived, a shake-up was inevitable. The strong-minded Ulsterman – he was mad as a box of snakes, some reckoned – was not shy of delivering blunt messages to all concerned, Rowe included. 'Tony didn't know anything much about rugby but he and John Baxter were very ambitious. A lot of people have spent all their careers at one club and can't see beyond the doors of that. I always remember our prop, Richard Gibbins, saying to me that, before I came, they thought foreigners started at Crediton.' The Chiefs might have stayed in happy mediocrity, believes MacLellan, had Bremner not pitched up. 'Without him it wouldn't have happened. He was the biggest change in Exeter rugby club, bar none. He had enough brass neck to say, "I'm going to do this."'

It took a while, however, for MacLellan to convince Bremner that a slightly more modern approach might pay dividends on the fitness front. In the end everyone wanted the same thing: to propel the squad to a different level. Craig Townsend, brother of the future Scotland head coach and still a member of the playing squad, offered to help out part-time on the strength and conditioning side. As much as the players cursed under their breath that training was getting harder and more frequent, they could sense a new era dawning. Suddenly there were club shirts, ties and even proper kit bags with 'Exeter' written on them. Rock and roll, boys, rock and roll.

* * * * *

Rowe had also come to another significant conclusion: Exeter needed a new name. 'I told people we needed to get more commercial. We can't be called Exeter Rugby, it's boring.' To help rustle up a few ideas a local newspaper competition was organised to allow supporters to have their say. Given Exeter's ancient Roman connections there were plenty of historical-themed suggestions – the Centurions was among them – but no standout winner. Then, one day at the County Ground, an old-timer slid along the bar and nudged Rowe's elbow.

''Ere, Tony, how's it going with that name thing?'

'Not very well. We just can't find anything that sounds right.'

'Why don't you just call them Chiefs?'

'Why would we do that?'

'It's an old tradition in the West Country. You call your first team the Chiefs.'

Rowe went away and did some more research. Sure enough, proud Devon clubs like Bideford, Barnstaple and Teignmouth all used to call their first team the Chiefs. So, crucially, had Exeter as far back as 1908. A commercial artist was swiftly commissioned and came up with a striking headdress design. Everyone loved it, without pausing to consider how the indigenous communities of North America might one day feel about it. Exeter's beautiful cathedral green was hardly the Wild West, but the vast expanses of Dartmoor and Bodmin Moor were a different matter. A hint of country and western? Rowe instinctively liked the idea and decided to rebrand the club for the 1999 season.

Initially, at least, few people really noticed. Only after the club's move to Sandy Park did a few supporters start turning up with feathered headdresses and tom-tom drums. Harmless fun or cultural appropriation? Once they had eaten their obligatory pasty and sunk their first pint of cider, most patrons seemed more interested in on-field matters. Anyone with the slightest knowledge of rugby could see Exeter had the makings of a decent side. Their long-time legends, Maunder and Green, might have stepped aside but the region was still home to remarkable individuals such as big Bob Armstrong, the prodigiously tough Navy forward who had been the Royal Marines heavyweight boxing champion. A deal was struck with Plymouth Albion to bring back the ginger-haired Armstrong, who had led the Combined Services against the All Blacks back in 1993 and become an adopted Devonian legend.

Bremner had already recruited two decent half-backs, the Cornish scrum-half Ricky Pellow from Worcester – still at the club as skills coach – and Bryan Easson from Scotland. It also helped when, out of nowhere, a couple of quality Kiwis rocked up. Blair Foote was a loose forward good enough to have represented the junior All Blacks, while Brian Meinung was a squat, cannonball centre who played rugby differently to anyone the club had previously seen. Standing at the bar one day, MacLellan looked around him and realised he was now one of the smaller people in the room. 'You could start to see this was potentially quite a formidable bunch of boys.'

Bremner, however, was taking no prisoners on the training ground, putting an extra onus on MacLellan to ensure the players' bodies were flexible and strong enough to take it. Increasingly they could be found lying on the stained carpet at the County Ground doing stretching and core strength exercises. No yoga mats were involved and, all too often, the players were easily distracted. Someone, normally Armstrong, would be in the back row, farting loudly. Another poor unsuspecting victim would invariably have his shorts yanked down. Stick a load of bored rugby players in a confined space and some things never change.

Out on the pitch there were also some eye-raising moments. Long before the Bloodgate saga that engulfed Harlequins in 2009, several teams at Exeter's level were bending the rules by using fake blood to help ensure that casualties – the players were often the last to know – could be temporarily removed from the field for a check-up. 'It was definitely going on,' recalls MacLellan. 'We did it. I remember turning up at the County Ground with theatrical blood capsules and using them. At the time it felt like it was part of the game.' On one infamous occasion, however, a member of the backroom staff got carried away and applied an absurdly large dollop of tomato ketchup to a pad before slapping it to a player's ear. The referee took one look at the mess and uttered the immortal line, 'Can I have chips with mine?!' Such was life in the early years of so-called professionalism.

Slowly but surely, though, results were starting to pick up. The team finished fifth in Bremner's first season and fourth in 1999/2000, with only Rotherham, Leeds and Worcester ahead of them. A hard-nosed forward core was developing in Armstrong, Rob and Richie Baxter and the excellent Gary Willis in the back row, and Bremner also loved the combative example set by Phil John, the former Pontypridd hooker. 'He opened guys' eyes to what commitment really was. He was unbelievable and the guys loved him. He was a great character.'

Third place followed in 2000/01 and, with the Australian Chris Malone prospering at 10, they finished in the same position the following year as well. Even when Malone moved on after a single season to join Bath in the Premiership, his replacement Tony Yapp proved a shrewd signing and would become the club's record points scorer. Alistair Murdoch, the ex-Wallaby back, joined from Worcester and Ed Lewsey, Josh's brother, arrived from Exeter University. In both 2002 and 2003 Exeter reached the Powergen Shield final at Twickenham, only to lose 35–26 to Rotherham and 26–20 to Orrell respectively. There had also been individual recognition for both Baxter brothers and Sluman in a non-Premiership XV against a strong Australia side at Welford Road in 2001. Bremner and Adrian Davies of London Welsh were invited to coach the home side and found themselves pitting their wits against a certain Eddie Jones, newly in charge of the Wallabies. The tourists were made to work for their 34–22 victory, although the older Baxter endured an awkward night in the line-out against his six-foot-seven-inch-tall opponent, Justin 'The Plank' Harrison.

Bremner, though, knew an inspirational leader when he saw one. 'Rob was an excellent captain and a good player. Jesus, he was a menace on the field. I remember my backs coach, John Roberts, saying to me, "Referees must have an awful time with Rob. He never, ever stops." It was hard to penalise him because he wasn't doing anything illegal but, as they say in Ireland, he'd bite the arm off you to get at the ball and make it difficult for the opposition. He was outstanding in terms of his leadership.' The Barbarians took a similar view and invited Baxter to lead them against the Portuguese national side in Lisbon in 2004. Just four years later he coached the Baa-Baas against the Combined Services, a distinguished double in anybody's book.

SIX

ROAD WARRIORS

Life in Exeter was being further enlivened by an increasing number of entertaining off-field characters. Among the new arrivals was a talkative, Cheshire-born lock called Chris Bentley, who turned up in the summer of 2004 with plenty of northern attitude, a philosophy degree from Liverpool University and an endless supply of priceless old-school anecdotes. As a 17-year-old, Bentley had joined New Brighton where he had learned his trade from several veterans of the formidable Waterloo side of the 1970s and 1980s. Laurie Connor, Shaun Gallagher and Nick Allott all had black belts in rugby's dark arts and the teak-tough Connor opened Bentley's eyes to a whole new world. 'Whoever we played he'd always be muttering, "I fucking hate these." He was proper old-school hard. He had a wrist support which he'd show to the ref, then he'd go back to the dressing room and put this steel plate down it. He'd usually be on the bench but if there was a problem he'd come on and deal with it.'

Most Tuesdays and Thursdays young Bentley would return home with black eyes and a split lip to show for his latest educational rugby experience. His league debut at Macclesfield was another eye-opener. 'Our tight-head prop Steve Dorrington told me, "If you don't punch their hooker at the first scrum I'm going to hit you." That was my job; I had to do it. Then I'd hide behind him.' A resourceful front-jumper, with lifting in the line-out now permitted, he also had to contend with the great Wade Dooley, who had also joined New Brighton but was struggling to dominate aerially because his teammates found him too heavy to lift.

Bentley's next move was to ambitious Orrell. Again it was to prove character-building. Wigan's backer Dave Whelan had decided to get involved in pro union in the north-west and Maurice Lindsay, the Wigan chairman, called Bentley in to see him. 'We see you as a young Andy Farrell, Chris. You're a proper leader.' Even Bentley himself was unconvinced but held his tongue: he wasn't about to turn down a contract offer worth twice the amount he had decided he would accept. It was certainly not a dull period: the squad's aim, for a while, seemed to be to discover how hard they could party during the week and still win at the weekend. Bentley also recalls their Australian coach, Jim McKay, taking a left-field approach to preparation. 'We had a big night out in Liverpool and were as hung-over as sin the next morning. Instead of talking about rugby he pulled out an old VHS video of surfers for us to watch. We're all sitting there thinking, "Who the fuck is this?"'

Orrell kept on recruiting as if there was no tomorrow, paying Premiership rates at a third-tier level and training at the JJB Stadium. In the dressing room it became a running joke that if your opposite number outperformed you, Orrell would buy him. In the case of the future England No. 8 Nick Easter, that was exactly what happened. One good game for Rosslyn Park and he was offered a contract to play in the north-west. It could not last indefinitely and, abruptly, Whelan pulled his money out.

The club went into freefall with two players, Adam Jackson and Simon Haughton, hanging around for two successive relegation seasons on salaries reputed to be worth £80,000 a year.

Amid all this madness, Bentley sustained a freak injury during a warm-up when, descending from a line-out, he caught a stud in Richard Wilks' sock and wrecked his ankle. He managed to engineer a short-term move to Biarritz but suspected his sojourn in France would be short when the coach picked a 22-stone prop in the second row ahead of him. Coventry subsequently offered him a deal but he was not keen, given they had just sacked a good friend of his. That left Exeter. He had few fond memories of playing against them for Orrell. 'We could never beat them. I was this gobby, bolshie kid who thought he was tough. Whenever I played Exeter you'd try and have a scrap. You'd pick on, say, Keith Brooking and about five people would hit you back. "Hang on," I'd say, "I'm fighting with him." They'd reply, "No, you're fighting with all of us." I liked that.' There was something about the County Ground that also appealed to him. 'The County Ground was iconic. They all had these red Nissan Almeras which they used to park all round the pitch. We'd play them and think, "This is cool."'

In late September 2003, finally, Orrell beat their tormentors 40–26 at the County Ground. Bentley could not resist the opportunity to rub it in with some choice verbals. 'Every time we scored I was shouting at Rob Baxter, "Get under your sticks, old man; you've got bandy legs, you're rubbish, you've got nothing." Rob doesn't remember it but, after four years of getting beaten up, it was so important to me to win.' It clearly helped when Bremner was deciding whether to offer him a contract in the summer of 2004. The coach indicated he was thinking of moving Baxter to the middle of the line-out, installing Bentley at the front and allowing him to scrummage on the tight-head side. Happy days, thought Bentley, and packed his bags for Devon.

He was so confident of making an impact that, when the local paper rang to ask for a few details about him, he told them everything: his battles with the Baxter brothers, the many physical scraps he had enjoyed. In the *Express & Echo* the next day the headline – 'Enforcer Checks In' – left nothing to the imagination. The general view within the squad was that if the Baxters read it, the new boy was as good as dead. There was much barely suppressed mirth, then, when the unsuspecting newcomer turned up late to his first training session at Exeter Saracens RFC, sporting a Biarritz tan and some flash French gear previously owned by Serge Betsen. 'Oi, lads,' boomed a voice from the back of the room, 'it's the fucking Enforcer!' As Bentley would find out, Exeter was not the place to go for a quiet life.

* * * * *

The club house just up the road from the County Ground was where most of the fun started. Among the residents were the Fatialofa brothers – Junior and Mark – and Tony 'The Beast' Walker and their door was never locked. The squad's student contingent lived just around the corner and Bentley swiftly discovered that match days followed a familiar pattern. 'We'd drink in the club after the game until it started to thin out, then walk up the hill to the Walkabout. Then we'd go across to Rococo's, even though we still had to pay to go in. There were other nightclubs offering us free drinks but we always went to Rococo's.'

With, at most, nine or ten players masquerading as full-time professionals, it presented a tricky challenge for the management. Increasingly it became common practice for the squad to train as early as 6 a.m. so the Baxter brothers could attend the session with the rest of the squad before heading back to work on the family farm. The pros would then be put through a skills session in the middle of the day to justify their supposed elevated status.

Even their playbook, though, made knowing reference to the club's amateur days and, specifically, the great Bob Staddon. The latter had been a silky-smooth attacking full-back but hated the fighting that frequently broke out. Legend had it that a 29-man brawl had once erupted in a game between Devon and Cornwall. Staddon was the only player not involved, preferring to keep at a safe distance and call out, 'Guys, why don't you all just stop it?' Within the current squad it was decided this was merely a cover story: it became accepted wisdom that, beneath the mild facade, Staddon was actually the toughest hombre ever to have played the game. When anyone ran a hard line back in towards the forwards it become known as a 'Staddon line'. Players would shout 'Staddon!' every time they were about to cut back against the grain. Soon enough, the in-joke began to apply to off-field activities. One end-of-season Sunday a group of players were in the Walkabout, ordering pints of snakebite and blackcurrant, when somebody yelled 'Staddon me in!' prior to chinning his pint. The event became known as 'Suicide Bob Staddon Sunday' and T-shirts with the letters 'SBS' scrawled on them in black marker pen were produced. To this day the squad's end-of-season social is still known as 'Staddon Sunday'. Harmless fun but also a perfect way to bond a disparate bunch of players.

The unorthodox recipe seemed to work. It was also no coincidence that Exeter were beginning to forge closer links with the Marines, based just down the road in Lympstone. Sir Clive Woodward's England had travelled down to the camp in the build-up to the 1999 Rugby World Cup and Exeter's attitude was simple: if it's good enough for England, it's probably good enough for us. Pre-season would involve assault courses, log runs and being flogged up and down Exmouth beach, all with the aim of pushing ever onwards and upwards.

With morale high and confidence rising, the Chiefs finished second in the league in 2004/05, even beating the eventual champions Bristol 23–12 at home in February after Bremner had delivered one of the more rousing speeches of his tenure. Those present remember him going round the dressing room one by one and exhorting every player, not least Bentley, to give his all. 'Bentos, if you haven't let them know you're the boss in the first 10 minutes you've failed. You've not just failed me, you've failed yourself and you've failed your mates. You need to get hold of Ollie Hodge and slot him.' Bentley and his teammates were fortunate the referee seemed happy to turn a blind eye. 'He let us get away with murder. I was going berserk, thumping everyone. The ref came up to me afterwards and said, "It's okay, I don't like Bristol."' The icing on the cake was a last-quarter try for the so-called 'Enforcer' after a fine run by his winger Sione Kepu. 'I was a bit of an opportunist and ran 20 yards to score under the posts. I was dancing around a bit, enjoying the moment, until I heard Rob Baxter yelling, "Put the fucking ball down!"'

What really galvanised everyone, though, were the away trips. With Exeter there is no such thing as a short hop, their West Country rivals Bristol or Plymouth excepted. For that reason, insisted the senior players, it was crucial to enjoy the ride, win or lose. Among the more popular sources of entertainment was the 'Thing to Bring' which involved turning up with a specific item for every coach journey. The squad would be split into teams with the gregarious front-rower Keith Brooking, who had inherited the role of fines master from the departed Armstrong, in charge of compliance. On one famous occasion Brooking ordered everyone to bring a magnetic pasty. The older heads knew about a local shop where they sold fridge magnets, including one designed in the shape of a pasty. Younger students such as Adam Staniforth and Haydn Thomas took the challenge more literally and turned up with real pasties into which they had hopefully inserted hastily purchased magnets.

With his fines book at the ready and carrying a large steel board, Brooking decreed that all magnetic pasties were required to stick to his board for 10 seconds to avoid a £2 fine. Witnesses still snort with laughter at the memory of the pasties starting to crumble and disintegrate as the whole bus joined in the countdown. Even on the rare occasions when the team travelled by train, the 'Thing to Bring' would apply. On one such trip to London, Brooking decided to put the relatively new drug Viagra on the list. MacLellan was working at a private hospital in Exeter at the time and, sensing a chance to avoid a fine, popped in to see the head pharmacist.

'This is going to sound slightly bizarre but could I borrow some Viagra?'

'What?'

'I'll bring it back on Monday, I promise.'

'It's a controlled drug. If this comes back to me I'm in trouble. Which means you'll be the one in trouble.'

MacLellan knew he was pushing the boundaries but his endless reassurances finally paid off. Feeling ever so slightly smug, he reported to the bus with the pills. Handing the precious blister pack to Brooking for inspection, he could tell the latter was impressed. 'Is this them? I've always wondered what they look like.' At which point there was a loud pop as Brooking burst one of the foil seals. MacLellan's entire professional life flashed in front of him. 'No-ooo! You have to put that back. This is my career. Actually, come to think of it, I don't have a career any more.' Too late. Already the pills had mysteriously vanished and the rest of the physio's journey up to London – 'How do I tell them on Monday morning that I've lost their Viagra?' – was painful in the extreme. Only much later in the evening did the blister pack make a miraculous reappearance, with the foil helpfully stuck down.

Every so often there were also initiations to be conducted. This usually involved an individual removing all his clothes, standing at one end of the bus, and downing a drink. The next requirement would be to run down to the other end of the bus and down another drink. Once four 'laps' had been completed it was time to sing a song. On the way up and down the bus there was also every chance of being whacked by clothes hangers or whatever else the rest of the team might have to hand. One week someone even went to Ann Summers and came back with a paddle.

Down, down, deeper on down. Increasingly Exeter were a drinking club masquerading as a rugby team. Joining the 'Hundred Club' – drinking 100 shots of beer, which equated to six pints, in 100 minutes – became a badge of honour. Another regular bus favourite was the drinking game 'Shithead', which involved getting rid of all your cards until one loser remained. The latter would have to stand up and say, 'I am the one and only,' at which point everyone else, in unison, would shout, 'Shithead!' The loser's team would then be required to sink a pint. The Baxters would invariably be together as would the two Tonys, Yapp and Walker. The latter pair were known as 'TNT', Yapp having previously been part of a combo named 'Fat Boy Slim' with Brooking. Another regular pairing were Richard Liddington and Alan Miller, known as 'Mandela' because they lived in a nearby block called Mandela House. On one infamous occasion 'Mandela' lost eight rounds of Shithead on the bounce. Not surprisingly Liddington and Miller – known to all as 'Mist' – started to struggle. Bentley recalls Rob Baxter being less than sympathetic. 'Rob used to love breaking people. He'd be on the bus going, "If you don't want to drink it just quit. Just say we're better men than you are." He was like one of those physical trainers in the Royal Marines.'

By now it had become a game within a game: Liddington urging Miller to hang tough, Baxter not remotely inclined to back down.

'Just say the Baxters are better men.'

'Mandela never quits, Mandela never quits!'

'Just say I'm a better man!'

'I don't think I can do this much longer!'

'Don't quit, don't quit!'

It forged a spirit which spilled over on to the field and endures to this day. Even now, almost two decades later, 'TNT' are still claiming to hold the upper hand over 'Mandela'. If people were ill, broken or otherwise unable to join in on the bus that was fine. At all other times, though, it was about sacrificing yourself for the greater good. A team that socialised and laughed together would be more inclined to look out for each other under enemy fire. Bremner, who used to enjoy sitting at the front of the bus with a bottle of wine himself, took the view that a few drinks were okay if no one got arrested. 'As long as I was not getting calls from the police or players' wives the following day I was more than happy that they enjoyed themselves.' One day, to celebrate Murdoch's impending wedding, the team stopped by for an end-of-season drink at a bar next to Exeter St David's station. 'The players will be here in a moment,' Bremner informed the landlord. 'They're just on the bus putting their clothes back on.' Exeter may not have been the best side in the land – yet – but they knew how to enjoy themselves.

SEVEN

CHARIOTS OF FIRE

With momentum starting to build, Rowe was also busy on the stadium front. The County Ground may have been the club's spiritual home but its limitations had long since become obvious. As far back as the mid-1970s, Bob Staddon and Andy Cole had been looking at plots of land where a new ground might conceivably be based, not least in Topsham where Exeter University's sports grounds are now based. 'If we could have sold the County Ground we would have gone,' recalls Staddon. 'Thank the Lord, we never did.'

John Baxter was among those who had argued for years that Exeter's entire future revolved around making the best possible decision for the long term. When the game went professional, he stood firm against those who thought it was a perfect moment to sell up. 'We were being pressurised to sell the County Ground to pay the players and make sure we got into the Premiership. Thank goodness the decisions we made when we were an amateur side were the right ones.' Over the years he had earned a certain reputation for his refusal to take the easy, popular option. 'The one thing I could do was bang my fist on the table. People knew I meant what I said.'

Given his two sons were playing in the first team, both naturally keen to play at the highest level possible, there was no shortage of debate in the Baxter household. Rob, for one, still recalls his dad's words of warning. 'I remember Dad saying to me, "The most important thing is not to rush, son. Let's just see what happens."

'To be fair to Dad and a few other boys on the committee, those decisions not to sell were really important when you look back now. The County Ground has been the key foundation for everything we've achieved. It would have been very easy to have lost it. It was on prime land in the middle of St Thomas. There were loads of opportunities to sell it a lot earlier for a lot less money.'

Father and son were also keenly aware that plenty of rival teams had sold their birthright and never recovered. 'An awful lot of clubs lost their crown jewels,' recalls Rob. 'They'd think, "We'll sell it now and move to a nice little ground on the edge of the city with a couple of little grandstands. It'll be amazing." Actually it's not. You've got no way of making any serious income. Once you've spent the money in the bank, that's it. You're done. The business acumen and drive to create not just a rugby club but a business here has been amazing but we still needed an asset to make it work. It could have been frittered away so easily so many times.'

By the early 2000s, though, things were finally coming to a head. Rowe was clear in his own mind that Exeter could be a Premiership club but he needed a stadium that fulfilled the minimum ground criteria. The city council, however, wouldn't let him expand the County Ground. They pointed out that, originally, the land had been sold to the County Ground and Athletic Company with a covenant stating no building over two storeys could be built upon it. Rowe's response was that if they didn't waive the covenant the club would sell the site for housing. It turned out that Exeter City Council wished to regenerate the

St Thomas area anyway and were keen to be helpful. It wouldn't be the easiest site in the world to clear but the club moving elsewhere suited all concerned. Rowe was sent a plan of the city marked with a few possible spots to which the Chiefs could relocate. One of the few options with sufficient space was a 23-acre site at Sandy Park Farm owned by the Pratt family, close to Junction 30 of the M5 on the outskirts of the city.

The ever-shrewd Rowe instinctively felt it was a good option. To fulfil his ambitions for the club it was essential to have a stadium that would meet the Premiership's strict ground criteria. It would also make a perfect conference centre; the biggest hotel meeting room in Exeter at the time could accommodate only 110 people. Nor could it be said, hand on heart, that the tired old County Ground was packing them in. 'You could almost namecheck the fans,' recalls Bentley. 'When we played away from home, you definitely could.'

The average home attendance when the club finally moved in 2006 was around 1,800 but many of them were reluctant to shift. Back in his earliest days in charge, Rowe had grown accustomed to being at the County Ground with his long-time business associate and friend Keiron Northcott and gazing sceptically around him. 'Keiron, there's 400 people here today. I bet when we check the turnstile money half of them haven't paid.' He took to hanging around by the turnstiles to see who was sneaking in for free. Those he caught were forced to come back through the turnstile and open their wallets.

He was equally conscious that, to make the move to Sandy Park worthwhile, the club's old home needed to be sold for the best possible price. Happily the UK housing market was approaching its absolute peak at that precise moment. Wimpey, Bovis and Bellway Homes were all interested in purchasing the 5.6-acre County Ground site, ramping up the price even further. It went to sealed bids, with Bellway offering to pay £11.5 million, significantly higher than the initial valuation of £6.5 million. Rowe advised the club's members to grab it with both hands. The deal was agreed and in 2003, a few weeks prior to England winning the Rugby World Cup in Australia, plans were unveiled for a modern 8,200-capacity stadium with a leisure centre attached. The blurb predicted 'a win-win situation for everyone – a historic opportunity to boost Exeter's emerging status as the sporting and cultural capital of the west'. There were a few, even so, who didn't fancy the idea of trekking out of the city to some windblown new modern stadium. As Rowe recalls: 'Some thought it was too far out of town by the motorway. But I just had a hunch it would all work out.'

* * * * *

By now anyone who had encountered Rowe knew better than to dismiss his 'hunches' out of hand. Perhaps the most extreme example was the hobby he had chanced upon prior to getting involved with rugby. Driving up the North Devon Link Road towards Barnstaple one day en route to a business meeting, he found the carriageway blocked. To pass the time, he pulled over at a local garage for a packet of fags. With time to kill, he wandered idly around the back of the building and came across a big fire engine with a bush growing out of it. Suddenly he was the five-year-old Tony again, standing on the street corner in Gosport and watching a similar fire engine, bell ringing, with a big wooden ladder and a big wheel on the back. Fire! Fire! His reverie was abruptly shattered by the voice of the garage owner behind him.

'Do you want to buy it?'

'What?'

'The fire engine. It's for sale.'

'Why would I want to buy that? No, thanks.'

The abandoned fire engine with a bush sprouting out of it,

however, became lodged in his consciousness. Just over a year later, by sheer fluke, he found himself back at the exact same spot, stuck in traffic with the link road shut because of an accident. Once again he decided he needed a smoke. Walking round the back of the garage, he fully expected to find the fire engine had gone. But no. There were now three of them. The garage owner, recognising a possible sales opportunity, popped out to say hello.

'Do you want to buy it?'

'No.'

'Well, if you do you've got to take those other two as well.'

'Eh?'

The siren call could be resisted no longer. By the time he'd returned to his car, Rowe had bought himself three wrecked old fire engines. Back at work everyone thought he'd lost his marbles. It required a friend with a big low-loading lorry to make three separate journeys simply to pick them up. Stripping them down and doing them up again was also going to be a major job, requiring dedication and effort. Shortly afterwards his fleet was further increased: popping down to a car auction in Exeter to buy a van, he returned with another abandoned fire engine which, it turned out, had previously seen service in Ottery St Mary. Two of the smaller fire engines he had originally purchased were also from Ottery, with one dating back to 1765. Before long it became an obsession. His collection grew to 16 full-size antique fire engines, with another 350 miniature models lining the walls of his office. Given his other lifelong interest – collecting British stamps – it was a wonder he found any time for rugby, let alone a relationship with Sharon, now his third wife.

Sharon, by coincidence, had grown up in a house which had backed on to the County Ground, looking at the rugby and speedway out of her bedroom window. How many people end up living with the person who sold their childhood view for housing? She and Rowe nevertheless got together and one evening in 2000, she told him she was pregnant. Rowe had just got in from work and was due back out to the Digger's Rest pub in Woodbury Salterton to meet the club's recent Samoan signing To'o Vaega. The newcomer was teetotal and did not smoke, while Rowe's then-lifestyle was appreciably different. 'I was drinking probably six pints of beer a day and smoking three to four packets of Hamlet. It wasn't good.'

Sitting opposite Vaega, and mulling over his previous shortcomings as a father, he made another instinctive decision. 'I'm going to give up smoking,' he said, suddenly. 'It's my last chance. My first two children . . . I lost them. I split with my daughter Kim's mother when Kim was about four. I want to enjoy watching my son grow up.' That evening he smoked his last Hamlet and cut back on his drinking. It has been worth it. Taking his youngest son, Morgan, to the school bus stop for a decade and a half has subsequently given him as much pleasure as any business deal.

Back at the rugby club, meanwhile, the world beyond Devon was starting to take an interest. Even the *Guardian* was curious enough to send its rugby man down west to find out what Exeter were up to. With five games remaining in March 2005 the Chiefs were a single point behind Bristol Shoguns (bears had not yet been spotted roaming through Clifton) ahead of a meeting between the top two clubs at the Memorial Ground. Promotion to the Premiership still appeared Bristol's to lose but the Chiefs were starting to believe they could throw a spanner in the West Country works. 'Plymouth would die if we went up,' chuckled Bremner. 'That's their worst nightmare. They'd close down in mourning for a month.'

Looking around the County Ground, however, it was still not obvious that Exeter were ready to take the giant leap. Pride of place in their trophy cabinet belonged to two Allied Dunbar Fair Play awards from the late 1990s. There had been a break-in on the Tuesday night but, in the absence of anything obviously of value, the thief had nicked the cigarette machine off the wall. With the move to Sandy Park still a year away, there was talk of sharing for a year with Exeter City at St James Park. Rowe, either way, reckoned the Premiership's leading officials were not terribly keen on welcoming a bunch of yokel upstarts. 'The Premiership clubs don't want you unless you're box office. Do they want us? Probably not. They might take Bristol but we're not terribly fashionable.'

There was a clear risk, too, of Exeter over-reaching themselves. Plenty of established clubs, from Moseley to Wakefield to West Hartlepool, had made that fatal error. The players, though, still fancied a crack at the high life. Murdoch, who had already endured the perils of over-ambition at Bedford and was now juggling his rugby with a day job as a pensions adviser, looked around the dressing room and saw no desire in there to turn down promotion should it materialise. 'We know there's a huge gap between us and the Premiership. Look at Worcester. They didn't lose a game last year and they've still been flirting with bottom place all season. But every single one of us would still want to test ourselves in the Premiership.'

In hindsight, it was probably just as well Murdoch's desire for instant gratification never materialised. Only one side was ever in it at the Memorial Ground, Bristol cruising to a 68–15 victory which featured a hat-trick of tries for the Argentine centre Manuel Contepomi. The end-of-season table saw Bristol promoted with 105 points, four ahead of Exeter in second place. In terms of clearing the final hurdle, the Chiefs clearly had more work to do.

* * * * *

The gap would also have to be bridged without one of their all-time warriors. By 2005 Rob Baxter was 34 and starting to feel his playing days were up. He was beginning to suffer from painful 'stingers', courtesy of a nasty collision against Penzance and Newlyn. 'We were in a driving maul and as we came out the other side I got my head clipped by someone running into me. After that, any time I got clipped in a certain way it would fire up again.

Sometimes I would be having two or three stingers a game.' He knew it was all over when, during a very gentle ball-handling drill in training, someone ran behind him and nudged his shoulder, causing one of the worst stingers he'd ever had. 'Now you'd have four to five hours' intensive physio every day until those symptoms were gone, the neck muscles had loosened up and everything was realigned.' He kept playing but it was increasingly a case of mind over matter and he played his 394th and final game for the club that April. 'In the end rugby became a bit of a pain. My hips and groin were starting to play up and I'd done both my knees. It got to the stage when I thought, "I'm still captain, I'm still in the first team, I'm still first choice, I'm coaching at Exeter University, it might not be the worst time to finish."'

Squeezing in the uni coaching, on top of playing and farming, was not entirely done for the pure joy of it. 'Unless you're a bit of a fool, most people realise that small family farms are not gold mines. They don't just sit there and pour thousands of pounds into everyone's pockets. In those early years rugby was an important source of income for us as a family.' With two young children, Annie and Jack, now at home, it made for a ridiculously hectic weekly schedule. 'You'd be at the gym in the morning at 6 a.m., then go and do a day's work and be back at training at 6.30 p.m. Three times per week. I'd combine that with coaching the uni on a Monday night. They'd have matches on a Wednesday; if they had an away game I could be back in the middle of the night.

'I still talk to Jo about it. When I was working hard to become a young coach, I'm not quite sure how she coped with two young kids. Sometimes I'd be on a bus on a Friday to an away game, play on Saturday and not be back until the early hours. Sunday would be an off day but then you'd do it all again.' All that investment in time and energy was to prove worth it in the end. 'It's nice to know it wasn't all for nothing. Jo knew I really wanted to do it but, at the time, it was pretty selfish in a lot of ways. Maybe it's what you have to do to give yourself enough opportunities to be either good enough or in people's minds when they start looking for coaches.'

Initially it was line-outs that intrigued him, although as Exeter's captain he was used to talking to the media or at dinners and was also involved in selection prior to Bremner's appointment. 'As we started to professionalise I started calling the line-outs. I started taking home the video analysis of opposition line-outs that Ian had clipped. I'd work through various ploys and decide what calls we'd use and that ignited an interest in coaching.'

When Sam Howard, who had been coaching at the university and playing for Chiefs, moved on, the opportunity arose for Baxter to do likewise. 'I was asked whether it was something I'd like to do. It felt like the next step on from what I was doing at the club. I really enjoyed it and it taught me a lot about coaching.' The students' enthusiasm was infectious and some future Premiership players – Haydn Thomas, James Hanks – emerged from the Exeter Uni pathway. 'It taught me what I still say to coaches now – to believe in what you see. If you see players doing good things you've got to trust it a little bit.'

When he had gone in to see Rowe to ask for his advice on what he should do next, however, the answer was not quite what he wanted to hear. The chief executive told him his best career option, coaching-wise, was to go away and gain some more experience outside the Exeter bubble at another Championship club. It was a blunt reminder that, in coaching, there are no guarantees.

The good news was that, in the short term, he was clearly a natural candidate to help coach the Chiefs' second team alongside Keith Fleming. In the first match of the new season they travelled up to London Welsh and enjoyed a good win while the first team came a cropper at home to Penzance. With the move to Sandy Park now barely nine months away, the onus was on the first team to crank things up as well.

EIGHT

THE HARDER THEY COME

The big question was how long Rowe's patience would last if his Premiership aspirations remained unfulfilled. Despite the fact the enthusiastic Bremner had signed a new three-year contract just 12 months earlier, pressure had been steadily mounting. In the December of the previous season, with Chiefs flying high, Rowe offered to increase his coach's playing budget to make promotion a reality. 'I'll give you a quarter of a million quid; go out and sign enough players to make sure we finish the season strong.' Bremner had spent Christmas in the office, phoning almost anything with a pulse, but everyone decent was under contract and he couldn't find the players he wanted. When Exeter had subsequently been hammered by a clearly superior Bristol, Rowe was less than thrilled.

In the summer of 2005, for the first time, Bremner sensed potential trouble brewing. He and Rowe had been great mates – even going on holiday together with their families – but this was clearly business. 'We used to have a meeting every year at the end of the season when we'd go out and get completely hammered.

"Tony," I said, "we'll get promoted sometime."' For the first time, he sensed Rowe was slightly dubious.

The new campaign began sluggishly. Rather than kicking off their final season at the County Ground with a flourish, something was awry. Inside the first four league games Exeter were soundly beaten 35–13 at Plymouth and 16–43 at home by Cornish Pirates. Opponents were beginning to work the Chiefs out and, tactically, rugby was also changing. In October, Exeter went up to the Stoop to face Harlequins, still on the rebound following their relegation from the Premiership the previous season. It was carnage. Ugo Monye contributed five of his side's 12 tries in a 70-point drubbing and both Bentley and Junior Fatialofa were unceremoniously hauled off early in the second half. The former was not entirely unhappy to see Quins rattle up even more points in their absence. 'Me and Junior were quite glad they carried on scoring. We were in the stands singing "The Mighty Quin" and chanting "Ugo!"'

The mood was darkening even before an inauspicious trip to Coventry, when the journey up to the Midlands took longer than expected. Because of the squad's delayed arrival, Bremner decided to call a team meeting before allowing his players to go and have their evening meal. By that stage, unfortunately, half the squad had already disappeared off into town in search of food. Bremner hit the roof, the players rolled their eyes and the atmosphere in the team room was as strained as the club's most loyal servants could remember.

The bad vibes swiftly reached the committee, who were advised the players were on the verge of open revolt. Rowe needed a swift upturn in results while Bremner's suspicion was that John Baxter was lobbying for his son Rob to take over. Morale-sapping home defeats to Otley and Plymouth did little to lift the gloom, with a 37–35 loss at Newbury two days after Christmas compounding everyone's frustration. Bonuses were on offer for either a win or a losing bonus point but Tony Walker, who had gone on as a replacement, gave away a late penalty at a line-out and the extra money was instantly blown. Walker copped plenty of heat on the bus home but, ultimately, the buck stopped with the head coach.

The final straw proved to be a 23–16 defeat to London Welsh in front of 830 spectators at Old Deer Park on 14 January 2006. It was the Chiefs' fourth straight league defeat, their worst run since November 2000, which left them in seventh place in the table. Sharp post-match words were exchanged on the field, Bremner letting his team have it within earshot of supporters before the players had even walked past the cricket square back to the dressing rooms. The players, by now, were growing disillusioned and sensed the Bremner era was coming to a natural end.

Despite the result they also saw no reason not to enjoy a few drinks on the journey home. Something inside Bremner snapped. Marching to the back of the bus, he exploded like a Northern Irish version of Mount Vesuvius. 'You'd much rather learn words to songs than play rugby,' he stormed, his anger lending a real edge to his Ulster rasp. By now it was clear he had lost the dressing room. Before he had even made it back to his seat at the front of the bus, the winger Gary Kingdom stuck on Bon Jovi's 'Livin' on a Prayer' – 'Woo-aaah, we're halfway the-rre!' – and the raucous choir was back in full cry. Everyone on board could sense the director of rugby's days in charge were numbered.

Sure enough, Rowe did not hesitate. On the Sunday evening he phoned Bob Staddon to ask if he was in a position to take temporary charge of the first team. Staddon, a retired teacher, offered to come back as manager with Rob Baxter as coach. By Tuesday morning it had come to pass. Bremner was called in and told his time was up. That same afternoon he was in a solicitors' office discussing severance payments. Rowe did not relish wielding the axe – Bremner had married Keiron Northcott's niece – but has never been the type to stand idly by. 'I could see things were faltering. I had a word with Rob and said, "Look, I'm going to let Mr Bremner go and I want you to step in as interim coach."' In Rowe's view, cutting ties with Bremner was the only way forward. 'We were a good first division club but the reality was that he couldn't take us that little bit further. I learned years ago in the Royal Marines that you're only as strong as your weakest link. If, however, you use everybody's talents collectively you're strong. He never quite got that. I actually liked the guy. You've got to acknowledge the fact he took an amateur club to a semi-professional club batting up at the top of the Championship. He's never spoken to me from that day to this and it was probably the toughest thing I've had to do. But if I hadn't got rid of him we wouldn't be where we are today.'

Bremner – then and now – felt differently. 'Despite circumstances I have great admiration for what they've done and what Tony and Rob have achieved. But when you fall out with Tony you fall out with him. He's that kind of a guy. It had happened in the past but I thought, "No, we're good mates, it couldn't happen to me." We did a lot together. It took me a long time to get over it. I'd put my heart and soul into it.' Perhaps most poignantly of all, he had spent many hours helping to design the rugby facilities for the new stadium. 'I planned all of the ground floor but I've never been there.' As countless top-level coaches have found to their cost, professional sport giveth but it also taketh away.

* * * * *

With Bremner no longer around, appointing Rob Baxter on a temporary basis was not the toughest call of Rowe's career. Baxter already had his own ideas about how best to go about winning rugby matches. On 25 February 2006, barely a month after being thrown the keys, his first big test loomed. Harlequins

– Monye and all – were due down at the County Ground to face the same team they had recently smashed by 70 points. The visitors were in for a shock. Exeter's notoriously heavy pitch was even damper than usual. Some even alleged – it was vehemently denied, of course – that big agricultural water bowsers had been quietly brought in two days prior to the game specifically to douse the five-metre strips closest to the touchlines and ensure Quins' dangerous wide men would have to plough through Devonshire treacle. 'They're not running round us,' Baxter told his players. He also stressed the importance of disrupting the Londoners' line-out. In the previous game, Quins had surprised Exeter with 'bookend' line-outs; instead of numbers 2, 4 or 6 jumping as tradition dictated, the modern variation was to station a prop at either end of the line-out which opened up more options.

Baxter was adamant that if the whole Exeter pack came across the middle of the line as one, the referee could not penalise them all. His midweek team talk was a hard-nosed classic. 'Look, if we all cheat we'll be fine. And, at scrum time, make sure we get the right shoulder through. Bentos, give your tight head everything you've got. If we can do that then I want you, Richie, to run straight at Andrew Mehrtens. When you get to him let him tackle you – and when he does, keep hold of him. Then the rest of you stamp on Mehrtens. Bentos, you sit on Nick Easter. He's more important to them than you are to us (cue snorts of barely suppressed laughter). Right, Fats. When you get the ball run straight at Will Greenwood, or whoever's playing 12. Elbows, knees, hurt him. Junior. You do the same. Everything's got to be hard, everything's got to be intense.'

The concluding message Baxter wanted to leave uppermost in his players' minds was simple: 'Boys, we've got to MAKE IT WAR!' There was only one snag: when the final page of his flip-chart presentation was finally revealed, it read: 'MAK IT WAR'. Mark Fatialofa's head instantly disappeared into his tracksuit top but his heaving shoulders gave the game away. His brother Junior was the same. Others tried and failed to keep a straight face as they filed out for their final team run, only for Mark Fatialofa to rise to his feet, punch the air and shout: 'Let's Mak it War.' The entire squad, by now, were in stitches. By kick-off the collective determination to 'Mak it War!' on their sodden pitch was so strong the result was almost preordained. Right winger Jason Luff scored a crucial 52nd-minute try and Quins were beaten 13–8, their only league defeat of the 26-game season. The Londoners were not happy, with Dean Richards unimpressed with the refereeing. Soon enough, though, disappointment gave way to magnanimity. The former Springbok captain, André Vos, made a point of visiting the home changing room to congratulate his opponents and tell them the better side had won. Richards also instructed each of his players to seek out their direct opponent and buy them a beer. The happy, thirsty Chiefs were rarely in the mood to decline such offers.

The feel-good mood continued until the end of the season. The players instinctively respected Baxter. Average A levels or not, he was proving far smarter than some had perceived him to be. 'Robert was a very clever boy at school. He could have been an academic,' insists Staddon. Fellow forwards like Bentley also knew him to be a keen student of the game. 'He wasn't the best player but he was a line-out nause like you'd never believe. He loved line-outs. Exeter's calls at the time were simple enough. If there wasn't a call they'd go off the top, they had a code for down and pop and if they said, "You decide," it meant drive. At Orrell myself, Sammy Southern and Phil Moss would sit in the wood-panelled changing room looking at VHS videos of Exeter. We'd sussed that they'd often say, "You decide," and were trying to work out if it was some sort of code. Did the scrum-half have open or closed hands? We spent about 40 minutes trying to figure it out. When I joined

Exeter I told Rob. He laughed and told me that "You decide" simply meant driving the line-out.'

Baxter, from the players' perspective, also appeared to be some kind of savant when it came to unpicking opposition confidence. Starving teams of possession could be just as unnerving, on occasions, as points on the scoreboard. Win the first three line-outs of a game, for example, and any rival pack would start to doubt themselves. There was also an emphasis, from the start, on getting the first three phases spot on. Bentley recalls spending hours walking through patterns to ensure everyone knew their roles inside out. 'Rob is massively heavy on structure. Even now they always know what their first three phases are going to be. Then it's heads up. He'd say, "Why are you standing there? I need you to be clearing this ruck over here." The level of prescription for the first couple of phases is extraordinary.'

Whereas Bremner had run the whole show, from ordering the kit to player contracts, Baxter began to delegate certain aspects to people with the requisite skills and let them get on with it. MacLellan, having spent time with Martin Johnson at Leicester, reckons there are comparisons to be made with the World Cup-winning captain. 'They're very similar types. Rob is more cerebral and verbalises things better. Martin was more direct but, in terms of rugby brains, they're on a par. As a player Rob was a bit light to have gone the next step but he'd probably have done better in today's game.' When it came to on-field ruthlessness, Baxter was tough enough, as his former Gloucester winger Mark Foster was advised even before arriving in 2009. 'My old teammate Will James used to play against Rob a lot and he said that if you didn't knock him out or kill him he would keep coming back again and again.' Johnson, though, was a competitor apart. 'We were playing Bath in the Pilkington Cup and needed to bring on a sub because Richard Cockerill was struggling with something,' recalled MacLellan. 'In those days the only way you could do that was through blood. I've come on in the middle of this huddle to patch up whatever I needed to patch up. Cockers has just put his head down and the next thing you know – bang – Martin has caught him under his eye and drawn blood.'

'What are you doing?'

'He needs to leave.'

'What?'

'Get him off the field.'

The increasing incidence of television cameras in the modern game demands rather greater restraint from today's captains, not to mention an increased duty of care towards their colleagues. It did not prevent Johnson from rising to the England manager's chair and MacLellan is among those who firmly believe Baxter can follow suit. 'There are different ways of being leaders. There are those who are quite vocal, those you'd follow over the top and those with a bit of both. If you were going to put someone in a senior role beyond the Chiefs, you'd look at a Rob rather than a Martin.'

* * * * *

At this delicate stage of Exeter's history, Rowe still felt he needed a director of rugby with a little more experience. Several names were considered – there was even talk of luring Graham Dawe from Plymouth – but in the end it was decided to go for Pete Drewett, who was in charge of England U21s at the time. Drewett had played on the wing for the club in his younger days, had studied to be a teacher locally and had shared a dressing room with Baxter, who was handed the role of forwards' coach. Drewett had also been heavily involved in player development at the Rugby Football Union and was an easy man to like. He ticked an awful lot of boxes.

It was also immediately obvious to Drewett that training needed to become more professional. 'There were a few lads they called professionals but everybody else was working. We were training on Tuesday and Thursday evenings and playing on Saturdays. I told Tony we had to get full-time players and train during the day. Tony backed it massively.'

The next requirement was a good fitness coach. The man he had in mind was Paddy Anson, a former Marine who knew the area well. To Drewett's mind, he would set exactly the right tone. Sitting in a black taxi en route to a Matt Hampson fund-raiser in London, he gave Anson a call. 'I've just got a job at Chiefs. Would you like to come and be our fitness coach?' Two days later, Worcester offered Anson almost twice as much money to stay but he had already given Exeter his word. It was an important signing: Exeter could now properly maximise their Marines connection, instil the same culture of one-for-all values and encourage a similar winning mindset. The squad were soon being put through their paces on the famous Lympstone assault course, no place for the flabby-chested or soft of heart.

After two away games to kick off the season, the finishing touches to the stadium were finally complete, allowing the new Sandy Park era to dawn on 16 September. Not too auspiciously, as it turned out, with a 13–13 draw against Coventry scarcely the stuff of legend. There was a solitary try for the hooker Sam Blythe plus a conversion and two penalties from Tony Yapp but the biggest plus was the attendance, an encouraging 5,234. Build it, it seemed, and the people of Exeter would come. In early 2007 the ground even staged its first representative game, England Saxons beating Italy A 34–5 with tries for, among others, Mike Brown (2) and Dylan Hartley.

These, even so, were still transitional days. On top of everything else Drewett had to lock up the gates leading to the stadium when he left every evening. Wrestling with the padlock and trying to avoid setting off the newly installed alarm, the new director of rugby began to appreciate just how many responsibilities were now piled on his plate. As he began the business of transforming the make-up of the squad, he also swiftly realised Baxter had all the makings of a top-class coach. Drewett encouraged him to continue coaching at Exeter University and became his mentor for his Level 4 RFU coaching course. 'I'd worked with the top 10 English coaches over the years and within months I knew Rob had it. Even in those early days I thought he'd take over one day. I even stood up at the end-of-season dinner and asked Rob to stand up too. In front of 300 guests I said, "I've been lucky to work with a lot of good English coaches but in Rob we are very, very lucky. I honestly believe Rob will be good enough to coach international rugby."'

Aside from Baxter's work ethic and sharp analytical eye, Drewett also noticed something else: the former was an excellent talent spotter. If Exeter had six props they were vaguely interested in signing, he would invite his assistant to compile his own report on them. It was not long before he began to trust his assistant's judgement implicitly. Exeter finished equal fourth in the table but recorded a memorable 29–0 win at second-placed Rotherham and were beaten just once in the second half of the season. They were also starting to recruit like a team with real ambition.

One of Drewett's first signings was a flanker who had been impressing for Coventry. Tom Johnson was a prime example of the late-blooming talent that is so often wasted in England. As a schoolboy in Cheltenham he had been a scrum-half and, coming from a services family, had ambitions to join the Parachute Regiment. He had pitched up at Coventry on the recommendation of a referee who had seen him playing for Reading – he attended university there – and had noticed his rare pace and fitness.

No one, least of all Johnson himself, ever imagined he would end up representing England, the first Exeter debutant to do so since Dick Manley in the freezing winter of 1963. What the former did sense was that Chiefs were a team going places. By pure coincidence Coventry had been the final visitors to the County Ground in May 2006 and Johnson was also in their squad for the opening fixture at their new home. It was obvious from their facilities that Exeter were serious. Johnson took one look at the ice bath – designed to accelerate the players' recovery – and by Christmas had agreed to move down the following summer.

From his first encounter with Baxter he became accustomed to a whole new level of detail. 'I'll always remember Rob saying to me, "We know you're quick with the ball in hand but I don't think your line-out's very good." He told me my weaknesses straight away.' It was exactly the same for numerous other players suddenly being approached to join the club. Soon it became a running joke in the dressing room. 'We had the 50 best blokes in the Championship,' recalls Johnson. 'We'd raided everyone.' Fine in theory, not always so good in practice. Bentley, who had returned for a second stint at the club after spells in New Zealand and Edinburgh, believes that, ultimately, there were too many players absolutely convinced they should be in the team. 'Some of the guys we'd signed didn't really fit in and there were some big egos. It all went a bit shit. In Pete Drewett's last season there were 52 players and everyone wanted to play. There was no tiering: pretty much everyone was aged between 24 and 28 and thought they were good enough to start.'

With the squad in need of some firm leadership, Drewett increasingly had his hands full. He was popular and a good man manager but not, by nature, a massive shouter. On the rare occasions he lost his cool, people remembered it. One day, after a particularly disappointing first-half display, he aimed a kick at a chair in the dressing room, only for his foot to end up wedged in the gap between the seat and the back rest. The team fell about, all the tension was released and they went out and played brilliantly in the second half. The players, though, were not huge fans of Paul Larkin as backs coach and Exeter's game plan, as Johnson recalls, was not hitting the spot either. 'We just tried to overpower everyone. Rob would have all eight of us forwards running around after the ball. It was very, very attritional.'

In a first-past-the-post league with only one team promoted each season, the odds were also heavily stacked in favour of the side relegated from the Premiership going straight back up again. Exeter were close but not quite close enough, losing a further brace of EDF National Trophy finals in successive seasons in 2007 and 2008. Most galling was the former, a 19–16 defeat to Cornish Pirates despite controlling large chunks of the game, but their subsequent loss to a Northampton side featuring Carlos Spencer and Chris Ashton underlined the difference that a sprinkling of class can make.

The new signings, consequently, kept on coming. For the start of the 2008/09 season, there was a raft of them: Matt Cornwell and Bryan Rennie from Leicester and London Irish respectively, the chunky prop Chris Budgen from Northampton and the lock Dan Tuohy from Gloucester. Slightly less heralded were a fly-half from Cornish Pirates named Gareth Steenson, the Irish forward Tom Hayes (brother of the Ireland prop, John) and a prolific winger from Launceston by the name of Matt Jess.

It was a decent-looking squad, captained from No. 8 by the ever-influential Richie Baxter. In his father's view, his younger son, who ultimately played a record 434 games for his local side between 1997 and 2013, scoring 126 tries, would definitely have represented his country had he been at a more fashionable club. 'He should have played for England, there's no getting away from it. He was too good for Exeter but he wouldn't let his team, his family or his club down. He was an absolutely outstanding talent.' His older brother, Rob, felt similarly. 'I'd be watching him play against international back-rowers in his late twenties and I don't think I ever saw him come off second best. He and a few other guys could have been in the international environment if they'd have been playing for more fashionable clubs.'

All it needed was one collective final push. Frustratingly, it was still not happening. In the season's two biggest league games, against Leeds Carnegie home and away, Exeter were beaten by one and two points respectively. Promotion was still mathematically possible, though, if they could win away in a rescheduled fixture at Moseley in mid-March. The league leaders Leeds were enduring a mini-wobble and had just lost twice, to Doncaster and Bedford, inside eight days. There was one complication. Exeter were also due to face Moseley in the semi-finals of the EDF National Trophy. The fateful decision was made to combine both games into a single winner-takes-all fixture.

Drewett cautioned Rowe against the idea but, financially, it made sense not to make two separate trips up to the Midlands. Rowe is a persuasive man and Moseley, for their part, were struggling to fit in all their games. With a couple of Chiefs players omitted because of England sevens commitments, it became a perfect ambush scenario. 'If it had been a league game we'd have walked it because they wouldn't have been interested,' suggests Johnson. Instead the Chiefs found themselves pitched into an intense cup tie against hosts who, despite having no promotion ambitions, were massively motivated by the possibility of a first Twickenham appearance in 27 years. By half-time Moseley were 25–12 up and there could be no arguing with the final 32–24 outcome. In the space of 80 minutes Exeter's season had fallen apart. 'It sounded brilliant because it seemed like we'd tick both boxes,' recalls Steenson. 'We'd win with a try bonus point and get to a Twickenham final. The players were keen; we didn't want to travel up twice. We just didn't get it right. The whole season just exploded in one day. Everyone was upset.'

Rowe was definitely in that category. He still liked Drewett but, once again, felt compelled to intervene. 'He's the captain in charge of the ship, the ship's going down, it's his fault.' For Drewett it was devastating news. 'I'll be honest with you, it was the saddest day of my life. I still absolutely love the club and it's in my heart and soul. I'm totally delighted that everything worked and that Rob has gone on to do better and better. The only sadness is that I'm not still involved.'

With Larkin also departing, it was not totally obvious who would take charge. The name of the former England scrum-half Richard Hill was mentioned and Rob Baxter spent a nervous weekend wondering about his own future. Would Rowe opt to start completely afresh? Within the squad, recalls Johnson, there were plenty of opinions. 'I think the players thought they'd get someone like Richard Hill in. Someone who'd coached in the Premiership before. It was definitely the harder choice to put Rob in charge. It certainly wasn't automatic. In the end Tony probably went with his gut.'

That was pretty much the truth of it, with Rowe spending the weekend deep in contemplation. The move to Sandy Park had increased costs substantially, as had the construction of the new North Stand to hoist the stadium capacity to 7,300. Yet aside from the local derby against Plymouth there had been barely any attendances above 5,000. Going out into the marketplace for an expensive 'super coach' was not really an option.

Maybe it could be made to work if Baxter had decent support around him? Robin Cowling, the former England prop forward, who had done much to help set up the club's highly promising academy, was already a trusted lieutenant. He was also firmly of the opinion that Baxter should be the next head coach. Cowling was as durable as they come. In 1978 he had spent 40 minutes scrummaging against France at Parc des Princes with a dislocated shoulder, declining to come off because England had already used their permitted number of replacements. He could tell a strong-willed individual when he saw one.

Two other experienced coaches, Rob Gibson and Ricky Pellow, were also involved with the youth conveyor belt. Rather than starting completely afresh, concluded Rowe, it made better sense to give Baxter his head. The latter was put in temporary charge but Rowe soon discovered that not everyone felt he should have the job permanently. 'Half my board of directors voted against it. Half the club were Baxters and half were against. You could have split the club down the middle. Not everyone loved John Baxter. There were two board members I know well who voted against it. I remind them of that every now and again.' With the board split, Rowe had the casting vote. 'I said, "We've got to do it." I remember calling in Rob to tell him. He thought he was in for the chop.'

Instead, on 7 May 2009, Rob Baxter took charge with Cowling as his temporary team manager. Barely a fortnight earlier the Exeter crowd had slow handclapped their own team during a 9–9 draw with Doncaster. Baxter's post-match quote to BBC Devon – 'I think you've got to be careful when everything becomes about promotion all the time' – did not necessarily sound like a man promising instant miracles. In Bob Staddon's view, though, appointing him was absolutely the right call. 'In my opinion it was no gamble at all. He's a leader.' That just left the small matter of identifying a suitable backs coach. Within a few days Baxter was back in Rowe's office with a proposal.

'Do you remember when we lost to Bedford down at the County Ground in 2006?'

'No.'

'Their number 10. Ali Hepher. He's at Northampton, coaching their academy.'

Given Baxter and Hepher did not know each other it was a sizeable call. They had, however, played against each other and Baxter vividly remembered a Cup semi-final during his first temporary spell in charge. Exeter were leading 35–34 but

Bedford had possession in the closing stages. With the referee reluctant to give a match-turning penalty, the instruction came from the Bedford bench that Hepher should attempt a drop goal. 'I hadn't kicked a drop goal for about five years but I got the call from the sideline to step into the pocket. It was from about 40 metres out but it snaked over somehow like some kind of heat-seeking missile.' Bedford won 37–35 to deprive Chiefs of another Twickenham date; now, three years on, Baxter was prepared to forgive if not entirely forget. Hepher had just been rejected for a job at another Premiership club when an unfamiliar number flashed up on his phone.

'Hi, it's Rob Baxter here at Exeter. Would you like to come down for an interview?'

'Er, yes. Sure, I'd love to.'

Baxter wanted an attack coach with Premiership and Championship experience. Hepher, who had featured in Northampton's European Cup final success against Munster in 2000, fitted those criteria and was keen to take the next step up the coaching ladder. The interview went well and as Hepher jumped back into his car to head off for a prearranged weekend in Newcastle, he suddenly did not care about the long trek ahead of him. In his stomach there was something he had not felt for a while: a fizzing sense of excitement. 'My mind was on fire. Ideas, what I could do, all the things I'd been waiting to get out there.' He had only been driving for a couple of hours when his phone rang again. It was Baxter. The job was his.

NINE

INCH BY INCH

A few minutes' drive from the County Armagh border separating Northern Ireland from the Republic is a small village called Killylea. It is only five miles west of Armagh but a very long way from the English Premiership or Ireland's national rugby side. Not that a young Gareth Steenson was remotely interested in rugby. His electrician dad John was a football guy, deeply involved with Armagh City FC, and Gareth played for mid-Ulster U11s. Tottenham Hotspur's scouts would occasionally come and take a look and a couple of his teammates were picked up by West Ham. Then there was his true passion: snooker. 'What I really wanted to be was a snooker player. On Sunday afternoons I'd come back from church and, with my waistcoat on, play on the small kids' table we had at home.' On other Sundays, for variation, there might be a trip over the border to mess around on his brother Johnny's jet ski. Johnny also loved his cars and, when he wasn't lining up reds to the bottom pocket, Gareth enjoyed going fishing as well.

Everything changed when he went to the Royal School, Armagh. They played rugby union and lots of it. One day, too, a new kid showed up. He had one arm in a plaster cast and spoke with a slow, deliberate accent which instantly set him apart. 'Hi, every-one, I'm Tom-my Bo-we and I'm from Mona-gh-an.' Everyone in the changing room waiting for PE was highly amused. More often than not, it stayed that way for the remainder of their schooldays. Tommy Bowe, it turned out, was extremely good value on and off the field. He was never picked for Ulster schools but still ended up playing for Ireland and the British & Irish Lions. Often it is the late bloomers who soar highest of all.

Thin lines, fine margins; it is what makes sport so compelling. Some youngsters have fame thrust upon them at an early age. Others have to traverse the road less travelled, humming Van Morrison as they search for the bright side of it. Steenson is a rarity; someone who has spent time in both camps. One minute he was captain of Ireland at the 2005 IRB Under-21 World Cup in Argentina, having helped steer them to the previous year's final against New Zealand. Inside 12 months he was on the scrapheap, unwanted by his home province and required to take a punt across the Irish Sea in Rotherham and Penzance.

To some extent it came down to luck, or a lack of it. In that same Irish U21 squad was another fly-half called Jonathan Sexton, a year younger but not short of self-belief – 'Johnny was a confident kid, you might say' – or competitiveness. The two strong-minded 10s from opposite sides of the Irish border roomed together for a month without becoming bosom buddies. Towards the end of the tournament, prior to a game against Canada, Steenson was pulled to one side. 'We want to give Johnny a run at 10. Can you play 12 and talk him through it?' Ireland won 77–3 and things were never quite the same again. Sexton went on to play senior Test rugby at fly-half for Ireland for more than a decade while Steenson was fated never to win a cap.

History might have turned out differently, too, had Ulster's kingpin David Humphreys not opted to keep playing until four months short of his 37th birthday. With Humphreys' younger brother Ian also in the background, Steenson never managed to play a single game for his home province. Whereas Bowe was promoted to the first team because of a shortage of fit wingers at Ulster and Sexton seized his chance at Leinster when Felipe Contepomi was injured, Steenson simply could not buy a break. Instead he was put to work in the Ulster branch office, registering all the junior players in the province, and turned out for his local club, Dungannon.

Something had to give and it was never going to be Ulster's management. In 2006 he was called in by Mark McCall, then Ulster's head coach, and told he was being released because David Humphreys wanted to stick around. Over 300 appearances and 2,600 points for Exeter later, it is now McCall who winces whenever their paths cross but at the time rejection was hard to take. 'It was very difficult to be told, "Either go and get a job or try something in the lower leagues." It's easy to sit here now but it was tough. Mark says he now uses me as a great example to his young players.'

There was nothing cushy or glamorous about his next move. Faced with the alternative of ditching his sporting dream and becoming a PE teacher, he was offered the chance to join Rotherham in the English Championship. He had never been to Yorkshire in his life before and his mother Helen caught a Jet2 flight to Leeds Bradford Airport to take a look around. He decided to give it a crack only for life to take an instant twist. On the very same day he agreed to move to England, his father was diagnosed with cancer. It was a deeply unsettling time, even though Steenson senior was subsequently given the all-clear. 'I have no doubt, knowing what I now do about mental health, that I had depression at that point, but it's character-building.'

Life at Rotherham was certainly not dull. In charge of the Titans was the full-throttle André Bester, who took one look at his diminutive fly-half and cut straight to the chase.

'Right, you're going to tackle.'

'Okay, André, I'll tackle.'

He also kicked everything in that 2006/07 league season, contributing 264 points as Rotherham finished second, just five points behind champions Leeds. He responded well to Bester's blunt, passionate style – 'He was a real straight-talker and, basically, an angry bloke' – and had his eyes opened to another way of playing the game. The team contained a strong South African core and had a serious pack, including Hendre Fourie who would go on to play flanker for England. 'He was a phenomenal player. He'd play for 60 minutes in the back row and then play the last 20 at tight head.'

Rotherham, though, were feeling the winds of financial reality and Steenson joined the Cornish Pirates for the following season, despite having only briefly visited the club – by then coached by Bentley's former Orrell coach Jim McKay – the previous March. No sooner had the decision been made than painful history started to repeat itself: his father's cancer had returned. Early in the autumn of 2007, the family were informed he only had three to four weeks left. Steenson would play on a Sunday, jump on the plane from Newquay back to Ireland the following day and then retrace his steps, emotionally drained, at the end of the week. Not only did the small planes cause him to develop a fear of flying – 'You'd be looking at the air hostess and she'd be shaking her head going, "Not good!"' – but his dad had always been his sporting mentor, pushing him to maximise his talent. 'The last game he saw me play was against Chiefs. It was the last time the Pirates beat the Chiefs in a competitive game and I kicked 21 points, missing only the final conversion.' After a 30–23 victory had been completed, his first priority, as usual, was to phone home.

'I'll see you tomorrow.'

'You missed one kick. Not great.'

'Yeah, but I kicked 21 points!'

It was the way the two of them had always talked but now the clock was ticking inexorably. 'We knew when I left that the next time I came back he'd be gone. It was a difficult time because Cornwall felt very far away.'

The only professional consolation was that he had started to catch the eye of good judges in England. When he went over for two tries for the Pirates as part of a 17-point haul in the return fixture against the Chiefs at Sandy Park in January 2008, it merely confirmed what Pete Drewett had felt since his England age-group coaching days. 'I first saw Gareth play for Ireland U21s versus England U21s. He'd also played for Ireland in the final of the U21 World Cup and was top scorer in the tournament. He was consistently scoring 200 to 300 points a season. We had Tony Yapp, who was also an excellent goal-kicker, but I thought we needed two of them because the time would come when we might need to win big games by a point. Gareth had just lost his father so it was a difficult time for him but I think we built a pretty good rapport. He could see we meant business.'

Steenson, however, had other options. Pirates were talking about a new deal and London Irish were also keen. 'The entire time I was over here my goal was to get home, get back playing for Ulster and play for Ireland. I made no secret of that. I met Brian Smith twice but I just didn't like London. It scared me. It was too big. Exeter, though, seemed to fit. It seemed to me the club was going to go places. It had the facilities, they were putting a big squad together and the biggest driver was there was an airport down the road. I could be home quicker than anyone who lives in London.'

With so many players vying for places, however, many reckoned he had made the wrong choice. 'At the Pirates they were saying, "You've made a mistake, you're not going to play." And the first year was a bit strange. We had 50 full-timers. It felt as if Pete had gone out and recruited all the top lads from Plymouth Albion, Pirates and everyone else in the area. We had three or four players competing for each position.' Steenson was soon slotting his goals but Drewett, as with Bester, felt less confident when the opposition had the ball. 'He had a fantastic kicking percentage success rate but he'll be the first to admit we had to do a lot of work on his defence.'

By the start of the 2009/10 season, though, with Baxter and Hepher in charge, the collective vibe was improving. It had begun in pre-season when the squad had been packed off to Dartmoor to be chased around by first-year Marines. They had already walked almost 80km in second-hand boots, completed various team-building tasks and slept outside for a night when the coaches told them to brace themselves for a full-scale night exercise. Already short of sleep, food and home comforts, the footsore players began to panic. At that precise moment they spotted some headlights heading in their direction. Then they heard a loud horn blaring. Only the management knew what was coming. It was the team manager Tony 'Beast' Walker, driving a big high-sided transit with 'Booze-bulance' written on the side. Out jumped the 'Beast' in full medical scrubs. 'Right lads, the piss is in the back . . . no one leaves till we finish all of it.' The inside of the truck was stacked, from floor to ceiling, with ice-cold beers and ciders. Walker was suddenly the world's most popular man. 'We had pizzas arrive, we had all sorts of stuff. You've never seen a group of guys so pleased to see you in your whole life.'

As they savoured the beers and forgot about their blisters, it was clear the wider object of the exercise had been achieved. The group were establishing a tighter bond and Steenson, who had spent all summer with an arm in a cast after breaking it at the end of the previous campaign, began to notice a growing number of people like himself: players who had endured significant knock-backs elsewhere but were determined not to let that define them. 'I think my whole career has been built on being told I wasn't good enough. If my wife was to describe me, "stubborn" would be one of the words she'd use. You've got to overcome things. If you're handed stuff you don't appreciate it. We were all a bunch of misfits. If you looked at our squad, everyone, somewhere along the line, had been let go by somebody. You could run through our entire XV and every single one had been told "No" at some stage. I think it was the biggest part of our persona for the first five to six years in the Premiership, the fact everyone kept saying we had no chance.'

* * * * *

Steenson's assessment was spot on. At full-back there was Phil Dollman, who had failed to secure a contract renewal at a cash-strapped Newport Gwent Dragons having previously played for Caerphilly and Bedwas. He was halfway through a PGCE qualification and was considering going into teaching when Exeter got in touch. He had a mullet and was wearing 'quite a tight T-shirt' when he first met Rob Baxter. 'The way Rob tells it, this flashy, chubby Welshman came down and he didn't quite know how to take me. I must have made some kind of positive impact, though.'

Dollman became Baxter's first Exeter recruit – and the director of rugby still rates him as his all-time best signing. A natural footballer who could play centre or full-back, he was exactly the loyal, un-starry but quietly impressive kind of team man that Baxter loved. 'Unselfish with a bit of commitment are probably the traits Rob's looking for. The coaches like to meet someone one on one so they get a better feeling of a player. They've seen their qualities as a rugby player but it's also about their qualities as a person.'

Then there was the persevering Matt Jess on the wing. The previous year he'd been working in Harvey's Bar in Launceston, helping out as a youth development officer in a school twice a week and playing for the local side. He'd previously been with the Pirates in his native Cornwall and the Dragons in Wales but had broken a leg playing for Ebbw Vale the season before, and suffered some complications. A prolific try-scoring season for the Cornish All Blacks, however, had attracted fresh interest from Stuart Lancaster at Leeds, Jim Mallinder at Northampton and, most memorably, Philippe Saint-André at Sale. 'He told me to stand up and asked how tall I was and what I weighed. I told him I was six foot even though I'm five foot eleven and also added a couple of kilos.' What he did have was pace, inherited from his Mum, Bernice, who was a sprinter of some repute around the Coventry area in her prime. 'She used to line up against all the boys. They'd go, "Bloody hell, Bernice is here today."'

Jess's auntie and uncle had moved to Land's End in the 1980s and, when Matt was three, Bernice decided it was time to relocate the rest of the family to Cornwall. Matt adored life in the south-west, so when Exeter got in touch he instinctively liked the idea. It took him a while to establish himself but his desire was apparent every time he touched the ball. He collected 16 tries in his first season with the Chiefs and, attitude-wise, there was no one who wanted it more. He suspected that was what Baxter liked most about him. 'When Rob sees someone who will fight and not give up he'll keep them. They might not be playing but he'll retain them because they absolutely want it.'

Even the club's kitman, Andy Worth, was famous for going the extra mile, particularly when he was informed the scrum-half, Clive Stuart-Smith, had swum an extraordinary number of lengths of the club's ice bath without coming up for air.

So insanely determined was Worth to beat Stuart-Smith's underwater record that Jess and other players ultimately had no option but to jump in and drag him from the water.

The 'Originals', as they would come to be known, also included Ben Moon, who had made his Exeter league debut in a 71–5 win over Sedgley Park in early October 2008. As a young prop, Moon, from Cullompton RFC, had represented his country at age-group level alongside Courtney Lawes and Joe Marler; when push came to shove he was as unyielding as the local quarry stone in his home village of Westleigh. His father Alan had been renowned for his strength in the local Young Farmers' tug-of-war competitions and Ben spent most of his time helping out with the calves on his best mate Dan's farm in nearby Burlescombe. 'My friends from growing up are all pretty level, farming people. They'll always say something to bring you down to earth, even after the biggest game of your life. Every time I see them the first thing they'll say is, "Good dropped ball at the weekend."' His mother and father ferried him around to endless games but, tragically, Alan would not live long enough to see his son go on to play for England or hoist the Premiership trophy. After an eight-month battle with lung cancer, he passed away at the age of just 52 but Moon is still motivated by his father's fierce desire to provide for his family. One glance at his taped wrists on a match day sums up his priorities. Before each game the loose head sits down and writes out the initials of his father, his wife, Laura, and their children Finlay and Mabel 'so I know they've got my back on the pitch as well'.

There were numerous other good players, not least James Scaysbrook and Mark Foster. Both already had Premiership experience with Bath and Gloucester respectively. Scaysbrook was a tireless flanker who appeared utterly impervious to pain and had previously featured in the England Saxons squad. Foster was a quick, strong winger who had represented England Schoolboys, had notched up 24 tries in 84 appearances for the 'Cherry and

Whites' and was reliably good dressing-room company. The way he saw it, he was simply a product of his upbringing: 'The Gloucester backline had so many personalities in it you had to have one just to survive. With an Essex boy for a dad and a Scouser for a mum, I already had plenty to say for myself.'

Foster, though, was also observant. He could see a club that still had a significant amount of growth in it and was socially tighter than most. 'Gloucester were a very mature team and had some serious world superstars. There was also a lot of money. When I got to Exeter there were only a handful of us who had come down from the Premiership. There were no egos at all, and it was a very level playing field. From day one, everyone had a chance of playing. There was no one being paid four times your salary. Everyone was genuinely friends; it was like a family. A lot of people had come from afar, their partners got on, the kids got on and Ali and Rob would regularly create opportunities for people to get together. Rob understood that to build a good rugby side you needed people who were genuinely willing to buy in totally and lay down their bodies – and beliefs – to each other in order to achieve the ultimate goal.' When Foster moved house to a place off Magdalene Road, half a dozen players turned up to help without being asked. 'Guys would do things not because there was anything in it for them but because it needed to be done. It was exactly the same on the pitch. If a ruck needed clearing, someone would clear it.'

There were also mood-enhancers like Brett 'The Energy Train' Sturgess from Northampton – he also answered to 'John Graft' – and the relentless Bentley, who could always be relied upon to keep the troops amused. Famously, during his first stint at the club, the team were gathered in a huddle at Bedford when Bentley exhorted all concerned to 'smash these southern shandy-drinking fools.' He instantly felt a tap on his shoulder from his hooker Keith Brooking. 'We're actually from further south than them, Bentos.'

None of this musketeering spirit was a coincidence. Commencing with Dollman, Baxter knew exactly the sort of players he wanted. Having to bide his time under Drewett following Bremner's departure had, in some ways, been a blessing in disguise. 'In hindsight what happened probably benefited me. It gave me a bit of time to sit and reflect. I hadn't been a head coach long enough. Whether I'd have been able to carry on pushing on is hard to tell.'

It had also allowed him to start poring over videos and assessing potential new players' strengths and weaknesses in detail. As long as they were open to being coached and still had improvement in them, they were welcome at Exeter. Hepher's arrival had also brought a fresh perspective. In Johnson's view, it was the missing link. 'Ali was the big piece in the jigsaw. There was something missing and Rob needed someone to challenge his way of thinking. We started to play a better brand of rugby.' Gradually it felt to Johnson, and others, that things were beginning to click. 'That's the beauty of what Rob and the coaches have done. They realised the collective is bigger than the individual and created the system to suit that.'

Specific targets were set for short blocks of games, sometimes with financial incentives attached. A perfect gym-honed physique was not necessarily required, either. Foster well remembers Steenson, in his early days as a fully professional rugby player, complaining about how much time he was spending in the gym: 'He'd say, "This is bollocks. I didn't sign up for this. I just want to go and play rugby."' Before too long the realisation dawned that, to keep pace with the Chiefs' ambitions, there was little choice. 'He's a lot better now. He understands his longevity is based around his ability to perform physically.'

The fly-half, though, remains very much his own man. Prior to leaving for every home game, from his early Championship years onwards, his pre-match routine has never wavered. First he heads upstairs to his bedroom and presses play on an ancient iPod containing all his favourite old tunes. As he showers and changes, a few classic tracks set him up nicely for what is about to follow. In the film *Any Given Sunday*, Al Pacino plays Tony D'Amato, a veteran coach trying to rouse the fictitious Miami Sharks American football team. Steenson has listened to his recording of the film's classic motivational speech so often he can recite every word. Every time he hears it on match day it still strikes a chord:

I don't know what to say, really. Three minutes to the biggest battle of our professional lives. All comes down to today.

Either we heal as a team, or we are going to crumble. Inch by inch, play by play. Till we're finished. We are in hell right now, gentlemen. Believe me. And, we can stay here and get the shit kicked out of us, or we can fight our way back into the light.

We can climb out of hell . . . one inch at a time.

Now I can't do it for you, I'm too old. I look around, I see these young faces and I think, I mean, I've made every wrong choice a middle-aged man can make. I've pissed away all my money, believe it or not. I chased off anyone who's ever loved me. And lately, I can't even stand the face I see in the mirror.

You know, when you get old, in life, things get taken from you. That's . . . that's part of life. But you only learn that when you start losing stuff. You find out life is just a game of inches.

So is football. Because in either game, life or football, the margin for error is so small. I mean, one half a step too late or too early and you don't quite make it. One half-second too slow, too fast and you don't quite catch it. The inches we need are everywhere around us. They're in every break of the game, every minute, every second.

On this team we fight for that inch. On this team we tear ourselves and everyone else around us to pieces for that inch. We claw with our fingernails for that inch. Because we know when we add up all those inches that's gonna make the fucking difference between WINNING and LOSING, between LIVING and DYING.

I'll tell you this: in any fight it's the guy who's willing to die who's going to win that inch. And I know if I'm going to have any life any more it's because I'm still willing to fight and die for that inch, because that's what living is, the six inches in front of your face.

Now I can't make you do it. You gotta look at the guy next to you, look into his eyes. Now, I think you're going to see a guy who will go that inch with you. You're going to see a guy who will sacrifice himself for this team, because he knows when it comes down to it you're gonna do the same for him. That's a team, gentlemen, and either we heal now, as a team, or we will die as individuals. That's football, guys, that's all it is. Now, what are you gonna do?

As the final sentence washes over him for the umpteenth time – 'Now, what are you going do?' – the metamorphosis is complete. Gareth the family man has been transformed into 'Steeno' the warrior Chief. A slightly built gladiator, admittedly, but match programmes list neither the dimensions of a player's heart nor the intensity of his desire. Nor the connection to his teammates and the potential power and energy that can generate. Jumping into his car for the five-minute drive to the stadium, it is time for one last musical cue: either the theme from *Mission: Impossible 2* or, latterly, *The Greatest Showman*. 'The word impossible is not in my dictionary,' wrote another diminutive playmaker, Napoleon Bonaparte. It has also been Steenson's motto for so long he has forgotten any other way.

TEN

THE MEMORIAL HEIST

By mid-December 2009, Exeter were sitting as pretty as a Devon scone – jam on top, cream below – at the summit of the restructured RFU Championship table, which now comprised 12 teams rather than 16. They had won their first 13 league games, most notably a 35–25 victory at Bristol, and were scoring freely. If ever there was a golden opportunity to secure promotion to the top tier of the English game and end the club's 139-year wait for widespread national recognition this was it. With the top eight clubs qualifying for the end-of-season play-offs, however, everything clearly hinged on their ability to peak in May.

Ali Hepher: At Christmas we decided to take the guys off feet and into the gym. We had enough points already to reach the top eight so a play-off position was already guaranteed.

Rob Baxter: Bristol came down around Christmas and beat us. I genuinely think they thought they'd done the hard bit. In some ways losing that game gave us a mental advantage.

Ali Hepher: During the period we put the guys in the gym we lost three games. They were the only three games we lost all season.

Rob Baxter: A lot of what we did wasn't just me. Paddy Anson wanted to push the mid-season fitness regime. If people came to me with a good idea I was more than happy to go with it.

Mark Foster: Guys were wrecked. We were doing as much training as we'd do in pre-season. Five or six weights sessions a week, running drills at far higher intensity than we normally did.

Rob Baxter: We never planned on losing some of those games. I knew our players were sore and tired from what we'd been doing but we had one really sticky game down at Plymouth on a frozen pitch. It should never have gone ahead and I thought, 'There's no way this will be on.' The players saw me talking to the officials and Plymouth were far more motivated. We lost 23–13.

Ali Hepher: Once we'd finished our 'pre-season' we started banging in big wins against people. We were fit, physical and everything was going well. Until, that is, we went away to Nottingham [for the first game of the play-offs]. It just went quiet. At half-time we were shot, we were done. We hadn't had a properly competitive game for so long. We couldn't handle it and lost 20–9. We didn't even pick up a bonus point.

Rob Baxter: We just rolled into the Nottingham game. It teaches you that you need to prepare for play-offs. Every other team had shut up shop for two to three weeks. It gave us a bit of a wake-up call. We thought our preparation had gone really well but in a way it was false because the other teams were preparing for the last eight. We thought, 'We've got to pull our fingers out here.'

Ali Hepher: We had a real tussle with London Welsh for 70 minutes and only beat Doncaster thanks to a late 40-metre penalty from Danny Gray. Then we went away to Welsh and lost 16–15 but finished top of the pool after putting 50 points on Nottingham at Sandy Park. Then we beat Bedford 37–8 in the semi-final.

Brett Sturgess: Rob's still got the note Nottingham left in our dressing room. 'Good luck but we'll see you next year.' They obviously thought we'd lose to Bristol. Rob has it up above his desk even now.

Rob Baxter: Those play-offs were hugely intense games. It wasn't a huge leap from there to the Premiership. Everyone realised they had a chance to get promoted. There were people out there killing each other.

Brett Sturgess: The overriding factor was that everyone Exeter brought in had a chip on their shoulders. They all had something to prove.

Haydn Thomas: Preparation-wise, the attention to detail during those two weeks was something we'd never seen before.

Rob Baxter: It was Ali who suggested shifting training to the evenings.

Matt Jess: It seems obvious now but, at the time, it felt like a genius idea.

Rob Baxter: We also made some huge decisions around selection. The biggest was around my brother. He'd completely detached his pec muscle against London Welsh. We gave him a couple of weeks off then brought him back off the bench in the semi-final.

Chris Bentley: Rich was a leader through example, not words. The doctor, Adrian Harris, saw him and said, 'There's nothing more you can do. You're fucked. We will repair it but if we do you're out for three months.' So for the latter stages of the season he played on without a pec tendon. He couldn't lift his arm above the horizontal. When he was tackling he had to kind of swing the arm in. It was all about pain tolerance. How much pain could he handle?

Rob Baxter: He made the call that he was all right to go but he was strapped up, pain-killered up and wearing a harness.

Matt Jess: I think there was an air of excitement as much as nerves. Two finals, you've got two chances. There was a sense of 'This could be our year.' Effectively it was still Pete Drewett's squad. You've got to thank him a little bit. I'd also been waiting to play Premiership rugby for a long time. To have that opportunity, to earn your right to play there with a West Country club . . . it felt massive. It felt like we were playing for the region. We had the Devon flag on our backs but we were representing Cornwall as well. We all wanted to prove ourselves. We also weren't entirely sure what the league structure was going to be the following season. Would there be automatic promotion? A play-off?

Tom Johnson: There was a massive monetary motivation. In the Championship I was on £35,000 basic. In the Premiership we could potentially earn £50–60,000. There were big implications for all of us.

Mark Foster: The day before the first leg at Sandy Park, Danny Gray caught Bryan Rennie with his head during an unopposed team run and fractured his eye socket in 15 places. It was ironic because 'Renzo' has one of the hardest heads you'll ever come across. He spider-cracked the whole thing and broke his nose as well. Ali turned to me and said, 'Right, Foz. Do you want to play full-back?' I hadn't played there since I was a kid.

Matt Jess: I'm not saying he couldn't play there but it felt different.

Rob Baxter: The game that won us the final was the first leg. We got a fair bit of criticism for not taking shots at goal and only having a 9–6 lead at the end of it. But I thought we put a real marker down. We weren't going to get pushed around; we weren't going to get bullied.

Mark Foster: There was a tacit agreement between me and Ali that, despite being more of a running player, I would play some percentage rugby and try and play the ball in their half. It was a wet night. I reckon I probably kicked 80 per cent of the possession I had, if not more.

Rob Baxter: We'd analysed Bristol endlessly. They had set plays for every situation: if this happens, we'll do this. I said, 'Guys, we're going to beat them at their own game.' The first leg was probably one of the most brutal games of rugby I've ever watched. The physicality of the collisions . . . it was Premiership level. After we went up we had easier games than that.

Ali Hepher: The two defences just smacked each other around. There wasn't much space. We tried to be aggressive by going to the corner and mostly didn't take our shots at goal. We were trying to send a bit of a message: 'We're coming after you, we're coming after you.' We wanted to be the aggressors. There are times on the field when teams score three points against you and you think, 'I don't mind that at all.' When they go to the corner, however, you're thinking, 'Shit, this is it.' It's about judging those moments.

Phil Dollman: It was so wet it was almost impossible to play any rugby. It was a really tight game and the weather was horrible. Somehow I managed to get man of the match because I made one break. The ball was fumbled out of the back of a line-out, Steeno gave me a switch, the defence just parted and I made it up almost to their try-line from where we eventually got three points. We played it to a tee.

Matt Jess: I was up against Lee Robinson. He was a big winger. I remember playing against him when I was 17 or 18 for Pirates against Plymouth. At the time Plymouth had a big backline, including him and Luke Arscott. He ran about three tries around me and I remember thinking, 'Oh my God, I'm completely out of my depth.' Since then he'd been playing in the Premiership at Bath. Give him too much space and he'd take you on and bump you off but, no disrespect to him, he wasn't the best kicking-wise. It was a bit of a game within a game, a mental challenge as well.

Tom Johnson: I came on for Chad Slade with 25 minutes to go. Luke Arscott broke through and managed to kick ahead towards our line. I corner-flagged and just got there before him. The crowd were going mad. In the Monday review Rob said, 'That was better than any try you've ever scored for this club.'

Rob Baxter: We only won by three points but it showed our lads that we could take them on in most areas of the game. It also gave me an insight into Bristol's mindset. I didn't see them changing much. It was almost like, 'We're winning games and this is how we win them.'

James Hanks: We knew we had more in us and that they didn't have that much more in them. We had an inner confidence that if we played well it was all set up for us.

Phil Dollman: We also played the underdog card well, despite the fact we were quietly confident in our abilities.

Ali Hepher: I was driving into work one morning thinking, 'Right, what's our biggest advantage over them?' I knew fitness was one. I'd been watching them all season. I'd been up to the Memorial Stadium six or seven times because I knew if we were going to get to the final we'd come up against them. I knew they weren't as fit. Then I thought, 'We've got the best kicker in the league. If we knock over a drop goal early on . . . boom.' We hadn't kicked a drop goal all season but we said, 'This time, if we get a shot, let's take it.' We went in with a good mentality. We said, 'Guys, score the first three points of the game and you'll have a six-point lead. Bang in another and you're a score ahead.' That way all the pressure and heat's on them.

Rob Baxter: What we didn't want was the rest of the team standing around and waiting for the drop goals to happen. So we just talked to the half-backs about it and didn't tell anyone else. If you look back you'll see everyone going flat out and then the ball dropping back to Steeno. Boom. That's why it worked so cleanly. He was under no pressure at all. You can't read anything from the other players' body language because they don't know.

Ali Hepher: Rob had also noticed that, all year, their hooker had walked on to the pitch when he was throwing. We held it back and didn't mention it, right up until that last leg. Then we mentioned it to the referee. It was a masterstroke. We got all over them in the line-out that night.

Rob Baxter: Their hooker, by the time he threw, was always a metre on to the field. So we mentioned it to the ref and his assistants before the game. At one stage the touch judge was physically trying to pull him back over the line. They're all little pressure things. We also changed our line-out calls from game to game. Bristol didn't. We must have stolen four or five line-outs in the second game. But I can't take credit for the attitude of the players. Over the course of the season they'd become a very tight-knit team.

Matt Jess: The first game was just about controlling it. The second one you knew you had to throw the kitchen sink at it.

Haydn Thomas: I was a bit nervy after the first one. I think Bristol probably thought they'd done it.

James Hanks: I was extremely nervous. My stomach was terrible. I said to the doc, 'I think I'm ill.' 'No, you're not,' he said. 'It's just a big game and your body doesn't want to carry anything extra.'

Rob Baxter: Even my wife said it felt different watching the lads warm up. It's amazing how many people have said what an emotionally charged atmosphere it was. When everybody gets themselves into that state it almost creates some kind of orb.

Gareth Steenson: Everyone was telling us we were going to lose but at no point did we think that. We were going to win.

Rob Baxter: We also did some cheeky things.

Ali Hepher: Ah, the champagne! I got the idea at Northampton from John Steele. He used to rile you up to get little bits. I knew there were little porkies he told along the way. I was discussing this with Rob. I said: 'Why don't we chuck something in just to get them going?' Rob goes, 'Yeah, brilliant.' Before the game he stood there and delivered it perfectly. You could see the lads thinking, 'Right, they can have this.'

Dave MacLellan (physio): We'd warmed up and had come back in. Everyone's fizzing and ready. Haydn Thomas gashed his head and I was patching him up thinking, 'He probably shouldn't be playing.' Then Rob calls everyone in. 'These fucking bastards think they've got it. I've just watched them deliver three boxes of champagne to their changing room. They think they've fucking won already.' You could feel everyone going, 'Right, they're having some.' Of course there was no bloody champagne, was there? It was a stroke of genius. We killed them in the second half.

Phil Dollman: We're lucky with our coaches. Ali's very sharp.

Rob Baxter: Even now I get a bit emotional about it. I looked into a couple of players' faces and thought, 'Shit, this has hit the mark this has. This is the final little bit that has topped them right up.' They were literally looking at me going, 'I can't believe a team has done that. I can't believe they've shown such disrespect.'

Matt Jess: I remember sitting in the corner with the back three. To this day I can't remember what Rob said tactically but everyone took the champagne thing personally.

Gareth Steenson: It must have worked for the front-row lads. I didn't hear it!

Matt Jess: The truth didn't hit us until we were all in the bus on the way home and started drinking champagne ourselves.

We were like, 'Hang on, someone's been playing a mind game here.' It was great reverse psychology. It wasn't them who brought the champagne, it was us.

Haydn Thomas: I genuinely believed it. I said to Ali afterwards, 'If they're not going to have their champagne we'll have it off them.' And he goes, 'There wasn't any champagne.' Bastard.

Ali Hepher: When it came off I was so excited that I told all the lads. We haven't been able to do it since.

Rob Baxter: We were well prepared and the guys just delivered. Our pack of forwards were like Trojans all the way through. I've got the game on CD and still watch it every now and again. Certain things stand out. On that day in those conditions if someone had said you can swap Gareth Steenson for any other fly-half in the world, Dan Carter included, there isn't one who would have done a better job. He knocked a conversion over from wide out, he kicked a penalty from halfway, he kicked those drop goals and controlled everything. He even made the break at the end that led to us scoring our try. You look at it and go, 'Could anyone have run the show better?'

Gareth Steenson: I felt confident coming into the game. I don't normally drop goals but they all flew over that night.

Matt Jess: It was the first time I've ever really felt, midway through a game, 'Do you know what? We're not losing this.' We just took control.

James Hanks: It was an incredible evening. It felt like we were never going to lose.

Gareth Steenson: There was talk at half-time of a bonus. 'Lads, there's an extra £1,000 in this for all of you if you win.' We were like, 'Have you cleared this with Tony yet?' Tony was so delighted afterwards I don't think he was that bothered.

Rob Baxter: There was only one moment when there was a swing. You could tell we were getting a big edgy. Someone kicked a ball out on the full, there was a scrum back and they got a penalty, from which they hit the post. Then they got done for a late tackle, we got a penalty where the ball landed and Steeno kicked it. It was a six-point swing in a matter of 30 seconds. We'd weathered the pressure and pushed on through.

Ali Hepher: We got to the stage where we knew we'd blown them up. We were screaming, 'Go now, guys. You've got them.' Then Steeno threw a dummy in his own 22 and went. It broke the whole game open and that was that.

Gareth Steenson: Listen back to the television commentators and, even when we're 20-odd points up with 15 minutes to go, we're still losing according to them. Out on the field I knew we'd won.

Bob Staddon: We were sitting quite close to Tony. He just couldn't watch.

Tony Rowe: About 20 minutes from the end I thought, 'I can't take this.' We were leading but I was so nervous. I walked down the grandstand and went outside into the car park. It was pissing with rain. I was walking up and down until I heard this huge cheer signalling the end of the game. I went to rush back inside but they wouldn't let me in because I didn't have a ticket on me. Eventually someone from the BBC came out and said, 'Hello, Tony. What are you doing here?' I said to him, 'Could you tell this guy who I am.' He turned to the steward and said, 'You've got to let him in, he's the chairman.'

Ali Hepher: The pack were amazing. Everything just worked and psychologically we were bang on it. They scored a try to come back into it but then we stole a line-out and, instead of trying to drive it over, Steeno kicked another drop goal. We just knifed it. It was the perfect killer blow.

Tom Johnson: I came off the bench for my usual 25 minutes and had a great time. All we had to do was add the finishing touches and make sure the nail remained rammed home. I just enjoyed it so much. We knew we were there long before Si Alcott's late try. We never thought we were going to lose. It was a completely surreal atmosphere.

Brett Sturgess: The campaign had lasted 50 weeks so there was definitely a sense of relief.

Phil Dollman: It wasn't relief at the end, it was joy.

Gareth Steenson: If there hadn't been play-offs, we'd still have won the league. There was no doubt in our minds we were a better side than Bristol.

Tom Johnson: I remember running around with Clive Stuart-Smith and Danny Gray. They left that year, so it was a little bittersweet in that sense.

Pete Drewett: I got invited up to the game by a mate. I was sitting up in the stands and at the end of the game I went over and shook hands with a couple of the directors. I was delighted. Then I sat in the corner and had a little cry. Tears of joy.

Ian Bremner: I was in Singapore. Despite the circumstances I have great admiration for what the club have done and for everything Tony and Rob have achieved.

Bob Staddon: They wouldn't present the cup on the pitch because health and safety said it was too wet.

Rob Baxter: The trophy was supposed to be awarded in the middle of the pitch but our fans were everywhere. Initially they were talking about getting us back out there. Then they said, 'We'll do it in the changing rooms.' But by the time I got back having done all the press, the changing room was empty. The players had all gone.

Tom Johnson: It was a big old party. The dressing room was great.

Gareth Steenson: It was quite nice, just being together inside for a few moments, before we went outside again to be with our supporters.

James Hanks: Those of us who had been there a couple of years knew that once we took that step the club wasn't going to look back. We knew it was going to be onwards and upwards for us all.

Tony Rowe: I phoned the club and asked how many people were already there. They said, 'It's rammed. They all want to know when the players are coming back.'

Rob Baxter: It was a huge day and, from what I can remember, a fantastic night.

Tom Johnson: It was a brand-new bus with a big U-shaped sofa of a back seat. You could fit 12 boys in there easy. We were drinking out of the cup all the way home.

Matt Jess: We'd only had the Championship trophy about two hours and someone dented it. We were having a look and suddenly it was, 'No! Oh God!'

Haydn Thomas: My playing shirt fell out of my bag when I was getting off the bus. I was really lucky someone handed it back. I'd have been devastated if I'd lost it.

Rob Baxter: My main memory from the bus was how many messages I got from agents offering me players. We barely took any of them. That was a key part of our planning. We had all the lads under contract. They all knew they were part of what we wanted to achieve the following season.

Tony Rowe: I make the players wear suits because of my military training. The suits were quite heavy and got absolutely saturated. I'd hired a directors' bus but the air con couldn't cope with all the steam. I had to sit on the dashboard with a cloth wiping the windows so the driver could see his way home. We eventually got back here and the place was a riot.

Haydn Thomas: It was mental. Tony put his card behind the bar and we got a good tab going.

Gareth Steenson: I remember Chris Budgen getting drinks from the top shelf.

Matt Jess: Steeno and Simon Alcott got a load of beers, sat in the middle of the pitch and drank until the sun came up. Fair play.

Gareth Steenson: We got back in between 4 a.m. and 5 a.m. Si and I walked through the door, put our fancy-dress outfits on for the next day's social and walked straight back out again wearing farmers' hats and swimming goggles. It was cold. We went straight to Tesco to get a case of beer but it was still only 5.30 a.m. and they wouldn't serve us until 6 a.m. We had to wait outside with the staff staring at us. Eventually, though, we made it back to Sandy Park. We took a couple of chairs out on to the pitch and sat on the halfway line with our case of beer and a couple of cigars. Then we met up with the rest of the lads in the Blue Ball pub at 8 a.m. I think we ended up going out to Exmouth on the train before heading back into town. I remember it being quite a nice day. We just bumbled around the city.

Brett Sturgess: We had vests made with 'Worthy Thursday' written on them in honour of our kit man, Andy Worth.

Tom Johnson: The next day I had to set off for my mate's stag night in Edinburgh. We spent the weekend at the Scotland sevens at Murrayfield, dressed in pink.

Brett Sturgess: There was a celebration parade on the Saturday but, at the last moment, I got called off the bus because my wife Heather had gone into labour with our first child, Noah. The only downside was missing the free beer at Tony Rowe's house on the Sunday. That doesn't happen every day.

Chris Bentley: We were on the piss non-stop. We had Staddon Sunday, Mad Monday, Terrific Tuesday . . . the lot. Rowey had a party at his house, the celebrations went on for days. Gradually it stopped being fun. The family guys started drifting away but the crazy boys carried on.

Rob Baxter: It felt incredible and then, very quickly, it felt very scary. All of a sudden the fixture list comes out and your first two games are Gloucester and Leicester. I remember thinking, 'Right, here we go.'

Tony Rowe: It was fantastic winning the Premiership but I will never, ever forget that night in Bristol. In a way we'd been working towards it since 1993. People wrote us off when we got to the Premiership but I never wrote us off. There was no way we were going back down.

RFU CHAMPIONSHIP FINAL SECOND LEG
Memorial Stadium, Bristol Wednesday 26 May 2010

Bristol (7) 10 Exeter Chiefs (15) 29
(Exeter win 38–16 on aggregate)

Bristol: L Arscott; L Robinson, L Eves (S Giddens, 63), J Fatialofa (J Adams, 40), T Arscott; A Jarvis, J Spice (capt; S Alford 43-49, 69); M Irish (M Vunipola, 59), D Blaney, W Thompson, D Montagu (D Barry, 63), R Winters, I Grieve, R Pennycock (J Merriman, 64), J Phillips.
Try: L Arscott. Con: Jarvis. Pen: Jarvis.

Exeter Chiefs: M Foster; M Jess, N Sestaret, P Dollman, P McKenzie; G Steenson, H Thomas; B Sturgess, N Clark (S Alcott 50), H Tui, T Hayes (capt), J Hanks (D Gannon, 63), C Slade, (T Johnson, 55), J Scaysbrook, R Baxter.
Replacements (not used): C Budgen, C Stuart-Smith, D Gray, M Cornwell.
Try: Alcott. Pens: Steenson 6. Drop goals: Steenson 2.

Referee: A Small (London). Att: 11,850.

ELEVEN

READY FOR THE CHOP

Tony Rowe had been planning for this moment for months. As far back as January, with the team riding high, he could sense things were coming together. He suggested to his board it was time to go and talk to Premiership Rugby. In 2006, when the possibility of promotion had first materialised in earnest, the club had found itself scrambling to satisfy the necessary criteria. Discussions had even taken place with the Exeter City football chairman, Julian Tagg, about a possible temporary ground share. 'We would never have survived,' reflects Rowe. 'This time we were ready. Everything had fallen into place.'

A phone call was duly made to the offices of Premiership Rugby Limited, situated in Regal House just down from Twickenham station.

'Can we come and see you?'

'Why?'

'Well, we might be promoted.'

'Okay, but why do you want to see us?'

'We've got a couple of questions.'

In company with his fellow directors Alan Quantick and Keiron Northcott, Rowe arrived at Regal House on the appointed day to meet PRL's chief executive Mark McCafferty.

'We think we're going to win the Championship this year.'

'Really? Do you think you'll beat Bristol?'

'Yeah, we think we might. And if we do, I need to know how much money we're going to get.'

'I'm sorry, we can't tell you that.'

'But we need to know.'

'We can't tell you exactly. All we can tell you is that you'll get 25 B shares and 5 A shares. If you want your P shares you have to be in the Premiership for two years and buy them from a club that already has them.'

'Oh, right. How much will that cost?'

'Sorry, we can't tell you precisely how much.'

The Exeter contingent could not believe what they were hearing. How were they supposed to compete with one arm effectively tied behind their backs? The brief silence was broken by Phil Winstanley, PRL's rugby director.

'Tony, I'm sure you've also read the promotion criteria document we sent you last July. You'll need to have a stadium with a sufficiently large capacity.'

'Yeah, but if we win we'll get the capacity up by the start of the season.'

'Sorry. You will need to have met all the criteria by the end of March.'

'So we've come up here and you can't tell us how much money we'll get. And even if we do win promotion that we might not get in?'

'As things stand, yes.'

'Right, thank you very much.'

Back outside in the street, Rowe was seething. 'Fuck it,' he murmured to Northcott. They had assumed, naively, that if they were promoted they would have time over the summer to upgrade the stadium. Now they had only a few weeks. On the way home to Devon it was decided to seek further advice. 'We came back and made a couple of phone calls to other Premiership chairmen. We were told we'd probably get less than a million pounds, possibly around £800,000. We all said to each other: "Fuck, that's not enough."' It was also less than half the amount the established sides were receiving.

Rowe, though, was not about to give up now. He phoned a company called Arena Seating to find out what might be possible.

'I want you to design a new North Stand.'

'When do you want it for? This summer?'

'No, we've got to start work now.'

He also phoned Olly, a local builder who had helped the club put the finishing touches to Sandy Park in 2006.

'Tony, it's pissing with rain.'

'I don't care, mate. I've got to get the foundations in.'

In eight weeks, miraculously, a new stand was designed and built. Nothing flash but there was no time for frills. All that mattered was ticking the necessary boxes, regardless of how unreasonable the demands might feel.

* * * * *

Once the deliciously warm and fuzzy Bristol afterglow had worn off, however, the 'to do' list was still daunting. Exeter might have reached the promised land but the quaint notion of a level playing field for newly promoted clubs simply did not exist in English rugby. Rowe was also unsure what ticket prices to announce. 'We didn't know so we checked what the other Premiership clubs were charging. Our Championship prices were around half the price.' While Exeter clearly needed to attract more bums on seats, the businessman in Rowe clicked instinctively into gear. Main stand season tickets, previously £280, almost doubled in price to £540, some £45 more than the equivalent price at Leicester. Locally there was a lot of grumbling but Rowe was having none of it. 'Whatever I've done in my life I've never wanted to be the cheapest. I don't like discount. I always think you should give value for money and I knew that's what people would be offered at Sandy Park.'

By the first weekend in September, in addition, Exeter would have to be competitive on the field. The good news was that the fitness staff had driven down to the Marines camp in Lympstone and managed to source a few discarded old ropes and other bits of second-hand gym equipment to furnish their gym under the stand. 'Most of the heavy ropes were rotten as hell but there were five or six in a pile out the back that were okay,' recalls MacLellan. 'We were scrounging stuff left, right and centre.' It reached the point where there was such a 'military boot camp' feel that newcomers felt slightly intimidated. 'We had a couple of physios who came in and said, "I don't like the feel of this. This is hardening men for battle." A few guys, particularly from overseas, would come in and say, "What is this?"'

The coaches and players, however, were bang up for it. As Steenson recalls, the off season was basically non-existent. 'Everyone now talks about five weeks of mandatory rest. We had two. I went on holiday to Tunisia and trained the whole time I was away. The excitement going into it was just so great. We couldn't wait. We were saying to each other, "We're going to be as ready as we possibly can." Guys were bouncing in to do fitness tests. Trust me, that's not normally a day people want to come in for.'

Baxter and Hepher had already decided that tiptoeing into the Premiership would be a mistake. Having waited so long to reach the top, Baxter was determined everyone would enjoy the experience. 'I'd seen so many teams and so many coaches talking about the Premiership being a dogfight, a battle or a marathon. I remember saying to our guys, "Forget all that. We've worked really hard to be here and we might only be here for one year. We're going to enjoy it and give it a really good go. We're not just going to try to win games 9–6." We deliberately didn't talk about how amazing it would be if we finished 11th. It took all the pressure off the players.'

From the start, they also pledged to take the game to their opponents and to accentuate the positives. Among other things, Baxter gave the squad a pre-season questionnaire to fill in. 'We asked them to come back with answers to three questions in particular: 1) What are going to be the important qualities for us to do well this season? 2) What do you want other people to see when they look at us? 3) How do you want to be judged yourself?'

The answers were illuminating and formed the basis of Exeter's entire approach. 'The things that cropped up the most were Attitude, Commitment and Enjoyment. That became our mantra for that first season. We had 'ACE' written up everywhere. The interesting one for me was 'enjoyment'. The guy who brought it up was our prop, Hoani Tui. He said it was really important to him to enjoy training and playing. He felt it brought the best out of him. He'd already talked to a few other players about it as well. Ten years ago nobody really talked about fun in professional sport. I never really expected a player to come back and say, "I think it's really important we enjoy it."'

How, practically, could this goal be realised? It was going to be a struggle to win every week, which is the simplest way to keep rugby players happy. Instead Baxter told his players that fulfilment would not necessarily be based on what the scoreboard said. 'We based blocks of the season around certain things. Right, in this block we're really going to show our attitude. In this one we're going to emphasise our commitment. In this one we're really going to show our enjoyment.'

Collectively, they also talked a lot about judging themselves on their levels of commitment. 'The biggest thing was how hard we trained. The next was how hard we could play and still be okay at the end of it. That would be our yardstick . . . whether we'd deserved to enjoy it. Probably our key defining quality is how we have sought to maintain that genuine enjoyment, which is aligned to how we think we should be performing.'

In practice that meant an intense summer for the players. 'It was like no pre-season I'd ever done before,' Johnson recalls. 'It wasn't harder. We just trained better, more specifically, more focused on our skills. Our old game plan was completely ripped up. From minute one we were walking through new game plans. "Right, this is how we're going to play." We knew that if we played Championship rugby in the Premiership we'd come straight back down. We had to fire some shots. People used to say, "That's mental." But you never know where your boundary is until you push it. We really pushed the limits of our attacking rugby.'

There was method in this apparent madness. From the outset Baxter agreed with Hepher that simply kicking the ball to high-quality opponents would be suicidal. 'I remember saying to Ali, "We need to have a bit of a policy here that we don't just give the ball to the opposition because they'll beat us. There's nothing wrong with keeping the ball. If we've got the ball, they haven't and that keeps us in the game.'"

And instead of Baxter acting as sole judge and jury as to how Exeter had performed, the players increasingly marked themselves. 'Initially I was always the judge in the changing room after a game. It was decided that we could enjoy some losses more than some wins if we'd played beyond what we regarded as our potential. Whether it was a win or a loss it was judged the same.'

* * * * *

The fixture list had further heightened the sense of anticipation. Not only would the Chiefs' opening game be at home but it would be a West Country 'derby' against Gloucester. As the significant September date approached, not many pundits exuded huge faith. Rowe held court in the Exeter Suite on the Wednesday before the game and could detect some scepticism. 'The whole world was saying, "You're lucky to be here." I was sitting there thinking, "You don't fucking know what we're going to do." I had great confidence in Rob.' Haydn Thomas, who had spent two seasons at Gloucester, was keenly aware of the looming challenge but also knew the Chiefs would be right up for it. 'What motivated us? We'd heard people like Austin Healey saying we wouldn't win a game. There was so much motivation from what the pundits had said. Almost everyone had written us off. It was fantastic.'

Mark Foster, another ex-Gloucester player in the Exeter ranks, was more than happy to put people straight in the *Guardian* on the morning of the game. 'This is a different place to what people expect,' Foster insisted. 'I've never been involved with a club where the players have so much emotional involvement. A lot of clubs are built around highly paid players who are not necessarily emotionally invested in the club. Gloucester is a very passionate place but the guys are primarily there to play rugby. At Exeter you totally belong. It's a real family. People pay lip service to it at other Premiership clubs but it's what sets Exeter apart. The work ethic here is frightening.'

He also reckoned that, despite a round one selection containing only a couple of new players – James Phillips and Luke Arscott had been recruited from Bristol – people were seriously underestimating the likes of Richie Baxter, not fit for the opening weekend but a massive influence on all around him. 'Richie astounded me from the moment I met him. He doesn't look like the biggest or fastest but I've never seen a man break so many tackles or hit so many people so hard.' At prop Chris 'Budgie' Budgen was also accustomed to putting his body on the line, having earned operational medals from Northern Ireland, Iraq and Afghanistan during his career in the Royal Welsh regiment.

Baxter, meanwhile, had a useful stat ready. Five of the previous six promoted sides (the exception was Leeds in 2008) had stayed up the following year. 'Every article you read has us finishing 12th and we've stuck a couple of them up around the place. The realism is that staying up would be an achievement. But I think the ambitions of the club and the playing staff are that we'd like to be a bit better than that.'

Rowe still barely slept a wink on the Friday night. The good news was that just over 9,500 supporters had booked tickets – 'We couldn't have got our pricing that wrong' – and the players' wives and partners much appreciated being invited, for the first time, to watch the game from the comfort of an unsold hospitality box. But what if stage fright intervened and the whole occasion fell flat? Even Rowe could not guarantee nirvana. 'We were a bit apprehensive. It's one thing saying, "We'll be okay," but we needed to find out.'

He need not have worried. The weather was glorious, the atmosphere sensational and the old County Ground felt like a parallel universe. Every second person seemed to have bought a pasty and, even before kick-off, the beer and cider was lubricating the voices of Exeter's excited fans. The Tomahawk Chop chant, which originated from Florida State University in the 1980s and was subsequently adopted by supporters of the Atlanta Braves baseball team and the NFL's Kansas City Chiefs, had found its way across the Atlantic to Devon. Suddenly grown adults in headdresses were roaring to the heavens and chopping their forearms up and down with an open palm to simulate a sharpened blade.

'Ooooh-Ooh-Ohhh, Ooh-Ooh-Ohhh!'

Sung in unison, with real feeling, it had a haunting quality. It also created a distinctive sporting identity and an accompanying soundtrack, as with Munster and 'The Fields of Athenry'. The Chiefs came steaming out of the tunnel, dressed all in black with a white swoosh across the chest. Despite the presence of seven England internationals, Gloucester were rattled even before Foster sprinted over to score against his former club after just five minutes. Having touched the ball down, the winger caught the eye of his old housemate, Luke Narraway, with whom he had played for both England Schoolboys and the Cherry and Whites. 'Anyone but you,' muttered Narraway. Foster grinned back and was still smiling at the final whistle. A perspiring Gloucester, 16–5 behind at half-time, had been beaten 22–10. While Steenson had kicked everything, his opposite number Nicky Robinson missed all five of his efforts at goal. Thomas also knew Narraway and, as the pair ran off beside each other at the interval, he noticed his former colleague was breathing heavily. 'He turned to me and said, "Will you guys just kick the ball to us?" We were playing so much rugby the opposition never had the ball.'

Up front, the Chiefs lock forward James Hanks also sensed a major mental hurdle had been cleared. 'To win was just the biggest relief ever. We knew in that moment we could compete, that we could do it. It was one of those days when everything was set up for us. It was hot, the crowd were right behind us and Gloucester didn't quite know what to expect. It was almost written.' As Mike Tindall told Thomas afterwards: 'Inside the first 10 minutes we knew it was going to be a long afternoon.' On BBC radio, the former England prop forward Gareth Chilcott was similarly impressed. 'Bath used to be the gateway to the south-west; now it's moved an hour down the M5.'

A pedant might argue that several formidable Bath forwards – Graham Dawe, Roger Spurrell, Victor Ubogu – spent their formative rugby years in the far south-west. And what about Phil Vickery, Trevor Woodman, Julian White, Stuart Hooper and the dozens of other top players who might have gravitated towards

Exeter had they become a Premiership side earlier? Imagine the pack they could have had. Baxter, though, was not about to get distracted. 'It was a fantastic occasion but we're not going to celebrate until we know we're here in the Premiership next year. If any boys had suggested a lap of honour I'd have thrown them in the changing room myself.' Hepher was also mindful Gloucester had not enjoyed much fortune. 'I think we got a bit lucky. There were four or five forward passes given against them. They were forward but on another day they could have scored more tries if they'd got their timing right.'

On the Monday morning Foster also received an insight into the coaches' attention to seemingly minor details. 'I did my debrief with Ali but Rob was in the office as well. After we'd finished he asked for a word.

'Foz, have you got a second?'

'Yeah.'

'Awesome game, you were outstanding. That's everything we want from you. That's why we signed you. You'll have a great future at this club.'

'Thanks.'

'There's just one thing. When you scored, you celebrated to the crowd. The reason you got the try was because of your teammates. When you celebrate, the first people you should celebrate with should be the team.'

It struck an immediate chord. Of course Baxter was right. More recently Foster has found himself working in finance and the lessons he learned at Exeter about teamwork and operating under pressure continue to serve him well today. 'I totally retrained as a chartered accountant and had to do 15 four-hour exams having not studied since 2002. That belief I'd developed when I was doing some of these horrific training sessions at Exeter was the only way I got through it. Normal people think, "I'm tired, I'm done." We were taught never to accept the end.' There was also another common denominator. 'Rob is a family man and very traditional with his values. It's very rare he hires single guys. Most of them are in long-term relationships or married with kids. That's the way he prefers the squad. He doesn't necessarily want the drama that comes with having 20 single guys out chasing girls in Exeter.'

* * * * *

For all involved, anything now seemed possible. Even Exeter's daunting first Premiership away game the following weekend against Leicester at Welford Road felt like a cause for real excitement rather than trepidation. Come what may, the Chiefs decided they would give it a lash. The same attitude had even extended to the directors' chosen mode of transport. Rowe had not felt the urge to travel to every Championship away game. In the Premiership, he told Sharon, it would be different. They would go everywhere. But how? Morgan, now aged eight, proposed a helicopter but that felt too ostentatious. Eventually it was decided to commission a company in Southampton to supply a small, tailor-made Mercedes coach. Sitting around the dining table on a Sunday in July, the conversation turned to what the vehicle should be called.

'We need a name for it.'

'What do you mean?'

'All commercial vehicles are usually given a lady's name.'

'Can we call it Sharon after Mum?'

'Er, no. I don't want to ask all my mates if they'd like a ride in Sharon.'

It was Sharon herself who suggested calling it 'Doris' on the grounds that was the catch-all description her husband often used whenever he temporarily forgot a female name. Within a couple of weeks Rowe discovered the number plate DOR 15S was for sale and his transport issues were satisfactorily resolved by the time the Chiefs headed up to Leicester on the second week in September. Rather more crucially, Baxter had kept faith with the same starting XV from the previous week, having been asked what he felt was a strange question in the press conference following the Gloucester game.

'Will you be resting up your first team for Leicester away because you've got Newcastle at home the following week?'

'No.'

'Why?'

'Well, most of our team haven't got any Premiership experience. I want them to be really good Premiership players. The only way you do that is to go to places like Leicester and experience it.'

Baxter could sense 'people looking at me as if I was a bit stupid' but, to him, it made complete sense. If you got in and played well, whether the Chiefs won or lost, you stayed in. Motivation was certainly not a problem and a belter of a game unfolded. Phil Dollman, wearing 13, exchanged passes with Foster to score a smart try and then added a second after neat approach play from Thomas and Arscott. Even the Welshman was taken aback. 'Before that, I couldn't remember the last time I'd scored two tries in a professional game.' In the second half Foster dummied gloriously past Alesana Tuilagi for another try and the Chiefs led 27–16 with 23 minutes left. A sensational result loomed until, as Baxter recalls, 'the crowd and the referee suddenly started thinking, "Hang on, this shouldn't be happening."' It remains a match Thomas and Hepher, among others, would dearly love to revisit. 'Of all the games we've been involved with, that's one we'd like to go and finish off,' confirms Thomas. 'They were fully loaded but for 65 minutes we had them beat.'

No matter. Leicester's scrum had gained the upper hand late on but, overall, the first fortnight had been highly encouraging. 'Leicester beat us 37–27 in the end but it didn't feel like that,' said

MacLellan, still involved on the club's physio staff. 'As somebody said, "This is Leicester. We've rattled their cage and, okay, a tiger has come out but we have challenged them." I think that game was a very significant one.' Steenson, meanwhile, was bisecting the uprights with regularity and could sense genuine belief flooding through the team. 'We all came away feeling confident. The following week, back at home, we beat Newcastle and thought, "Here we go."' Never had a promoted side, despite the shortfall in funding, looked so instantly at home at the top table.

PREMIERSHIP – ROUND 1
Saturday, 4 September 2010, Sandy Park
Exeter 22 Gloucester 10

Exeter Chiefs: L Arscott; N Sestaret, P Dollman (M Jess, 45–55), B Rennie (Jess, 55), M Foster; G Steenson, H Thomas (G Cowley, 73); B Sturgess (B Moon, 68), N Clark (S Alcott, 50), H Tui (C Budgen, 56), T Hayes (capt), J Hanks (D Gannon, 68), T Johnson, J Scaysbrook, J Phillips (C Slade, 50). Try: Foster. Con: Steenson. Pens: Steenson 4. Drop goal: Steenson.

Gloucester: O Morgan (T Taylor, 23); J Simpson-Daniel, M Tindall (capt, T Molenaar, 61), E Fuimaono-Sapolu, L Vainikolo; N Robinson, D Lewis (J Pasqualin, 66); N Wood (A Dickinson, 54), S Lawson (O Azam, 68), P Capdevielle, D Attwood, A Brown (W James, 68), P Buxton (A Strokosch, 48), A Qera, L Narraway.
Tries: Simpson-Daniel, Taylor.

Referee: R Debney (Leicestershire). Att: 9,562.

TWELVE

SOUTH COAST OFFENSE

For as long as he can remember Ali Hepher has seen things differently to most people. From his first year at comprehensive school in Northampton it came naturally. One day he and his classmates were given an exercise in which they played tennis against each other but were told they could ignore the lines. 'Everyone else just hit the ball back but I immediately hit it 20 metres left where no one could receive it. I just instantly knew.'

His games teacher immediately grasped that Hepher's spatial awareness might be useful on a rugby field, even though the latter had never played the sport in his life. Before he knew it, Hepher had been picked at fly-half and named captain. Self-effacing by nature but quietly competitive, he instinctively loved the idea of a game which, for all its physicality, had a chess-like tactical element.

Problem-solving already ran in the Hepher family, who had relocated to the East Midlands from the north-east when Ali was only three years old. His father was a project engineer who worked for the company that designed warning systems for the Eurofighter. When it came to sport, he was a keen armchair fan but his wife had been good at sport – netball, tennis, hockey – without having a particularly competitive edge. It created a decent mix of genes and Ali and his brother Simon both ended up representing Saints' first team.

The former's career at Franklin's Gardens was complicated by the presence of Paul Grayson but, having shared in Northampton's narrow European final success over Munster, he was picked to go on England's tour to South Africa in the summer of 2000. Unfortunately, in 2002, he ruptured his ACL playing in a second-team game for Northampton against Wasps, catching his studs as he turned to try and prevent Ayoola Erinle cutting past him on the inside. It was to be the end of his Saints career but at Bedford he relished playing under Mike Rayer and, having also been tutored by Wayne Smith and Ian McGeechan, began to feel he might have something to offer as a coach.

Again, though, Grayson's presence blocked his subsequent route upwards from the Northampton academy. 'I also knew I didn't have a big enough name to go straight into the top end of the Premiership.' When Baxter's call finally came he was desperate for an opportunity to blend Smith's rugby understanding, Rayer's man management and Geech's forward thinking – 'Back in the 1990s there were things he was introducing that were changing the laws of the game because they were so good' – into a coaching style he could call his own.

Even before he headed west he felt the Chiefs could do with thinking differently. 'I'd played Exeter the year before when they were competing against Northampton. They were picking and going from the middle of the park. I was saying: "You're not going to be successful in the Premiership doing it that way." Rob's mentality, though, was slightly different. Against Northampton he felt he couldn't afford for us to have the ball. If you've got the ball you're not defending. So it was a combination of me finding a different way for us to keep the ball which Rob agreed with.'

Hepher had always enjoyed American sports. In particular, he loved the annual documentary series called *America's Game* which profiles every team to have won the Super Bowl. Holed up alone in a flat in Exeter, Hepher trawled through 30 editions to see what might work in a union context. Often his NFL research would spark something: not necessarily a fully formed idea but a 'what if' thought that might lead somewhere else. 'It was often a case of "That wouldn't work for us but what if we did this and this?" Some coaches are notebook coaches. They want the secret answer and then they jot it down. I'm more "That makes sense" or "If we tweak this, that could work." One day Rob stuck up a clip of the Tampa Bay Buccaneers who had won the Super Bowl in 2002 with a famously hard-running full-back called Mike Alstott. We just said, "This is how we want you to carry the ball." On the sideline you could hear Warren Sapp shouting, "Alstott up the gut." When Sam Hill was younger he'd be our Alstott. We'd all shout, "Hilly up the gut."'

He was also a big fan of Bill Walsh's so-called 'West Coast Offense' which helped turn the San Francisco 49ers into NFL champions in the 1980s. It was all about creating space through passing the ball and angled running, with the aim of creating defensive mismatches. To Hepher's mind it made a lot more sense than simply running headlong into the nearest hunk of opposition muscle. 'My biggest pet hate, even when I was in the academy at Northampton, was old-style "wrap" rugby. It was just dated. Once you are physically matched you get done. So many times I'd watch Premiership games and teams' whole attack would be concentrated within the width of the posts. There would be nothing anywhere else, which made it really easy for the defence.'

All of this was bubbling away inside him before he had conducted a single Exeter training session. Soon enough, he could contain himself no longer. 'Midway through that first year in 2010/11 we had some incredibly hard-working forwards. We'd hit it up, then send the forwards repeatedly round the corner. The backs would be waiting on one side, would run out of space, reload all the way back and then we'd hit another forward. The forwards would be carrying about 30 times and the backs were carrying five times. I told them we had to be more efficient and smarter. If we've got backs over here, let's get them the ball. Let's balance it up so we're getting 12–15 carries out of each of our backs and spreading the load. Your carriers are going to be better and it's a two-sided attack, which gave us options both ways. That allows you to say, "Wherever you defend us, we're going to go to space." You can't defend everything so there's going to be an option for us somewhere. It's then about us making the right decisions to pick the lock. That's essentially it.' To make it feel specific to Exeter, Hepher suggested calling it the 'South Coast Offense', given the club's proximity to the coastline of south Devon. The name stuck. 'We still use it but we're on about version 110 now.'

Making sure the players were fully engaged with the basic calls that underpin every rugby playbook was another priority. At Bedford, Hepher had worked with Andy Key, who had previously spent many years at Leicester. The Tigers had a list of calls which could, if required, be linked together. 'Rum and coke' would be one example. A 'rum' would be a switch and a 'coke' would be a miss pass. There were similar variations based on fruit juice and sandwiches. What type of food or drink could Hepher use? One night he had a eureka moment: what about different varieties of curry? 'There were obviously the different meats – beef, chicken, pork – and your different dishes – tikka, korma etc.' The players liked it immediately. After a while it became so popular that half the club teams in the West Country nicked the idea as well.

Crucially, though, a move would never be entirely set in stone. 'It doesn't necessarily mean the pass is definitely going to a certain place. There's never an absolute. It's more a case of "I'm doing this and I'm an option if my opponent doesn't defend me." Alternatively, if a guy on my inside opens up a slide I can drop it into him, or put a short pass to someone else if he's heading into a hole. Or, if everyone's jammed in tight, there's another option out the back.' I like to do my attack strategies like flow charts. Maybe it's my maths side coming out.'

Hepher's thirst for innovation also extended to Exeter's kicking strategies. He wanted to find a way to train his on-field generals to find space and make the right decisions under the kind of pressure they would experience on match day. A few days later he had another brainwave: what about those military sniper targets that pop up and down? 'I wanted pop-up targets that I could operate remotely from behind. I'd knock one down and – boom – suddenly there'd be a space there. I phoned up a company who supplied them but was told they could only be sold to the military.'

Which was when the idea of lights on chairs popped into his head. 'When a light came on you had to kick to it. Then you could use different colours to represent different types of kick. Then we flipped it. Rather than the lights coming on, you had to kick to where it had just gone off, as if it were space that had just opened up.' His latest wheeze has been to try and persuade Premiership Rugby to allow him to switch on the digital pitch-side advertising hoardings and run a little stick man up and down the sideline to replicate a sprinting winger.

Permission has not yet been approved in case he crashed the system prior to a big televised game but it underlines Exeter's desire to think outside the box. Strong in the arm, thick in the head? Tired old rustic stereotypes have never applied at the Chiefs.

* * * * *

The newcomers could certainly never be accused of being dull. Very soon they were starting to become every neutral's 'favourite' team. More than that, they were making people feel good: they were fun to watch, gave everything and attacked every game with infectious enthusiasm. There was partly an element of needing to play attractive rugby to put a few more bums on Sandy Park's pale blue seats but Baxter was also adamant the Chiefs' debut season had to be savoured. 'Some of you don't understand,' he would tell his squad, not even attempting to disguise his own emotions. 'We've spent 15 to 20 years building towards this year in the Premiership. We are going flat out and we're going to enjoy every fucking second of it.'

Even heavy defeats such as a 40–13 loss at Harlequins in late September proved hugely valuable. Exeter had started poorly, lost a couple of players to the sin-bin in the third quarter and were a distant second by the final whistle. Baxter instantly sensed it was a pivotal moment: how would his mentally shot players react to their first thrashing? Early the following week they all debated it for almost two hours, with Baxter keen to highlight the importance of losing bonus points.

'Guys, when you're the away team, these are a massive advantage to you.'

'Er, how come?'

'Look, everyone expects to beat us, especially at their place. You all know that.'

'Yeah.'

'Okay, so what is going to make them a bit edgy and panicky? It's us being within seven points. One mistake and we've caught them. So here's what we're going to do. In every away game from now on we're going to play as if we've got a seven-point lead. If they kick a penalty we're still winning 7–3. We've still got something to fight for. That's how I want you to look at it. Even if we're 14 points down, play like we're only seven points down.

At that point most teams, against us, will start chucking their subs on thinking they've got a sufficiently big lead. That's when we can really go after them.'

The room went quiet as everyone wrestled with the mental maths. Baxter really wanted them to buy into the idea. The following week involved another big away game at Northampton, whose big pack were always going to be tough to crack. With 11 minutes left the Saints were 27–9 up and coasting, only to lose Jon Clarke to the bin and concede a pick-and-go try, scored by Budgen. The Chiefs dominated the closing minutes and a try in the left corner by Arscott, converted by Steenson, earned the visitors the unlikeliest of bonus points. Baxter could not have been more delighted. 'We went after them and they were relieved to kick the ball off the pitch. At home, at Franklin's Gardens. Our lads celebrated like we'd won the game. I think it sowed a seed. It's very rare now that we lose by more than a score. If you hang in there sometimes a team will break because they can't get rid of you.'

Just as Baxter had also hoped, it fostered a belief that nothing was impossible. The following month Exeter went up to Saracens and won 23–9 to record their first away Premiership win, courtesy of a spectacular late 40-metre try from Sturgess. Even when David Strettle caught up with the charging prop there was no stopping him. 'Rob says Strettle rode me in like he was a jockey. He still describes it as one of his favourite moments.' Again the celebrations were raucous and heartfelt and, talking to the Saracens players subsequently, Haydn Thomas received some interesting feedback. 'The Saracens guys were saying how much they learned from us that day: how much it clearly meant and how much we put into it.' Brendan Venter, their coach, admitted his side had been outfought in every aspect. It was Sarries' only home league defeat in a season which saw them crowned domestic champions at Twickenham the following May.

That same autumn there was also the novelty of a first European away trip. Those who were in Bourgoin still smile about it a decade later. Not only did the Chiefs play well and record a 34–19 win but their hosts had kindly laid on a free bar afterwards. For players such as Johnson, after years in the lower leagues, it was too good an opportunity to turn down. 'The French plied us with food and booze and we just thought, "This is the life."' They were still in party mood when they returned to the team hotel where, as Foster puts it, 'some of the shit going down was absolutely ludicrous.' The crowning glory was when the doors of the hotel lift opened and Sturgess, who had disappeared on a reconnaissance mission down to the kitchen, was caught red-handed with numerous bottles of wine and – ever the caring teammate – handfuls of croissants for breakfast.

It was all part of the learning curve, which proved steeper in some cases than others. There was a particularly entertaining example the following season when Ben White, the club's excitable Australian back-rower, got carried away during a one-sided Challenge Cup game against Cavalieri Prato. 'Take that, you French bastards,' he screamed at one point, only to turn around and find his teammates crying with laughter. 'Mate, they're from Italy!'

By Christmas 2010 it was already clear the Chiefs had done enough to stay up. Their ranks had also been boosted by Jason Shoemark, who had won a solitary cap at centre for the All Blacks. Even their mountainous Fijian back, Sireli Naqelevuki, was now dwarfed by his six-foot-five-inch-tall, 21-stone compatriot Nemani Nadolo. The latter's stay, unfortunately, proved short and ill-starred; by May he had been released from his contract having been arrested for drink-driving and banned from driving for 18 months. He had also been registered under his Australian passport which led to Exeter being docked two points and fined £5,000 for unwittingly fielding too many non-Kolpak players.

Some of Exeter's home-grown players, however, were starting to make people sit up and take note. In one home game against Northampton, for example, Exeter scored 27 unanswered second-half points to win 30–9, with the pacy Johnson among the try scorers. The flanker was a few months short of his 28th birthday but, suddenly, people were talking him up as an emerging talent in the frame for England Saxons. 'After I'd raced half the length of the pitch and scored, Luke Arscott and Phil Dollman were jumping on my back going, "You're off to the Saxons!"' Sure enough, at the end of the season, Johnson marked his first appearance in the white of England with a try against the Barbarians at Twickenham.

At the conclusion of their inaugural 22-game campaign in the Premiership, meanwhile, Exeter finished eighth, above Wasps, Sale, Newcastle and the relegated Leeds Carnegie. It was emphatically not what the majority of pundits had predicted at the outset. Rowe was also quietly delighted to have confounded the view further up the M5 that Bristol might have been worthier additions to the league. 'They didn't expect to lose the final but seemed to forget it was their chief executive, Steve Gorvett, and myself who'd proposed that "home and away" play-off system. There had been a proposal to stage the Championship final at Twickenham but we said, "Hang on a minute; who gets the money at Twickenham? You'll only get a crowd of a few thousand and it'll cost us money to go there. Why can't we have home and away finals?" After they lost that play-off final, the relationship between us and Bristol was a bit frosty. Their chairman, Chris Booy, said to me, "We won the bloody league; you should never have got promoted." It took them a few years to get over it.'

* * * * *

Exeter's supporters, meanwhile, were enjoying a magic-carpet ride of pure, undiluted joy. Everyone loved the Chiefs' apparent lack of fear. The club's increasing aspirations, though, did not translate into a glut of signings. Once again Baxter declined to rush out in the summer of 2011 and buy endless new players, although he did slightly change his team's mission statement. It was only a slight tweak, the 'ACE' acronym that had worked so well the previous season now amended to 'GRACE' with 'Graft' and 'Respect' bolted on to 'Attitude', 'Commitment' and 'Enjoyment'. Baxter wanted to emphasise that further improvement was still very much required. 'We added "Graft" because a lot of guys had bought into the idea there was nothing to stop us from working hard. "Respect" was not just about wanting respect from people, it was also about showing respect to the competition and how hard we needed to work to compete in it.'

There was, accordingly, plenty of pre-season sweat and toil with Baxter still keen for his players to be fitter than their opponents and consequently more able to run them off their feet. 'It's funny now when I read people saying, "Exeter have always played a forward-orientated game." In our first few years in the Premiership we ran the ball from everywhere.'

Baxter also sat the squad down and shared the remarkable, inspirational story of an American father who competed in full ironman events with his disabled son. 'This guy can do a full ironman dragging his son along with him on a bike, swimming with a rope in his teeth. There's no reason we can't dig a bit deeper.' Foster, who had broken his leg in an Anglo-Welsh Cup victory over Leicester in January, had already received an insight into how intensively Exeter rehabbed their players. 'I was in a cast for six days and then, suddenly, I'd be in an air boot. Paddy Anson would say things like, "Right, we'll warm up with 10 lengths of casual butterfly." I'd never been so fit in my life. Guys were coming back into training like complete machines.'

From the minute the Chiefs arrived in the Premiership, the aforementioned Anson had also introduced a culture of sweeping out the changing rooms, home and away, which has since been copied far and wide. As their team manager Tony Walker put it: 'We wanted to be a team and club who, when we went somewhere, people would say, "They're a good group of guys." Anson also famously wore a singlet on match days for an entire season, regardless of the weather. The rationale was simple: none of the players could then moan about being cold or wet when the worst winter weather whipped across the draughty expanses of Sandy Park. On match days, the locals reckon it is consistently two degrees cooler up at the stadium than it is in the centre of Exeter.

At other times Foster and his teammates would be given killer indoor sessions, specifically tailored to increase their resilience: 'They would sit us down in the dark in the gym, watching *Gladiator* in silence. Then, three at a time, they would take us into the back gym and tell us to start exercising on a particular piece of kit. If they thought we were going fast enough we could move on a station. If not, we had to move back a station. There was no time limit, you just go flat out for as long as you could. It was all based around the premise that if you were absolutely done at 80 minutes could you still keep going? It was why we were so good late in games.'

Exeter being Exeter, it also became a blueprint for some of the squad's more lively social gatherings. As Foster recalls: 'We basically turned it into a drinking game. People would have to be naked with goggles on, fish a dumb-bell off the bottom of the ice bath, come out and drink three pints on the head, do burpees in the shower and then go into the changing room and do Double Dutch while drinking WKDs. At the end there would be a game of "Aftershock Pong" – every time you missed you had to have a shot of vodka.' Foster also remembers one particular social where James Phillips and Simon Alcott, the day's enforcers, turned up wearing gas masks and spray packs – normally used to kill garden weeds – full of vodka. The giant ex-Bath lock Peter Short wore black speedos, a black cape and a black eye mask.

'What have you come as?'

'A sexy panda.'

'Oka-ay.'

It was the former Bath contingent, allegedly, who also introduced the risqué try celebration which involved squeezing the genitals of any Exeter player who scored a try. Given an increasing number of the club's games were featuring on television it could not continue indefinitely but, for a while, it was a popular in-joke. The management turned a blind eye, convinced a happy squad was much more likely to be a successful one.

What was invariably tougher was keeping fringe squad members onside when they weren't playing. In the view of his former teammate Chris Bentley, Baxter has grown steadily more adept in this crucial area. 'We'd go for a Sap-ucchino up at David Lloyd and suck the life out of it. The team's shit, the coaches are wrong, fuck 'em all. Now they don't sulk. They've got so much better at investing in the guys outside the 23. There is a real brutal honesty around selection and if you've got good characters you can handle that honesty a lot better.'

The results were there for all to admire. On the second weekend of September 2011, the Chiefs were officially top of the English league table for the first time. The season, admittedly, was just two games old but, for Rowe, that was just a minor detail. He had the newspaper cutting framed and stuck it on the wall behind his desk. Exeter went on to finish in the top half of the table for the first time, beating Leicester home and away in the process, and reached the Challenge Cup last eight. Fifth place also qualified them for a first appearance in the following season's Champions Cup. The determination that had characterised the squad through the Championship was still there and even fit players such as Matt Jess were pushing themselves like never before. 'We'd train on the dunes and the beach at Exmouth in pre-season, when the sun was at its highest. I remember after one session being dropped off at Sandy Park on a Friday. Everyone was absolutely done. Phil Dollman had only walked about half a yard when he sat down in the middle of the car park. He couldn't move. It was all about the Marine mentality: resilience, teamwork, testing the boundaries. Can you stick at it? We'd look into each other's eyes and know we'd worked hard. You'd take yourself to your absolute limit – and then you'd go beyond it. That would transfer to the pitch.'

For Jess, from the outset, there was also an element of wanting to show the rest of the league that the lack of a lofty reputation was no barrier to being a good, tough, consistent performer. 'I think a lot of us wanted to prove to people we were worthy of playing in the Premiership. We all had a point to prove. Motivation wasn't a problem. Individually everyone wanted the same thing.' The occasional beer was certainly not going to hurt. 'I remember back in the day Leeds having a drinking ban when Neil Back was in charge. I was told that one of their lads went out to the local Wetherspoons, ordered a pizza and a Coke, but someone saw him in a pub and he got disciplined. What's that going to do to your team?' The only question now facing Exeter was how much higher they could soar.

THIRTEEN

MODERN FAMILY

The missing ingredient from Baxter's perspective was the relative lack of top-level experience in his squad. Scouring the Championship for rough diamonds and polishing up other clubs' disaffected cast-offs was all very well, but international-calibre leaders and players were harder to come by on Exeter's still-modest budget. Not only that but the Chiefs' loyal club captain, Tom Hayes, was beginning to feel his age and had an increasingly sore back. The time had come for Exeter to consider something they had never previously felt the need to pursue: recruiting their first top-drawer, seasoned southern-hemisphere international.

But which one, exactly? This was a big call in every respect. Baxter did his due diligence and pored over hours of video footage before, finally, dialling a number in Australia. Within moments of answering the phone at home in Sydney, the Wallabies' second row Dean Mumm had a fair idea Exeter might be an interesting place to go and play.

'Do you like a drink?'

'Sorry?'

'Do you enjoy a good time?'

'Er, yes!'

In hindsight, Mumm came to realise it was a great interview question. 'You get to see whether people are honest or full of rubbish because, sooner or later, you'll work it out anyway. Rob didn't want to talk to me about the game so much but he was truly interested in me as an individual and how I would fit into his environment. You get the sense he has already made up his mind about your qualities as a player before he speaks to you. The interview is more about culture than rugby.'

Mumm was also intrigued by Baxter's blunt assessment of Exeter as a club that, as things stood, was probably punching above its weight and needed to make further improvements. Having spent his entire career in Super Rugby with the Waratahs, he also liked the idea of experiencing a new environment. He had recently married Sarah and neither of them had been to Exeter before. Was it worth a punt? The Mumms decided it was an opportunity they should embrace.

That said, both of them felt a long way from home having flown into Heathrow and caught the train down to Exeter. Here they suddenly were, in a temporary apartment in a totally unfamiliar English city. Sarah was also pregnant. Within a couple of months, cruelly, the couple's supposedly life-enhancing UK adventure took a deeply distressing turn. Mumm received a call at training from Sarah, telling him she was being rushed to hospital with stomach cramps and to brace himself for every couple's worst nightmare. Their daughter Sophie was indeed born prematurely at just 21 weeks and stood no chance of survival. Around the same time his Exeter teammate Chris Budgen and his wife Tina also lost their prematurely born twin boys, Rhys and Taylor. Rugby was suddenly the least important thing in the world.

* * * * *

Mumm's first game, for the second team away at Harlequins, was another test of character. Maybe it was a deliberate test to see whether the friendly Aussie incomer – whose grandfather Bill had won a cap for New Zealand in 1949 – was as refreshingly ego-free as he appeared. The glamour, either way, was not easily discernible. 'I'd never done a bus trip on the day of a game since I was about 12. Let alone on a Monday. And then we played the same night and drove home! That's not how professional rugby works in the southern hemisphere. You fly to the game, stay overnight and fly home the next morning.'

Sitting at the front of the bus with the junior kids who were living in the club's academy house, the 28-year-old Mumm began to feel about 108. 'I quickly realised how much the club and the players are on social media. I decided I'd better sign up for a Twitter account. When you're an old bloke, you've got to fit in somehow.'

The other big thing that struck him was the quality of the players in Exeter's extended squad. Jack Yeandle, Ben Moon, Dave Ewers, Jack Nowell, Henry Slade, Luke Cowan-Dickie . . . if these blokes were second-graders, the first team must be handy. 'There's some serious talent here,' thought Mumm as he gazed out of the coach window at the dark, unfamiliar English countryside on the long journey home.

Mumm was not wrong. Rowe and Exeter had been required to jump through a sizeable number of RFU hoops a few years previously to establish a fully funded academy set-up in Devon and Cornwall; now it was starting to bear fruit. In particular there was a cohort of local lads who had something about them. Jack Nowell, Luke Cowan-Dickie, Henry Slade and Sam Hill had all been born within a few months of each other in 1993; by the summer of 2012 they were helping England U20s win the Junior World Championship. Cowan-Dickie had been the first to make his Chiefs debut aged just 18, and Hill was the same age when he took the field against Wasps in January. In October, in an LV= game against the Ospreys, a 19-year-old Nowell made his first appearance and was picked to feature in the Premiership for the first time against London Irish the following month, his introduction coinciding neatly with Exeter's first away league win of the season. He had already played for Redruth and Plymouth and was immediately nicknamed 'James O'Connor' after the precocious Wallaby teenager who had burst on to the international scene. As Steenson now says: 'They were very similar in the way they ran and I've no doubt Jack modelled himself on him.'

Slade and Yeandle were both blooded in a game at London Welsh in November 2012; as players they could hardly have been more different – the thoroughbred athlete and the unyielding hooker – but in their differing ways they had both had to battle to reach this point. Slade had failed to get picked for Devon U15s, overlooked at fly-half in favour of a mate of Sam Hill's from Crediton called Rob Avery-Wright. 'We were moving house at the time so I went back to my grandmother's house. I think it was the last time I cried. I cried all night, I was gutted.' Short, slight of stature and with slight OCD tendencies, he resolved to train harder. Nature also began to take its course. 'I didn't grow until I was 16. Then I finally got my pubes and started playing for Devon U17s and U18s. It is tough when you're younger but in the long run it benefits you. I always found that if you're smaller you have to get your technique right to keep up with the bigger lads. Then, once you've caught them up size-wise, you're ahead.'

Slade had been sitting on the floor in the clubhouse at Ivybridge, tucked below the wilds of Dartmoor and just above the gentler South Hams, when dreams of playing for England initially stirred. The eldest of John and Jayne Slade's three sons – his mum also took in respite foster children – was a wide-eyed 10-year-old in November 2003, the perfect age to be swept away on a tide of World Cup-winning euphoria. Watching the final in the clubhouse he recalls Jonny Wilkinson's winning kick vividly: 'I was sitting under a table and when he kicked the drop goal I jumped up and smashed my head.'

As he got older he also began to empathise with the way Jonny liked to feel totally prepared. He, in turn, spent all his spare time outdoors practising his goal-kicking. There is a strong farming background in his family – pigs and sheep on his mother's side, dairy cattle on his surveyor father's – and no shortage of fields to roam. 'Pretty much all my grandparents and uncles have got farms. I nicked a set of posts from school and put them up in one of Grandad's fields in Plympton and used to practise my kicking there. I had to give them back eventually but I was 18 by then and kicking up at Exeter.'

Then, five days before he was due to start his A-levels at nearby Plymouth College – where he briefly coincided with the Olympic diver Tom Daley – another major obstacle emerged. One of his best friends was diagnosed with Type 1 diabetes and invited Slade to jab his own thumb to measure his insulin levels. By coincidence, it turned out he also had the condition, necessitating regular insulin jabs. Before training sessions and matches his blood sugar levels would have to be tested to help his body function properly. 'You have to keep an eye on it and control it but, if you do that, there's no reason you can't do whatever you want.'

In the circumstances, it required a good deal of resolve to press on with his rugby ambitions. 'I'd always wanted to be a rugby player but I'd never really known if I was good enough or if it might be a possibility. There was no one I could point to and say, "Well he's done it," and try and emulate him. Everyone was from up-country – London and those sorts of places.' That only changed when his school coach, Scott Williams, took him aside after a session and asked him if he had ambitions to play top-level rugby. 'I said, "Yeah," but that I had no idea how to go about doing it.' Williams and a couple of other coaches, Richard Edwards and Rich Thomson, did their best to give him the necessary support. 'They gave me the realisation that I could do it. I was always fairly rigorous in terms of going to the gym and doing kicking practice but I never realised I could be good enough to do it full-time. Those guys made me realise I was.'

Yeandle was also from local farming stock. Until he was 14, he was more familiar with the rolling hills and hedgerows of the countryside between Thorverton and Crediton than with the game of rugby. 'One day at school they didn't have a hooker and asked me to play. I didn't know the rules but I still got shoved there.' Only after he enrolled at Cardiff Metropolitan University did he start to make any serious progress, forced to sink or swim in the uncompromising world of Welsh club rugby. He even ended up being picked for England Students, despite having spent a fair chunk of his time in the pubs and bars of Cardiff. 'I finished university as a fatty. I'd rolled up weighing 95 to 96kg; I was over 20kg heavier when I left. I'd never done any weights before and the conditioner said I needed to get some weight on me. I managed that but then carried on going. I got fat, started losing my hair and looked awful. Older than I do now.'

Somehow, straight out of university, he got a contract at Doncaster. 'I'd never been there in my life. Anything past Bristol you get a nosebleed. I remember my girlfriend, now my wife, getting a bit emotional when I said I was signing for Doncaster. She's from the Teignmouth area and was working at Exeter College at the time.' It worked out fine in the end, as his partner had predicted it would. 'It was weird. I was cleaning out my old bedroom at home and found a handwritten letter from her. She said, "You'll be fine, you'll go there for a season and then Chiefs will sign you." That's exactly what happened. It was unbelievable.'

The day Yeandle signed for Exeter was another strange but true story. He was enjoying Doncaster but had popped back home for his mother's birthday. His phone rang and, completely out of the blue, he found himself talking to Rob Baxter. In retrospect he reckons Baxter was probably scrolling through footage of his Doncaster teammate Alex Brown and, by chance, noticed the bloke next to him. 'He invited me in for a chat which turned out to be a full medical screening. I was still wearing jeans and T-shirt and was sweating everywhere because it was a warm day. I'd left my missus in the car saying I'd be 10 minutes. In the end she had to sit there for almost three hours.' It was to prove time well spent: Yeandle has never looked back. 'Playing professionally down here has done me the world of good. It's taken some weight off me and made me watch my diet a bit.'

The list of promising young players did not end there. Dave Ewers, the huge Zimbabwe-reared back-rower from the Ivybridge academy set-up, was back from a formative season on loan to the Cornish Pirates. The aforementioned Brown, the alert ex-Bedford scrum-half Will Chudley and the former Scarlets lock forward Damian Welch, soon to become known as 'The Wizard' by his teammates on account of his dexterity in the air, had also arrived. The number of fresh, motivated squad members seemed to be growing by the day.

* * * * *

To help develop this pick and mix of potential talent, Baxter had also introduced some wise old heads from further afield. Kai Horstmann had already been around several blocks at Harlequins and Worcester, had a tight hamstring and, at 30, was thinking about knocking rugby on the head. It was only the fact his wife was from Exeter that persuaded the couple it might be worth resisting the lure of France, which was also an option. 'It tempted both myself and my wife but by that stage I was already drinking more vino than I should have done.'

The 1905 All Blacks kick for goal during their match against Devon at the County Ground. Dave Gallaher's tourists won the match 55–4, which an incredulous sub-editor reported as a 55–4 victory for Devon.

A vintage postcard featuring the County Championship replay between Devon and Durham at Exeter in 1907. The Championship was shared between the two teams. *Getty Images*

~ DEVON v DURHAM, EXETER 1907

Right and below: Eight Devon players were selected to face the touring All Blacks at Redruth in 1973, among them John and Paul Baxter.

CORNWALL AND DEVON
RUGBY FOOTBALL UNIONS

CORNWALL
AND
DEVON
v.
NEW ZEALAND
TOURING XV

REDRUTH
TUESDAY, 2nd JANUARY, 1973

OFFICIAL PROGRAMME   15p

CORNWALL and DEVON

NEW ZEALAND TOURING XV

	Cornwall and Devon				New Zealand Touring XV	
	(As originally selected)			Back	T. J. MORRIS (Nelson Bays)	15
					K. F. KARAM (Wellington)	
15	*R. S. STADDON	Full Back		Right Wing	G. R. SKUDDER (Waikato)	14
	(Exeter and Devon)				B. G. WILLIAMS (Auckland)	
14	†K. C. PLUMMER	Right Wing		Right Centre	B. J. ROBERTSON (Counties)	
	(Bristol, Penryn, Cornwall and England)				I. A. HURST (Canterbury)	13
13	T. PALMER (Captain)	Right Centre		Left Centre	R. M. PARKINSON (Poverty Bay)	
	(Gloucester, Truro and Cornwall)				M. SAYERS (Wellington)	12
12	R. FRIEND	Left Centre	)	Left Wing	G. B. BATTY (Wellington)	11
	(Plymouth Albion and Devon)				D. A. HALES (Canterbury)	
11	R. WARMINGTON	Left Wing	}	Stand Off	R. E. BURGESS (Marrawatu)	10
	(St. Luke's College and Devon)				I. N. STEVENS (Wellington)	
10	N. BENNETT	Stand Off		Scrum Half	G. L. COLLING (Otago)	9
	(St. Luke's College and Devon)				S. M. GOING (North Auckland)	
9	A. PEARN	Scrum Half		Prop	S. McNICOL (King Country)	1
	(Bristol and Devon)				L. CLARK	
1	†C. B. STEVENS	Prop				
	(Penzance-Newlyn, Cornwall and England)			Hooker	R. A. URLICH (Auckland)	2
2	J. LOCKYER	Hooker			K. M. NORTON (Canterbury)	
3	P. BAXTER	Prop		Prop	K. K. LAMBERT (Marrawatu)	3
	(Exeter and Devon)				G. J. WHITING (King Country)	
4	J. SCOTT	Second Row		Second Row	P. J. WHITING (Auckland)	4
	(Exeter and Devon)				A. M. HADEN (Auckland)	
5	J. BAXTER	Second Row		Second Row	I. M. ELIASON (Taranaki)	5
	(Exeter and Devon)				H. H. McDONALD (Canterbury)	
6	A. COLE	Flanker		Flanker	I. A. KIRKPATRICK (Capt.) (Poverty Bay)	6
	(Exeter and Devon)				A. I. SCOWN (Taranaki)	
8	A. HOLLINS	No. 8		No. 8	A. R. SUTHERLAND (Marlborough)	8
	(Exeter and Devon)		{		B. HOLMES (North Auckland)	
7	P. J. HENDY	Flanker		Flanker	A. J. WYLLIE (Canterbury)	7
	(St. Ives and Cornwall)		}		K. W. STEWART (Southland)	

† International.   * Trialist.

Reserves : **16. J. J. Cocking** (St. Ives and Cornwall), **17. G. Thomas** (Penryn and Cornwall), **18. J. Trevorrow** (St. Ives and Cornwall), **19. N. Diment** (Exeter and Devon), **20. K. W. Trerise** (St. Ives and Cornwall).

Touch Judge :
V. C. MARTIN (C.R.O.R.S.)

Referee :
E. M. LEWIS (Wales)

KICK-OFF : 2.15 p.m.

Touch Judge :
R. A. EDDY (C.R.O.R.S.)

The way they were. Exeter's team, including John Baxter (front row, far left), Bob Staddon (front row, fourth from left) and John Lockyer (middle row, far left), for the Devon Cup final against Torquay Athletic in April 1971. Exeter won 35–3.

The main stand at the County Ground. *The Tribe, rugbynetwork.net*

Rob Baxter plays his last game at the County Ground in 2005. *Phil Mingo/Pinnacle Photo Agency*

Gareth Steenson passes the ball during the Championship playoff final match, first leg, between Exeter Chiefs and Bristol at Sandy Park on May 19, 2010. *David Rogers/Getty Images*

The party starts in the Chiefs' changing room after defeating Bristol in the Championship final at the Memorial Stadium on 26 May 2010 to secure promotion to the Premiership for the first time in their history. *Stu Forster/Getty Images*

James Phillips wins the ball for Exeter as the Chiefs make their Premiership debut against Gloucester at Sandy Park on 4 September, 2010. *Hamish Blair/Getty Images*

Richard Baxter (left), John Baxter (centre) and Rob Baxter pictured on their farm in Devon in 2020. They played over 1,000 first-team games for Exeter between them. *Phil Mingo/Pinnacle Photo Agency*

Tom Johnson and Jack Nowell hold the Triple Crown trophy after England's victory over Wales at Twickenham during the 2014 Six Nations. *David Rogers/Getty Images*

Dean Mumm lifts the LV=CUP after beating Northampton Saints at Sandy Park in 2014. *Mike Hewitt/Getty Images*

The Chiefs parade through the streets of Exeter with the LV=CUP trophy.

Phil Mingo/Pinnacle Photo Agency

Jack Nowell at Newlyn Harbour. *Tom Jenkins*

Tony Rowe celebrates receiving the Freedom of the City of Exeter in September 2015 by driving a flock of sheep through the city centre. *Gary Day/Pinnacle Photo Agency*

Gareth Steenson kicks the match-winning penalty against Wasps
in the 2017 Premiership final at Twickenham. *David Rogers/Getty Images*

Champion Chiefs. Jack Yeandle (left) and Gareth Steenson (right) lift the 2016/17 Premiership trophy. *Dan Mullan/Getty Images*

Thomas 'the Tank Engine' Waldrom celebrates at full time with his two sons. *Phil Mingo/Pinnacle Photo Agency*

Tom Johnson, Ben Moon, Matt Jess, Haydn Thomas, Phil Dollman and Gareth Steenson: the 'Originals' who have all shared the incredible journey from the Championship to the summit of the English game. *Phil Mingo/Pinnacle Photo Agency*

Kai Horstmann lifts the Anglo-Welsh Cup after a 28–11 victory over Bath at Kingsholm on 30 March, 2018. *Jordan Mansfield/Getty Images*

The brains trust: Rob Baxter is surrounded by his coaching team at Ashton Gate, 17 October, 2020. *Phil Mingo/Pinnacle Photo Agency*

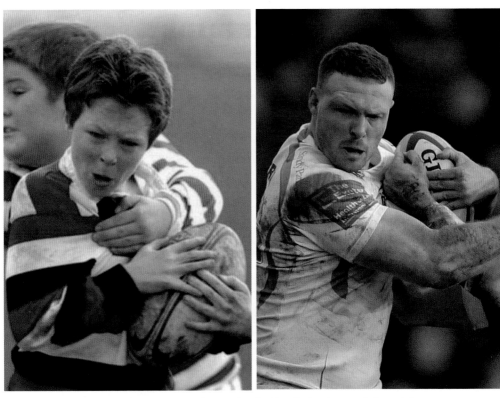

From Teignmouth RFC to a crucial cog in the Chiefs' pack, Sam Simmonds dynamic impact at No.8 saw him named European Player of the Year in 2020. *Andy Styles (left) and Henry Browne/Getty Images (right)*

The Maunder family celebrate with Sam after an England Under 20 match.
From left to right: Jack, Felicity, Sam and Andy. *Courtesy of theMaunder family*

Olly Woodburn soars over the line to score a remarkable try
against Bath at Sandy Park in March 2020. *Dan Mullan/Getty Images*

The King of the North: Scotland captain Stuart Hogg in full cry for Exeter. *Bob Bradford/CameraSport via Getty Images*

Power play: the strength of the forwards is the heartbeat of the Exeter game plan – demonstrated perfectly by Harry Williams, who scored crucial tries in both the semi-final and final of the 2020 Champions Cup campaign. From five metres out, the Chiefs' pack are virtually unstoppable. *Dan Mullan/Getty Images*

But there is grace allied to power as Henry Slade glides in to score a game-changing try in the 2020 Champions Cup final at Ashton Gate. *Tom Jenkins*

Master and Commander: 23-year-old captain, Joe Simmonds, roars in delight with Jack Yeandle after referee Nigel Owens finally signals full time in the Champions Cup final. *Tom Jenkins*

The 'impossible' dream comes true. Exeter Chiefs are crowned champions of Europe. *Tom Jenkins*

In howling wind and pouring rain, Jonny Gray steals a Wasps line-out on Exeter's five-metre line in the Premiership final at Twickenham. Eighty metres later, captain Joe Simmonds bisects the Wasps' uprights to secure a 19–13 victory for the Chiefs.

Phil Mingo/Pinnacle Photo Agency

The Devon Double. Ten years after they clinched promotion from the Championship, Exeter complete the fairy tale by adding the 2019/20 Premiership trophy to their European Cup triumph. *Phil Mingo/Pinnacle Photo Agency*

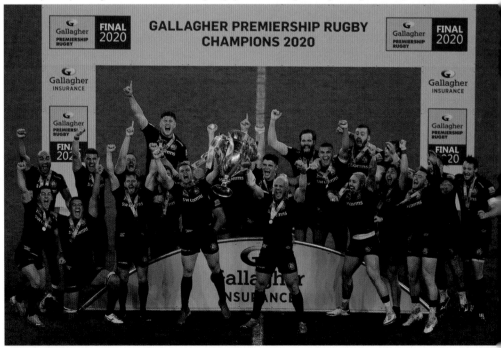

He was also disappointed that, having played 171 games for Worcester over seven years, his club were still not fulfilling their true potential. Had he retired or moved abroad, he would have left with a sense of regret and a significant amount of pent-up angst. 'Looking back, it would have been a disaster; I'd have walked away with a huge amount of frustration inside me because I hadn't been able to influence the club to get to where I thought it should be.'

There was also a nagging sense of dislocation from southern Africa. Like Ewers, his formative years had been spent in Zimbabwe. His German-born father, Heiko, was a surgeon and his mother Ann's family had two farms before Robert Mugabe's land-reform policies changed everything. Horstmann, packed off to boarding school in England, had to sit and watch the political situation deteriorate from afar. 'I remember opening a newspaper and seeing a picture of my mum demonstrating on the streets of Harare. I rang home and spoke to someone who told me she'd subsequently been locked up. She was held for four or five days and was pretty shaken up. There were 40 or so women in one cell. She said it was the most horrific thing she'd ever experienced.'

Now here he was in Exeter, with a stern-looking head coach standing over him while he did his medical. No one could be entirely sure how much mileage remained in his legs and Horstmann could tell that Baxter – 'I need to check this guy is still in one piece' – still needed convincing. 'He watched every bit of it. It was really daunting, particularly when I was shaking like a shitting dog on the squats.' Somehow he passed the test, only to rupture a hamstring in his first week at the club. At Exeter most players are already in the gym between 7.00 and 7.30 a.m.; those sidelined by injury are expected to arrive even earlier and go home later. For Horstmann, it underlined the precariousness of sporting life. 'Luckily it was my other hamstring but I was thinking, "Is this it?" I was living at my wife's parents' house and we were looking for a place to buy. You do have those low moments.'

Nor did Chiefs have a tiny squad with limited competition for places. Even Steenson, previously an automatic choice at fly-half, was now feeling insecure. The previous season he had lost his starting place to Ignacio Mieres and the Argentine had also started the 2012/13 season well. When Chiefs blitzed Sale by 40 points in their first game of the season with Mieres at 10, Steenson began to feel increasingly frustrated. 'It was very, very difficult. I'd go out and do kicking sessions with Nacho. He'd attempt 20 kicks in the session and kick two of them. Then in the match he'd kick everything. I'd think, "What's going on here?"' He began to ponder whether, at 27, he might be better advised to head elsewhere. 'Everyone gets frustrated if they're not playing. What I've learned as I've got older is that you don't need to play every game. At the time the bloke was playing well and the team was playing well. If you take your selfish head off, there's not a lot you can say. It was frustrating but it gave you a bit more backbone.'

The Chiefs' new centre, Ian Whitten, could empathise with those kinds of emotions. Like Steenson, he had found the road to satisfaction at Ulster blocked after winning a solitary Irish Test cap on tour in Canada in 2009. Wholehearted, strong and a tireless trainer, he was another unselfish player who made those around him look better. Exeter, though, was proving a totally different environment. At Ulster there had been a non-drinking culture; his first proper away bus trip with the Chiefs was a very different story. The Chiefs had just lost at Northampton, but on the long bus ride home the beers began to flow. Not being entirely familiar with all the arcane rules and assorted forfeits, it wasn't long before Whitten was extremely drunk and had been parted from his clothes. Sensing the opportunity for a wind-up, the senior players persuaded Tom Hayes, as captain, to text

Rob Baxter down at the front of the bus to ask if he fancied participating in the joke. 'Yeah. No problem,' came the reply. Soon enough Whitten was being shown a message, sent from Baxter's phone demanding the player report immediately to the front of the bus.

'Oh no! I'm going to get sacked. What have I done?'

'You're right. What have you done? You're a disgrace.'

'Oh no. I'm in big trouble.'

'Look, there's only one way you can get out of this. Take this bottle of water and this apple up to the front of the bus with you and you'll be all right.'

'Are you sure?'

'Yeah, it's the only way.'

Just as he prepared to rise unsteadily to his feet, however, all the chatter suddenly died away. Down at the front, Baxter had not only risen to his feet but was heading down to the back of the bus where the naked Whitten was cowering.

'Ian, stand up and come here.'

'Rob, I've got a bottle of water and an apple for you.'

'Ian, look at me.'

By now the tension was palpable . . . until Baxter grabbed a beer from Tom Hayes, skulled it, pulled off his own top and gave his quivering centre a big, manly hug. 'Go and enjoy yourself, Ian,' he urged, before disappearing back down the bus. Whitten, a colossal weight released from his bare shoulders, could scarcely believe he had 'just naked hugged the coach of the rugby club.' When the bus finally arrived back in Exeter, a further toast or three was clearly in order. At 2 a.m. Scaysbrook, Steenson and Whitten were still out in town with a couple of bottles of vodka on the table in front of them. Far from being sacked, the swaying Ulsterman had fallen on his feet. Eight years later, the loyal, hard-running centre is still going strong in Exeter's midfield.

Steenson, always among the ringleaders when it came to back-of-the-bus entertainment, has been similarly durable. Egged on by Richie Baxter, he was now known as 'The Music Man' in tribute to the trademark song – 'I am the Music Man, I come from down your way . . .' – he would invariably sing. Rare was the rendition which involved keeping all his clothes on. 'There's a theory that if you're having a few drinks on the bus you don't want to spill your drink on your clothes. The best way to do that is not to have any clothes on. I blame Richie as the instigator, the quiet assassin that he was. Richie would sit in front of me, quiet as a lamb, and then gesture at me to get my shirt off.' Whitten, his fellow Ulsterman, tells it slightly differently. 'When I first arrived he was the life and soul. Him, Brett Sturgess, James Scaysbrook, Richie Baxter, Tom Hayes, Jessie, Sireli . . . they'd be in the back of the bus holding court. Steeno would have no clothes on and be singing "The Music Man" on most of the bus trips. Then he became a father. Karen must have said to him, "You're a dad now; you can't be taking your shirt off all the time."'

On one infamous occasion, having played in Newcastle on a Friday night, the decision was taken to drive back home through the night. Three different drivers were involved and players literally rolled off the bus at 7 a.m. Gradually, though, the on-board partying grew more sedate. As one seasoned regular put it: 'The bus journeys became less Wild West and a little more south-west. We'd have a couple on the bus but it was more like a wine and cheese party.' Around 2004 there would be an all-in party virtually every weekend. By 2010 it was more like once a month. These days it is more like every couple of months. 'It's more serious now but there's still the element of enjoying yourself, being a good team man and enjoying a good craic together,' confirms Whitten. 'We don't do it as often but that ethos has always remained.'

Rationing the number of blowouts made sense. Even for Steenson it felt perverse to be recruiting top internationals such as Mumm yet still carrying on like a pub team: 'We'd had Sireli and Shoey but Dean was our first superstar current international. He seemed to fit. He wasn't a misfit but he was a down-to-earth bloke who'd sit with the academy lads or whoever. A lot of our fellas saw that. We were all aspiring to be internationals and it was great to see someone like that buying into the culture. He fitted the way we played but he was also dynamic. We kind of needed to make that shift. At that stage we were still very "heavy" in terms of the way we were looking to play the game.'

* * * * *

The 'work hard, play hard' mantra, however, still did not prohibit an officially sanctioned blowout every now and again. It was just a question of identifying the most suitable dates. European away weekends were always circled in the diary well in advance, a good example being the club's first taste of Heineken Cup rugby in the autumn of 2012. The Chiefs had been drawn in Pool 5 alongside the defending champions Leinster and had to open their campaign in Dublin at the RDS. Few in Ireland expected anything other than a comfortable home win. Their team had lost just once in seven years at home. Instead the pink-shirted visitors – were they Munster in disguise? – gave the star-studded home side such a run for their money it was still 6–6 with quarter of an hour to go. Mumm, experiencing his first European club fixture, came off the bench and could sense the belief around him. 'It wasn't a team that held on for 60 minutes. It was a team that ripped in and kept scrapping.'

In the end it wasn't to be. Ben Moon conceded a penalty at a ruck, Johnny Sexton kicked the goal and Joe Schmidt's side, containing 11 internationals, squeaked home 9–6. The Chiefs were disappointed but not downcast and Sireli Naqelevuki, a giant character in every sense, arrived at the players' bar afterwards clutching a bottle of whisky in one huge mitt. A security guard politely told him he was not allowed to bring the bottle in. After a moment's contemplation, the giant Fijian got himself a glass, poured himself a pint of whisky and began to work his way through it. A big night was clearly in the offing: many already felt Sireli's greatest talent lay in persuading others to empty their glasses. As Whitten put it: 'What a character he was. He was an unbelievable man at making people drink and not having anything himself.'

Mumm could barely believe how the evening unfolded. Before the players had disembarked the bus back at the team hotel, Rob Baxter stood up and issued his instructions for the night. 'Excellent effort, boys, against top opposition. If you've got an injury take care of yourself, otherwise I expect to see everyone else changed and back on this bus in 15 minutes.' Back in Australia, players would creep out in small groups, not always with the management's permission. Not here. Baxter was even talking about a roll call to ensure every fit body was involved.

Within 15 minutes, sure enough, the whole squad was back on board and en route to Temple Bar. From there it was on to Copper Face Jacks for more craic. Mumm glanced around him and noticed how much unsung team men like Scaysbrook, Chris Whitehead and Carl Rimmer were relishing the experience. 'The road for them to get there hadn't been paved with gold. They'd experienced a number of clubs to get where they were. I'd been lucky and enjoyed a smooth journey to the top. For these guys the door had been shut many times. It gave them a resilience and a grit and they fought hard for their positions. It made training a bit narky sometimes but that was the way of it. I think Rob likes to see someone who has had a turn in their journey.'

Rimmer's story definitely sat in that category. Having grown up in the Midlands and turned out for Nuneaton and Coventry, the former bricklayer was coming to the end of his time with the Cornish Pirates. He had just been voted players' player of the year but, at 26, had reached a career crossroads. 'I'd called it time at the Pirates, not because I had somewhere else to go but because it was too far away for my wife and me to live there. It wasn't really a career at that point, it was a hobby that paid a bit of money.' He was a week away from having no career whatsoever but Baxter had seen something he liked.

Was it possible the boss had some special instinct possessed by no one else? Even Rimmer was not entirely sure. 'You couldn't really put your finger on it. The older I got, the more I started to wonder if he was truly a genius. Or was some of it luck with the core group he started with? If it is the former, he's definitely done it bit by bit. Yes, he values hard work but he's a big one on character. You can tell that by the people he's brought in. Time after time they're big characters who thrive in that environment. Whether he can pick that out straight away I don't know.' In Rimmer's case, it transpired that Baxter knew exactly what he was getting. 'I was under the impression he'd spoken to me because of a chance encounter with a friend. "No," he said. "We've looked at nine full games you've played in." That was more analysis than we'd been doing on our own team.'

The new arrival also soon found himself with 30 instant new mates once he'd survived his initiation in the Undercroft bar at Sandy Park. 'I still think some of the best places for initiations are dark cellars with no windows. I think they still do a bit of it. The advice given to us was, "You can go through dressed but I wouldn't advise it." Any clothes would have been nice. I came out the other side a different man.' It was not unknown, either, for players being initiated to be locked inside the kit van prior to being led in one at a time, dressed in black-and-white-striped outfits, for their court session.

When it came to culture shocks, meanwhile, something else had struck Rimmer's fellow new arrival Mumm. The range of different accents in the dressing room was extraordinary: the Chiefs seemed to have half the world covered. 'It was quite a melting pot of cultures. Everyone in Australia, from Sydney to Perth, has the same accent basically. When you've got people from Coventry, Cornwall, Devon and London and then you throw in a couple of Argentinians, Fijians, Kiwis, Australians and the Welsh . . . it was an eye-opener for me. They were all genuine characters, not carbon copies of media training. There's a real sense of identity and people give a tremendous amount. You really got a sense that people were trying to do something greater than themselves. If you got a bit ahead of yourself you'd be absolutely caned.'

The practical jokes could certainly be savage. Horstmann was among the victims, having his boxer shorts stolen for 21 consecutive days after training while he was in the shower. He was forced to keep buying new ones until, finally, he was presented with a stack of 21 miraculously retrieved pairs that had been tucked into a concealed space in the dressing-room ceiling. On another infamous occasion Haydn Thomas, one of several players who enjoyed their country pursuits, shot a squirrel and hid it in the Welsh prop Craig Mitchell's pocket.

Another striking example involved Tom Johnson, by now a fully fledged England international after making his debut on tour in South Africa in June 2012. His Exeter teammates were delighted for him, up to a point. 'How much money are you getting to go on this tour? Ker-ching!' The stick was merciless but Johnson knew he had no option but to suck it up. 'It kept you really grounded, in a nice way. If there's any arrogance or you don't buy into the team, the team won't buy into you. We've got people on all types of spectrums. Trust me, there are some right weirdos.'

Eventually, though, it was time to get even with Brett Sturgess. The prop had relentlessly teased Johnson for having lips like a fish, in retaliation for his teammate constantly delivering chocolate to his house. 'I'd come out of my front door and there would be Easter eggs or some other type of chocolate. I think he enjoyed seeing me put on weight and then having to work it off.' Johnson, though, now had a more elaborate plan involving a large sea trout, sourced via Jack Nowell's family fishing connections and smuggled into the dressing room. Suitably armed, Johnson crept up behind an unsuspecting Sturgess and whacked him around the chops with it. Game, set and catch.

* * * * *

The winter of 2012/13 was significant for other off-field reasons. Once Exeter had completed two years in the Premiership, they were entitled to approach a club who had been outside the Premiership for a similar period and apply to buy their all-important P shares. Exeter, consequently, had the choice of approaching either Bristol or Leeds. Rowe had a fair idea what Bristol's unimpressed reaction would be. Sure enough, their West Country rivals indicated they would fight any attempted deal in the courts.

Leeds, on the other hand, were on an increasingly slippery slope financially. A deal was struck to buy the shares for the stipulated price of £5 million. The solicitors completed all the details on the afternoon of Monday 10 September and the money was transferred. In the nick of time, as it turned out. The following day an emergency PRL conference call was arranged to discuss whether the league should shift its television rights from Sky to BT Sport. With a major financial uplift involved – the agreed figure of £152 million over four years was 50% higher than the existing TV deal – the clubs all voted in favour.

It meant that, overnight, Exeter's newly acquired P shares had soared in value from £5 million to almost £9 million. Not surprisingly, the phone lines between Exeter, Leeds and Twickenham glowed red-hot for a couple of days. 'Leeds wouldn't believe we knew nothing about it,' says Rowe. 'But we didn't. It came out of the blue 24 hours after we'd completed the deal. I'm not usually that lucky.'

If Exeter needed further proof the planets were aligning in their favour, this unexpected windfall was surely it. The timing was certainly opportune for Rowe as he sought to keep pushing the club's finances forward. Promotion in 2010 had been a game-changer but the economy had slipped into recession. 'I was quite confident it was working but the finances weren't brilliant because we weren't getting the full amount of money. By 2012 it had also become apparent that, to maximise revenues on the conference side and accommodate Chiefs' expanding requirements on the playing side, the stadium layout needed tweaking. The 3G training pitch adjoining the main ground was wearing out and serious thought was being given to establishing a new training ground a mile away at a 12-acre site on Old Mill Lane.

It was decided, in the end, to go in a different direction. A new enhanced grass Desso pitch was ordered and the idea of a separate training centre scrapped. A seven-year bond was also launched in 2013 to raise the necessary £9 million for the building alterations. Crucially, it meant Rowe did not have to put up the existing building as security. Exeter were still a members' club and there was no desire to jeopardise their primary asset. Rowe may have been fortunate over the P shares but it remained his belief that the club's rise was also partly down to prudent housekeeping. 'It wasn't luck. Sometimes people get luck mixed up with opportunity.'

Those who had worked closely with Rowe over the years also knew him as a hard taskmaster. It was certainly an education for Bentley, who worked for the club in commercial sales for six years having retired from playing. 'Rowey and Keiron Northcott went around all the clubs to see how they did things and then designed a club that was going to be a moneymaker. It's a conference and banqueting centre that, 16 weekends a year, hosts rugby games. There's only been one rugby club in the UK that's dragged itself up by its bootstraps into the Premiership and succeeded. Rowey drives hard, perhaps too hard at times in my personal opinion, but at the end of the day you can't fart against thunder. He's done it. It wouldn't have happened without Tony or Rob.'

Baxter could certainly be relied upon to go the extra mile purely out of his absolute love for rugby. Bentley recalls the time the club held a BMW-sponsored competition with a first prize of an hour's coaching session with the head coach. 'He was really excited because, with the first-team players, he'd never normally do more than 20 to 30 minutes of coaching at a time. He went on for an hour and a half. We had to stop him in the end, he was just loving it. He's almost autistic with it. He just gets it.'

What Bentley also came to understand was that, by accident or design, the Chiefs were in an enviable position geographically when it came to attracting sponsors and players and retaining season-ticket holders. 'It's an apex predator. In terms of top-level professional sport, there is nothing else down here. If you go south of Bristol there's nothing apart from cricket in the summer. If you're a young kid in Cornwall or Devon you want to be a rugby player. It wasn't difficult, sponsorship-wise, for me to say, "You're either with us or you're taking your clients 90 minutes up the road to Bristol." If they said, "Bristol's cheaper," then I'd say, "Well, crack on then."'

Players from other clubs were also now being offered the chance to live and work in a part of the country where millions of people go on holiday. Not every fan was delighted, however, by the increasingly punchy prices for tickets and hospitality in an area where average salaries were well below those in bigger metropolitan areas. 'We had this really difficult bloodletting one year. We had to go to a number of season-ticket holders and say, "I know you've supported the club since you were 10 but you've got to move." It caused a huge amount of bad feeling. People still wanted to pay £10 admission and £200 for an advertising board. We were saying, "We've now got a global audience in the hundreds of millions and we've got to compete on price for players. It's a business." All supporters are equal but some are more equal than others. If someone's going to give me £50,000, I can't say "off you pop behind the posts". They have to sit in the middle of the grandstand.'

Saying 'no' to Rowe was notoriously hard, even for popular employees. On one infamous occasion Bentley had done something wrong and was called up to Rowe's office to be shouted at. Bentley, though, decided he would stand his ground until the issue under discussion had been properly resolved.

'Right, fuck off.'

'No, I'm not going to fuck off.'

'Fuck off out of my office.'

'No, Tony, until we've dealt with this I'm not fucking off.'

On it went for a while longer, the decibels rising steadily, before Bentley stormed off, slamming the door behind him. At which point all the blood drained from his face as he realised he had just spent a full five minutes swearing at his chief executive. Fortunately, Rowe liked the way he'd stood up for himself. The occasional sharp word was merely par for the course. 'He'll go to bed that night and not even remember it. For Tony it's gone. For me it's etched in my soul.' By the summer of 2013, with Exeter having once again just finished in the top six and an ambitious crop of local youngsters pushing the established players, it was increasingly clear that Rowe's vision – he disliked the words 'fairy tale' – was gaining momentum.

FOURTEEN

PROPER JOB

The summer of 2013 marked another fundamental turning point, both for Rob Baxter and the Chiefs' ambitions. In June, with Graham Rowntree and Andy Farrell away with the British & Irish Lions in Australia, the England head coach Stuart Lancaster invited Baxter and Paul Gustard to join his coaching panel for the two-Test tour to Argentina. It was an honour for Exeter to have their head coach involved, although he was already among the club coaches Lancaster consulted most frequently. The squad was a decent one, too, featuring a 20-year-old Billy Vunipola, Courtney Lawes, Joe Launchbury, Mike Brown and Joe Marler among others. Both Tests were won convincingly but it was Gustard's approach to coaching defence that really caught Baxter's imagination.

The key was to engage the players' interest. To make it happen, Gustard was not averse to the odd gratuitous ploy. If, for example, he wanted to highlight the importance of defensive spacing, a selection of pictures of naked breasts would appear on the screen. Some were generously wide apart, others sat up a little higher or sank slightly lower. The pick of the bunch, it was suggested, were spaced just right. Not exactly PC but it seemed to get the desired message across. Baxter spent a few entertaining nights out with Gustard and saw how well the squad responded to the proactive defensive gospel he preached. According to one senior player, the former was a different man when he returned home to Exeter. 'He saw how it was done, came back and said, "Right, this is how we're doing it from now on."'

Baxter also sensed it was time to start raising expectations among his players. He and Hepher sat down in pre-season and decided they would break away from Exeter's beloved notion of the collective always looking after the individual. 'We wanted it to be more about the individual looking after the collective. We had all our good young players – Henry Slade, Jack Nowell, Sam Hill, Luke Cowan-Dickie – coming through together and I remember saying to Ali, "How long do you think it's going to be before some of these players look at me and go, 'Is this how Rob's going to be every time we lose?'" Or is he going to say, "Come on, guys, we should have fucking won today."'

The more he thought about it, the more obvious it was that a shift in mindset was necessary. 'I could see the older guys thinking, "Whoa, this is different." I knew it would cause a bit of disruption in the squad as a whole but the younger players I spoke to were quite excited about it. I said, "We're going to remove the comfort blanket of saying, 'It's okay, lads' when we lose a game. From now on we're going to tell you if we should have won."'

Baxter's other deliberate move was to stick up photos of other teams winning the LV= Cup, Premiership and Europe, with silverware glinting in the sun and umpteen bottles of champagne being sprayed. Turning to his players, he asked them how long it would be before they hoisted a trophy of their own. 'What is next for us, guys? We're a semi-established Premiership side. What are we really going to aim for this season? Are we going to aim to top out? What are our goals?' Exeter's Premiership apprenticeship, he felt, was at an end. 'If you miss a line-out lift because you haven't been switched on in the line-out meeting I shouldn't be saying, "It's all right, mate, that's okay." It should be, "C'mon, mate, that's cost us the game."' It was a subtle but crucial gear change. 'We changed our philosophy from it's all about "We" to it's all about "Me". It put extra pressure on individuals to be good, to be responsible and to help the group. Since that day we've probably driven that more than anything else. "What is my individual responsibility? How do I show you that I'm prepared to help you become an international player? How do you show me that getting a cap is really important for you?"'

It helped that Chiefs were still recruiting shrewdly. Don Armand, like Horstmann and Ewers, was another exiled Zimbabwean. His parents, Wade and Adele, had a farm on which they grew plants and flowers for export to Europe via Holland, specialising in an ornamental plant called hypericum with red berries and small yellow flowers. When Don was 12 they had been forced to abandon their land. There had been shoot-outs on neighbouring properties and farmers were being murdered. When workers on his father's farm started to be beaten up, the family had no choice but to move to Maritzburg in South Africa.

With money already tight, crop disease subsequently scuppered the family business and his parents split up. Armand managed to obtain a bursary to study psychology and HR at the University of Cape Town and his rugby coach John Dobson helped him to get the amount of the bursary increased. After making the Stormers squad and playing for the first Western Province team in over a decade to win the Currie Cup, he was not massively keen to leave South Africa to play rugby in England but a couple of good friends insisted the vibe at Exeter would be similar to UCT. His mentor Dobson also advised him to give it a try. 'I think you can go over there, give it a good crack and play for England.' At the time Armand just laughed at him.

The only snag was the weather. 'I'd never been to the UK before. Never wanted to go. Everyone tells you it's a miserable place. You think England is a mud island, that it's always raining 24/7. I got here in boots, jeans and two jerseys, just in case.' Sure enough, it was cloudy when he arrived in London but by the time Tony Walker had driven him down to Exeter it was hot and sunny and he was sweating profusely in his woollen jumper. Having trained and played with Jean de Villiers, Bryan Habana and Schalk Burger at the Stormers, his first priority was to check out the standard of player he would now be mixing with. 'The first person I saw was our front-row forward, Lloyd Fairbrother, doing a simple hand drill and dropping the ball. He also had a terrible mullet. Everyone was laughing at him. I thought, "Goodness me, what have I joined?"'

Trying to stay composed despite the perspiration dripping down his back, he dumped his bag in the first available space he could find in the dressing room. 'I just plonked myself down in what I later discovered was a prime space. One or two guys were giving me sideways looks . . . I'd just blown in from another country and all the riff-raff were supposed to start in the other changing room. It was only a couple of years later that someone said, "We saw you walk straight into the senior changing room." I'd always wondered why people had helped themselves to bits of my kit. But they embraced you, there was no hierarchy and it was quite easy to find your feet. It wasn't like an army barracks where sometimes you get the sense the seniors stick to themselves.'

* * * * *

What the club did have was an intense new ex-military forwards' coach accustomed to driving high standards. Before becoming a professional player with London Scottish and Northampton, Rob Hunter had served in the army with the Royal Engineers. He had also coached the successful England U20s side and knew all about the talents of Nowell, Slade, Hill and Cowan-Dickie. Not only was he a former colleague of Hepher at Northampton, but the pair even had a north-east connection. Hepher's mother had grown up in Harbottle, just south of the Scottish border, and his grandmother, in her latter years, was nursed by Hunter's mother who came from down the road. The pair had made the link in the late 1990s after Hunter's mother had walked into the cottage hospital in Rothbury where she worked and spotted a Northampton teddy bear on the bed.

'Why have you got that?'

'My grandson's playing for Northampton.'

'My son's playing for London Scottish.'

Hunter also did not come from a stereotypical rugby background. Hailing from rural Northumberland, he was more into climbing and basketball and had barely played rugby before he joined up. 'I was watching on the edge of the pitch in Germany, having only ever played one game in my life. They went a man down and asked if I wanted to join in. That was it.' After his playing career ended, he and Hepher ran the academy at Northampton together. 'We talked quite a lot in that period. There was always a feeling we'd work together at some point.'

Shortly before following Hepher to Exeter, though, Hunter went to watch Exeter play a European pool game away in Clermont. It proved an instructive journey. 'They got absolutely thrashed and Jack Yeandle played in the back row. Even so, with 78 minutes gone, you could still hear the supporters Tomahawk chopping and the lads were still throwing themselves at it. I thought, "That's a club I'd like to be involved in." They weren't worried they were outgunned; there were a lot of easy things to like. We already wanted to come down here but that was a massive factor.'

Having moved down to Devon, something else swiftly became clear. 'When I first arrived there seemed to be farmers and fishermen everywhere. Everyone works very long hours. With Rob, absolutely nothing is done for show, for style or because someone's read in a manual you should wear a tie. He's very natural in how he manages you, which means you know where you stand all the time.'

There were a few quirks, though, that Hunter struggled to get his head around. At the end of every training session the forwards would routinely separate out into four pods and practise their restarts, with points awarded for how high in the air the ball was intercepted and whether it was successfully caught. There would be much hollering, whooping and laughing rather than obvious po-faced attention to detail. Hunter, after a while, could stand it no longer.

'For fuck's sake, fellas; do you want to do this properly?'

The players looked at him quizzically. For a couple of minutes they dutifully went through the motions, talking in subdued whispers, not remotely enthused. There was only one thing for it.

'Okay, okay, you win. Do it your way.'

'Yes! Hooray! Catch, catch, catch!'

Hunter had just learned an important early lesson. This was a squad who thrived when they enjoyed their work. Even Mumm felt the need to have a quiet word with his forwards coach and put him straight. 'Dean taught me not to take myself too seriously. I was super-intense when I first came here.' Make it fun and, instantly, the Chiefs would come alive.

The players, too, were also fast discovering that Mumm was a top man. It was no surprise to anyone that he had captained Australian Schools. Even to a well-travelled player like Armand, his leadership qualities stood out. 'Mummsy was different. Very composed and less emotional. He wouldn't mind saying what needed to be said but he'd lead from the front. You'd only hear from him if you gave away a stupid penalty. Otherwise he'd play hard, knowing other guys would follow.'

Mumm, for his part, was being increasingly struck by Baxter's innate common sense – 'I've learned more life lessons from Rob than I have from any other coach' – on a range of subjects. When he was officially installed as club captain, Mumm's teammates joked that his biggest challenge would be spending six or seven unbroken hours in the car with Rob driving up and back to the start-of-season launch at Twickenham. On the contrary, it proved a revelatory trip. 'The river runs deep with Rob. He didn't turn the radio on once, and we just talked the whole way. We spoke about a whole range of subjects; there was even a foray into physics. He's very varied in his knowledge. It's not often elsewhere in the world that a captain and a coach spend that long getting to know each other. He's also got a tremendous moral compass in the way he leads and rarely compromises on that. There aren't many world leaders you can say that about at the moment.'

* * * * *

If anyone had come to see rugby as a strictly relative pursuit, however, it was assuredly Mumm. Nothing anyone could endure on the field could begin to compare to the emotional trauma the Mumm family were continuing to suffer. Sarah had become pregnant again six months after losing Sophie but had also been diagnosed with a condition which can involve the cervix dilating too early during labour. It was an understandably tense time for all and, cruelly, it led to further heartbreak.

The couple's first son, Henry, was born at 28 weeks but contracted an infection and survived for just nine days. The only time Dean was able to cradle his son in his arms was to hold him as he passed away. 'There was something special about being able to hold Henry, even for a short time and in such heartbreaking circumstances.' All Mumm's teammates could do for their colleague was to offer their unstinting support. 'We had a funeral for Henry in the crematorium chapel in Exeter. My mother-in-law and sister-in-law were there but one of the defining moments for me was that every single member of our squad, regardless of age or life experience, turned up and stood there with us, knowing we didn't have family in the area. Every single one of them came past and acknowledged myself and Sarah. Not many places would do that. They even changed training to make sure everyone was there, dressed in full suit.'

What do they know of rugby who only rugby know? Bravely, the Mumms decided to try for another baby and Sarah fell pregnant once more. For Dean, the anxiety was ever-present, rugby only a partial release. By now, though, it was the summer of 2015 and he had been selected for the Wallaby squad for the World Cup being hosted by England. Having played Fiji a couple of days previously he was sharing a room in Bath with Kane Douglas when, in the middle of the night, his phone rang. Sarah's waters had broken in hospital in London after 36 weeks of pregnancy. 'I was fumbling around in the dark, stressing, and he says, "Mate, just turn on the bloody light. You're having a baby!"'

It was to be an extraordinary week all round. Baby Alfie was born by Caesarean section and was immediately placed into special care with breathing difficulties. Dean had also just been appointed to lead the Wallabies for the first time against Uruguay. Sarah knew how much the honour meant to him and urged him to play. Somehow he had the presence of mind to skipper his country, score a try and lead Australia to a 65–3 pool victory at Villa Park. To complete the fairy tale his parents were able to take Alfie back to their temporary flat in Notting Hill the following week. Dean and Sarah are a truly remarkable couple: having returned to Australia they also lost twin girls, Grace and

Ella, at 20 weeks before little Rupert Mumm was born in March 2020. The family's continuing work on behalf of the Borne Charity, which raises funds for research into premature births, comes straight from the heart.

* * * * *

Some other emotional individual tales were also unfolding behind the scenes at Chiefs. Surgery to repair the 33-year-old Tom Hayes's neck problem had proved unsuccessful, prompting the lock's return to south-west Ireland. Playing against Bath in the LV= Cup semi-final in early 2014 – a game which saw the Chiefs finally break a frustrating 12-game streak without a victory against their neighbours from Somerset since their 2010 promotion – the reliable James Hanks also suffered a serious neck injury which would end his career. 'I basically compressed my neck and bruised my spinal cord. It took 10 to 15 minutes for any feeling and movement to return and a couple of months for my co-ordination to come back. I was very lucky that it wasn't really life-changing.'

Three or four months later, however, a specialist advised him his rugby days were over. In his heart of hearts he knew already. 'I remember speaking to Rob and saying, "I don't think I could put myself through that again anyway." Your initial emotion is relief that you can crack on with your life. Then, six months later, it hits you: actually, this is pretty shit now. You've gone from being pretty good at what you do and being respected to starting from zero again.' Mentally exhausted and deflated, it took him a lengthy period to bounce back. 'I'm sure my wife would say I was a nightmare to be around for a couple of years while I was trying to deal with it. You're battling with a lot of conflicting emotions at the same time as adjusting to the real world. It's not easy. I think boys these days are possibly more aware of it than we were. There's also more support around.' In addition to readjusting to life outside the Exeter 'bubble', even watching rugby as a spectator was a trial. 'I went to England v Italy at Twickenham with a couple of friends. Mike Brown got injured and briefly it looked as though he was badly injured. It brought back some horrible memories. For a while I was a bit angry with rugby.'

The injury also robbed him of an opportunity to play in the 2014 LV= Cup final, the biggest game in Exeter's history up to that point. The final was even being staged in Exeter and presented a perfect chance to secure the club's first piece of silverware, the Championship trophy aside, since Baxter and co. last lifted the Devon Cup 18 years previously. Unbeknown to their visitors from Northampton, the former Saints academy coach Hunter reckoned he knew how to beat his old club regardless of weather or venue. 'They were a big strong pack at the time and I remember saying, "The way to attack these guys is to attack them at their perceived strengths. You go at them at scrum and maul."' Within four minutes the popular Chris Whitehead was driven over from a line-out just as their coach had predicted. 'Damian Welch caught the line-out, we did a little move and you could almost see the lads thinking, "Bloody hell, that feels pretty good. This works. Let's do it again."'

By the time Mumm charged over for a try in the third quarter, it was apparent the hosts were not going to be denied. Kai Horstmann supplied the pass – 'I gave him an offload and was pretty chuffed he caught it' – but retains even clearer memories of his fellow Zimbabwean, Don Armand, making his presence felt. 'Don had just come off the bench and put in a hell of a hit on their No. 8 GJ van Velze. I was right next to him and could hear the gasp of air – oooph! – being forced out of him.' With Slade kicking the goals from fly-half, the final scoreline of 15–8 did not remotely flatter the Chiefs. Horstmann still reckons it was a pivotal moment. 'The stars were just aligned and the atmosphere was amazing. We hadn't won any silverware before but that Sunday you could see us all going, "Bloody hell." The whole belief process is crucial. If you're passionate but you're not confident you're pissing in the wind a bit.'

It may not have been the most prestigious trophy in world rugby but it also felt to Mumm like a coming of age. 'The stadium was full and people were excited. Not many mid-strength or light beers were going around that evening.' Among those glowing with pride was Tony Rowe. 'Aside from our promotion titles, we'd never won a senior trophy. I remember Dean and I cuddling each other on the pitch. "You know what, Tony," he said to me, "in all my career I've never ever won a cup." I know in the great scheme of things it was the LV= Cup and everything's relative. But we were on our way. That was the start to some degree.'

Nowadays an open-top bus ride around town for winning the LV= Cup would be seen as, well, over the top. For Exeter, though, it felt justified. 'It just typified what it meant to them,' confirms Mumm. 'It was completely surreal for a foreigner. We didn't do that sort of stuff.' Only when he was subsequently invited to switch on Exeter's Christmas lights did it dawn on him how much the locals were savouring their team's success.

The downside was that it encouraged the entire club to rest on its laurels. In Rowe's words: 'We fell off the rest of that season. Psychologically the guys thought, "We've done it." I know the coaching staff learned quite a lot from that.' There was certainly a steep decline: nine of the Chiefs' last 12 league games of the 2013/14 season ended in defeat and they finished a modest eighth in the table. The worst loss was undoubtedly a record 55–12 home defeat to Sale in mid-April. Even long-time students of Baxter's team talks such as Dollman could not remember the head coach looking so angry. 'It's tough to describe Rob as volcanic because he never really gets like that. It's short and sharp. He'll fly off the wall maybe, but it's very irregular. When it happens, you've just got to stand there and take it.'

Baxter was certainly in the mood to deliver some home truths. 'It was the one time I thought, "We've really let ourselves down." They walked through us like we were tissue paper. It was our record defeat in the Premiership and it taught me something. When the batteries run dry emotionally there's almost nothing you can do about it.'

A distinctly awkward sub-plot was also about to materialise. Baxter had received an evening phone call from one of his most trusted players. It swiftly became apparent why the player felt unable to air the problem in the following day's team meeting: he had just found out his wife had been having an affair with another squad member. Not only that but the other player involved was married and his wife was part of the same friendship group.

It was the second time something similar had occurred at Exeter in the space of a couple of seasons. Baxter knew he had no choice but to act swiftly. 'I phoned the player in question and told him I wanted to see him the next morning when no other players were around. I told him to stay away from the club until I'd thought about it further.' In the event the outcome was not long delayed. 'The more I thought about it, the more I came to the conclusion it had to be a cut-and-dried decision. I phoned him up and said, "That's the end of your time at Exeter." It wasn't nice and not something you feel good about doing but some things cut across everything you talk about and how you expect the players to treat each other.'

At least the elephant in the room had been addressed. The departed player was nicknamed 'Voldemort' on the grounds his real name could no longer be mentioned, while nudge-nudge references to 'the Exeter Swingers' were made for a while. The coaches wanted their players to feel free to open up to each other emotionally but, clearly, there were limits.

LV= CUP FINAL
Sandy Park, 16 March 2014
Exeter Chiefs 15 Northampton Saints 8

Exeter: L Arscott; F Vainikolo, P Dollman, J Shoemark, M Jess; H Slade, D Lewis (H Thomas, 72); B Moon, C Whitehead (L Cowan-Dickie, 66), H Tui (A Brown, 68), D Mumm (capt), D Welch, D Ewers, B White, K Horstmann.
Replacements (not used): C Rimmer, R Graham, D Armand, G Steenson, S Naqelevuki.
Tries: Whitehead, Mumm. Con: Slade. Pen: Slade.

Northampton: B Foden; K Pisi, G Pisi, J Wilson, J Elliott; G Dickson, K Fotuali'i (A Day, 77); A Waller (R McMillan, 65), M Haywood, S Ma'afu (T Mercey, 49), S Manoa, C Day, C Clark (B Nutley, 53), P Dowson (capt), GJ van Velze.
Replacements (not used): E Waller, J Craig, W Hooley, F Autagavaia.
Try: Manoa. Pen: Dickson.

Referee: A Small (RFU). Att: 10,744.

FIFTEEN

TOOT, TOOT!

'Would you like a muffin?'

Occasionally in life a player and a club are made for each other. As Rob Baxter stood at the motorway service station counter with Thomas Waldrom, it was already evident the pair were on the same wavelength. What the ex-England and Leicester No. 8 didn't yet know was how far he could push his luck. 'I don't want to look like a pig,' he thought, pondering his two options – poppy seed or chocolate. 'I know, I'll go for the poppy seed and a coffee to look half healthy-ish.' Baxter, though, had spotted his telltale hesitation.

'Look, I don't care. You can have anything you want.'

'Sod it, I'll have the chocolate muffin, please.'

'That's more like it.'

Thus it was, with his 31st birthday on the horizon, that Waldrom agreed to become a Chief on a three-year contract. With his wife away in New Zealand and his teammate Julian Salvi babysitting the kids, he hadn't even told Salvi – who would also move to Exeter the following year – whom he was going to meet. He had a sixth sense, however, that it might work out from the moment Baxter arranged to meet him at a motorway services in the Midlands. 'I knew exactly the one he meant because that's near where the Cadbury's factory is.' In hindsight, Waldrom reckons his honesty on the chocolate muffin front was music to Baxter's ears. 'I think it was what he wanted me to say. He wanted to see what the real person was like. After that he let me get away with a little bit more than other people. He knows I work hard but that I enjoy the odd sweet treat as well.'

Neither man knew just how beneficial a marriage it would prove. With a good few years clocked up in two hemispheres and a famously well-upholstered frame, the 'Tank' might not have seemed an obvious fit for a Chiefs side seeking a harder edge. So much for lazy preconceptions. There is a case to be made that, along with Naqelevuki, Mumm and, subsequently, Stuart Hogg, the Kiwi did much to alter the way others perceived Exeter and, just as crucially, how the Chiefs regarded themselves.

By the time he left the club four seasons later in 2018, Waldrom had not only scored 51 tries in 101 appearances for the Chiefs but also generated a ton of stories. Few, if any, players have set the bar so spectacularly high when it came to playing professional sport while still indulging a sweet tooth. After a while his teammates discovered he had cookie jars strategically dotted around Sandy Park for whenever the munchies struck; among other locations he had secret supplies of biscuits tucked away in the laundry room and the team manager's office. 'Not many people knew about it. Me, June in the laundry, Rob Hunter. Eventually it got a bit out of control. By the end we were going through five or six packets a week.'

More often than not, he would recruit Tomas Francis, the Wales international prop, as his partner in crime. As Ian Whitten recalls: 'They were terrible for each other, the two worst guys to sit beside each other. Towards the end of Tank's time they'd get out of the Friday team run and go for a cream tea together in Topsham. They didn't care.'

Waldrom, predictably, was also an enthusiastic member of the 'Cookie Club', the invitee-only group of players who would gather once a week for ice-cream sandwiches, home-baked biscuits or, in the No. 8's case, mini banoffee pies and a doughnut cake. The Cookie Club's founders – Damian Welch, Dave Ewers and Ben White – instantly knew they had a potentially top-class new recruit. 'I told them I was definitely the sort of guy who could add a lot,' recalls Waldrom. 'I called myself the marketing manager. Getting married, having kids and playing international rugby were great, but getting into Phil Dollman's testimonial Cookie Club cookbook was a highlight of my career as well. I do enjoy a rocky road.'

Waldrom also seemed to have a sixth sense when it came to avoiding the club's head of strength and conditioning, Mark Twiggs, whenever the latter appeared to take body fat measurements. 'Twiggsy would get the calipers out to do the fat test and Tank would disappear,' recalls Whitten. 'For a whole year he never found him.' Even when cornered, the big man had an excuse ready. 'I always said I was allergic to the end of them. It gave me a red rash and I couldn't do it.' It was more fun than confessing that, in reality, Twiggs was in on the joke. 'Behind closed doors he was really good. He knew how much I trained. We ended up doing the test once a year, instead of once a month.'

In truth, Waldrom was fitter than he let on. Back home in the Hutt Valley just outside Wellington, he had always enjoyed his athletics, specialising in the shot put, hammer and discus, and done plenty of road running. His elder brother Scott represented the All Blacks and his family – his father was a prison officer at Rimutaka Prison in Upper Hutt while his mum worked at the supermarket up the road – loved their sport. 'I'd do a lot of secret training but when the other boys at Exeter asked me if I'd done anything I'd say, "Nah." My plan, though, was always to be one of the fittest players when I came back in for pre-season.' The proof was there for all to see when he and Don Armand did some pre-season fitness testing at Exeter University. 'I knew I'd done all this training but Rob came out to watch. I did really well and I could see Don thinking, "Shit, he can actually run."'

Exeter's decision to sign the former Hurricane from the Tigers was already paying off. With Richie Baxter having finally retired in May 2013 and the prodigiously strong Dave Ewers better utilised in the management's view in the blind-side flank role in certain match situations, there was a need for someone, in addition to Horstmann, to add a bit of back-row craft and dynamism. In some respects Waldrom resembled one of those old-fashioned football centre-forwards with an instinctive nose for goals. Off the back of a close-range scrum or maul, few players in history have been more deadly. As he put it: 'It's hard to put into words the feeling you get from five metres out. Maybe I'm looking a couple of steps ahead of everyone else. That's what I'd like people to think about me: that when the pressure comes on I make the right decisions.'

Within a fortnight of arriving, the Tank knew he had made a good career decision. His relationship with his previous director of rugby, Richard Cockerill, had been fraying and the Tigers' training regime was getting to him. 'The days are gone when you go and do 100 sets of bench presses. That's not me. At Leicester that's what they did. That was the culture and if you don't buy in you don't last very long. I probably lost my way a little bit.'

Exeter offered just the pick-me-up he was seeking. 'You're a professional sportsman but you've got to have a bit of fun as well. If you let things get to you, you end up in a dark place. You're probably not going to see a six-pack on me but I love what I'm doing.' Waldrom's five England caps in 2012/13 also suggested he was far more nimble on his feet than many realised. In his first season at the Chiefs, he topped the league's scoring charts with 16 tries; his overall career tally of 54 tries in 158 Premiership games was only five short of Neil Back's all-time record for a forward. In Exeter they will also forever remember him fondly for his sense of off-field fun, not least the pre-Christmas social in 2015 where the squad headed out into town dressed as elves, reindeer, snowmen, gingerbread men and Father Christmases. The big man went as a seasonal turkey in full festive costume, his teammates having long since nicknamed him 'Thomas the Turkey' on account of the alleged volume of wobbly skin beneath his chin. Having bought himself a fleecy costume online – 'There was an inflatable one but I didn't think I could trust the boys' – the ever-game Waldrom was the undisputed star of the show.

* * * * *

Hunter's arrival, meanwhile, had helped to strengthen Exeter's resolve to be a pack who made their presence felt without forgetting the importance to the team of scoring plenty of tries as well. Hepher and Hunter also knew each other well enough to appreciate that simply coaching their own little areas and ignoring the bigger picture would ultimately prove counter-productive. Hunter's time at the RFU had made him particularly alert to that common trap. 'In English rugby there's a lot of "silo coaching". People think, "That guy's a forwards coach, that guy's a defence coach etc." Here we have a vision for the game and everything serves that. The set piece doesn't sit in isolation: it serves the attack. I say to Ali, "What do you want?" Being dominant up front is not an end in itself, it's to create space.'

From Hunter's perspective, it still made certain things non-negotiable. 'If you're a forward coming into Exeter Chiefs there are two or three things you need to know. One, you're the beating heart of the club. We squeeze the life out of teams. There's a responsibility that comes with being a forward here. That's super-important. But you also need to understand how to get from your goal-line to your 22, how to get to the five-metre line and then how to get over the opponents' try-line. Understanding how to get from point A to point B is the key to everything. For example, having a 100 per cent line-out isn't one of our targets. It's not necessarily a stat that wins you the game. What we do want to try and do is to get pace in the game. Ball-in-play time, high-intensity minutes.'

As the LV= final had underlined, however, there was no point in looking a gift horse in the mouth. Hunter was almost pinching himself. 'For three or four years I sat in the stand thinking, "I can't believe this." No one was putting any numbers in against us. There was a particular team in the league who'd try everything to stop our maul and we'd still score three or four tries every time we played them. They'd whinge and moan about it but they'd only be putting three or four guys in against eight. If they'd put eight guys in, we'd have moved the ball.'

It is another reason why Hepher feels that those accusing Exeter of being one-dimensional have not been paying sufficient attention. 'My biggest pet hate in punditry is when people say, "They've got no Plan B." We've got thousands of plans. We've got a whole menu to pick from. No two plans are the same. It depends on the opposition, what they're doing and where we can expose them. Then it's about looking and finding it. If they're all here, we're going to hit over here and vice versa. The plan constantly changes and moves depending on the opposition. Yes, we're organised but we want to be organised so we have all these different options available to us.'

It is a flexible strategy which, as Hepher recalls, stretches way back to the pair's shared days at Northampton running the second team. 'One day a southern hemisphere player stood up and said, "Can we not just run everywhere?" Rob and I just looked at each other and our mouths dropped. What happens if everyone decides to run to the same place? The whole idea of how we operate is that it's all heads up. If I know there's space over there, this is my best option to get the ball there. If there's space around the ruck I can do this. If there's space down the blind side I can do that. Through the middle, over the top . . . I've got options for them all. The call will come and everyone will instantly know what's happening. It's built very much around a number 10's eyes. If your 10 is having to look around him constantly it's a lot harder. The whole essence of it is to make a 10's job as easy as possible. When 10s come here they play very well. They've got enough on their plate without taking on the entire organisation of 15 men. If the other 14 know their jobs, the 10 can pull the strings exactly as we want.'

Additional variations can also be bolted on depending on the weather or the state of the pitch. A farmer who employs a different plough, harrow or hedge-cutter on the back of his tractor, depending on the time of year or the job in hand, would instantly recognise the similarities. 'You can typecast us as a tight team,' shrugs Hunter. 'But I look at it and think, "It's pissing down and cold for the middle four months of the year but it's not going to be like that all season."

'People say, "What are they going to do when it dries up?" Well, we're going to score bonus points and run the ball.' He has a similarly flexible view when it comes to forward roles. 'When I look at a pack I don't really look at 6, 7, 8 or 1 to 5. You clearly need props but I look at who's going to give us "hot ball" , who's going to supply a big clear-out, who's a big lifter, who's going to be a big set-piece forward or a line-out pillar? Who's the stop-and-chop tackler, who's going to pressure the ball? Sam Simmonds is a great example. The only thing he doesn't really do as a seven is scrummage on the side of the scrum. That's because he's the quickest and most electric carrier. Why wouldn't you put him on the ball at the back of the scrum, with your two biggest, heaviest back-rowers on your props where they can be most effective? It just seemed to make a lot of sense. It wasn't an epiphany moment. It was more, "Ali wants us to score lots of tries, so we need to be able to pass, run, carry and get the ball over the line in the most effective way." That's probably the key to it.'

If this sounds like three men combining to solve an endless Rubik's Cube, that is not a million miles from the truth. Over the years Hunter has frequently disagreed with Hepher – 'We fight like cat and dog about pretty much everything' – but the pair of contrasting perfectionists have come to realise that, along with Baxter and the other coaches, they possess a range of complementary skills. 'In the early days we probably all saw things differently at times. The three of us are very different in temperament and style and there are a lot of advantages in that. When we disagree as a three, one of our strengths is that everyone gets on with it.' The modern history of Exeter might have looked very different had Hepher not introduced a few extra layers of tactical subtlety but, as a combo, he believes he and Baxter dovetail nicely. 'We see the game in different ways. I tend to see it wider while he's focused in on the breakdown, line-outs and forward play. We'll come at it from different angles but, along with Rob Hunter, we'll always find the best route. Rob's bright and he is pretty clear about what he wants.'

The other distinguishing characteristic is the trio's work ethic. Many clubs have a small army of backroom staff coding games. At Exeter, Baxter has always done it himself. 'Rob codes the games on the bus, as opposed to any analyst doing it,' confirms Hepher. 'No other directors of rugby do that. As a result we've always been able to find out the reasons why we've lost. We've never got to the stage of "I don't know where to go here." Rob knows exactly who's playing well and who's doing what. It explains why he often sees things that others don't see and is so good at recruitment. He knows exactly what they can bring. Ultimately it's all about improving players. That's something we've done all the way through. If we can improve players we're going to be a better team.'

Might this just be the underlying secret to Exeter's rise? Baxter reckons it is. 'If someone said to me, "What's been the key to it all?" I'd say it's because I've also been the analyst. I took the role very seriously and became totally absorbed by it. To this day I've done all our senior games. It takes at least five hours but it doesn't half make sure you stay on top of things. It would feel wrong and alien to me now if I didn't do it. I like being able to walk in and know, if a player asks me a question about any element of the game they've been involved in, that I can tell them.'

Collectively, too, it helps keep his finger on the squad's collective pulse. 'I feel like I know exactly where the team is at. You can tell immediately when players are a bit off or physically a bit tired. It gives you so much more insight into how the team are operating and the type of player you want to recruit. You can see exactly why they might fit in and how they compare to the lads you've already got.'

Rare, too, is the occasion Baxter says anything in public he has not already said in the confines of the dressing room. Aside from a 2013 game at Sale, in which he managed to get himself yellow-carded shortly after coming off the bench and Chiefs threw away a 13–5 half-time advantage, Horstmann cannot recall the head coach losing his temper away from Sandy Park. 'We ended up losing the game 21–16 and Rob properly lost it afterwards in the dressing room. But mostly he's got an amazing ability to motivate people without really raising his voice.'

Agents have grown equally used to receiving requests from Baxter for three full games of footage of their player – followed by a subsequent call telling them where improvements could be found. Once a 'hot list' of three candidates has been established, it is all about identifying which one will be the best fit. One long-standing member of the Chiefs backroom staff says he can recall only two players whom he did not particularly enjoy being around in his lengthy association with the club. The captain of the first all-female crew to row the Pacific, Laura Penhall, has spoken of the importance of not choosing individuals who share precisely the same 'get up and go' mentality. In terms of personality types, it is important to have some 'cool blues' and 'earthy greens' in there as well. Meshing them together – supposed misfits and all – has unquestionably been one of Baxter's major strengths. 'I say to the players, "We don't mind you being as odd as you like or what you do away from here. You can drive whatever car you like, you can dress how you like, you can be solitary or spend all your time with people. But when you come in here what makes us strong is that we all go in the same direction."'

If there is a Baxter 'philosophy', this collective buy-in lies at its heart. He denies, even so, deliberately setting out to recruit responsible family men rather than nightclub-loving singles. 'People over-analyse our recruitment. We don't go looking for the family guy but what we are looking for are the qualities that radiate from that sort of person. We probably pick that up from their rugby before we've even met them.

'You'll see if someone has a hissy fit every time something goes against him. You'll see if he's a guy who will get his head down and work. You'll see if he is a guy who wants to get off the floor. You'll see from his body language whether he's a guy who wants to stand and fight. You can see the things that exasperate them but you can also see what they're good and bad at. Then you can ask them some very simple questions based around what you're seeing. That tends to let you know if they've got any self-awareness or any ability to be coachable. If I show a guy three or four clips and say, "Are you seeing what I'm seeing?" and they do, you know they're someone you can work with.'

Certain physical prerequisites – 'I've got a template' – are also part of Baxter's thinking for each position. Never mind if, to some, these seem unnecessarily rigid, particularly in the case of late-developing younger players. Exeter sides, regardless of quality, will invariably be hard, strong and fit. The Chiefs, more than any other club, have mined the Championship successfully over the years and Baxter's instinct seldom lets him down. 'The most important thing about coaching is believing what you see with your own eyes. But if you want to believe what you're seeing you have to look. And spend time looking.'

If that means working around the clock, so be it. John Baxter has long been accustomed to not seeing much of his elder son during the rugby season. 'Rob lives next door but sometimes the only time I see him is on TV. He goes off at about 6.30 to 6.45 a.m. and he's not normally back until 6.30 to 6.45 p.m. If it's wintertime it's dark at both ends of the day. If he has a day off he's normally doing work or has to go off somewhere.' Hunter, similarly, has long been staggered by Hepher's level of commitment. 'The thing I most admire about Ali is the depth of his preparation and organisation. He doesn't get tired. Mentally he doesn't let up. He never thinks, "It's okay to be poor this week." That's probably the case for all three of us but it's true of Ali, in particular. He absolutely won't stand for the ball not being presented well on the training pitch.'

Underneath his laid-back exterior, Hepher can indeed get wound up by small, avoidable errors, both during training and games. 'I'm a big believer in pushing high standards in every little detail of what we do on the training field. It's absolutely crucial. I get frustrated by simple two-on-ones not being finished or whenever we're sloppy.' Performance rather than outcome alone is what really counts for him. 'It's not the winning and losing . . . we've always kept that separate. If we've played well and lost we'll congratulate the guys. Equally if we've won and could have been better we'll say so. We have high standards.'

Hunter, for his part, puts increasing thought and effort into how best to keep the players happy in their work. 'When I first arrived at the RFU there was a skinny guy sitting in the corner. He was a brilliant sports psychologist called Matt Tombs and nobody was really using him. I'd never really had access to someone like him. Suddenly a whole new world opened up. He taught me about the importance of consistency of message and looking at how you can work with the player, rather than the player working for you. Once you start approaching it from that angle, I learned a lot. It's about educating the coaches.' These days Tombs pops into the club a couple of days per month and Jack Nowell, among others, uses him regularly.

Small but significant examples of player-led decision-making also separate the Chiefs from other clubs. One has been the so-called 'design committee', chaired by Hepher, who took over the responsibility for what the players wear when representing the club. It has certainly made Rowe's life easier. 'The last time a director had an input into the players' clothing we ended up with a blazer and grey flannels. I took a lot of stick for it and it was nothing to do with me.' The team manager, Tony Walker, also used to get it in the neck. 'We were making decisions and players were always kicking off about it. So we set up a fashion committee. Ali Hepher thinks he's Gok Wan so we call them "Ali Hepher and his Gok Wan clan".' A distinctive example of their work were the country gent green tweed jackets which coincided with the club's 2017 Premiership success and player complaints have virtually dried up. When it comes to the black home match-day kit, though, change is resolutely resisted. Walker says the rationale is simple. 'There are questions as to why we don't put any colour on it. What would happen if you tried telling the army to change their colours? They'd tell you to bugger off. We wear black. Why change it? If someone from the army walks down the road you recognise immediately who it is. We want people to say, "There's a Chief."'

Other small behavioural wrinkles were also gradually ironed out. The coaches had noticed, for instance, that Rowe came down from his box to mingle with the players on the pitch after the final whistle only if the match had gone well. 'Like anybody, when we won I'd get excited and go down to the pitch afterwards. One day Rob said to me, "It's great you come down, it's good for the lads to see you. But I've got one piece of advice. You can't just come when we win. You've got to come when we lose as well."' Even the chairman is not immune from the occasional home truth.

* * * * *

One aspect of Baxter's job, though, never grows easier. Letting players go, particularly those who have given unstintingly to the club over many years, remains by far his least favourite duty. Keeping everyone happy and permanently employed is impossible and some ex-players remain bruised by the experience for years afterwards. For Baxter, it can be equally painful. 'People don't see the human bits behind ending contracts. There haven't been many players who have been happy to leave. My role is to make the decisions no one else wants to make. I can't just take the soft easy calls and allow us just to drift along as a rugby club. That's me not being fair.' In the end it has to be about the ongoing development of the team, rather than anything personal. 'The only way I can justify it to myself is that I'm doing it for the good of the other players. What really looks after a player is being part of a successful team. That's ultimately how

I justify the tough calls. I've had guys in tears and I've had guys who've made me cry with some of the things they've said when they've left. There is nothing tougher than letting a good guy go. We've had players who have given their heart and soul to the club. Some of them have seen how tough it is for me and said, "C'mon, Rob, it's all right. I've fulfilled dreams here I never thought I would have." When they talk to you like that, it's even tougher. It's easy to let a guy go who's done nothing and just wants to go somewhere else for more money.'

Fairy-tale endings, sadly, tend to be elusive. In theory it should have been a special moment for both the Chiefs and Tom Johnson when the flanker was selected to go on England's summer tour to New Zealand in 2014. Instead, it was to prove the beginning of the end of his late-blooming career. Earlier that same season he suffered a stinger against Saracens and began to experience recurring pins and needles down his arm. The timing was awkward: he had just signed a new three-year contract with the club and England were still picking him. Johnson prided himself on training hard; suddenly he barely had any strength in his arm and his self-belief, even as an England player in the Chiefs squad, began to dwindle. 'I never fully trusted that I wouldn't get dropped. In my mind it was always, "Have I played well enough to play next week?"'

If he was to make the 2015 World Cup squad, however, there was simply no alternative: he had to go on tour to New Zealand. He now regards it as a mistake: 'In hindsight I wish I'd never gone. I was probably only 70 per cent fit in terms of my neck and my strength. I stood in front of the haka and had a great experience but I would probably have been better staying at home.' He was to start only three more league games for Exeter before having to retire in 2017 and has since become a personal trainer.

Another of the fabled 'Originals' was also winding down. At his best Haydn Thomas was a splendidly quick-witted scrum-half, good enough to be called up to the England squad to face the Barbarians. He could also be relied upon to go the extra mile as the team's social convenor, organising events such as the themed bike-gang outing, not to mention the 'hare and hounds' social where the younger players had to set off first and be pursued around town, at one-minute intervals, by 'huntsmen' who each had to down a shot of port before setting off.

With more disposable income ready to be spent, the outfits grew ever more ambitious. Instead of 'Let's get someone paralytic', it became more a case of 'How imaginative can we be?' Among the more ingenious ideas was Thomas's personal favourite when, for an end-of-season outing, the squad dressed up as the toy soldiers from *Toy Story*, complete with green face paint. 'It was a good idea, except that the suits were plastic and it was an incredibly hot day.' All was fine until they were invited back to the home of the owners of Otter brewery and saw the swimming pool. Off came everyone's clothes – no problem there – but the moment the players hit the water so did the paint. As Thomas recalls: 'I'm not sure what colour the pool was beforehand but it was definitely green when we left.' Too much Otter was also the catalyst for an infamous outing to watch Somerset play cricket in Taunton, with the entire squad dressed as 1970s tennis players. 'We'd been at the brewery since 9 a.m. and then rocked up at the cricket. I thought it was going to be a Twenty20 match but we'd misread the fixture list. I didn't realise you could hear a pin drop.'

Within the squad, though, people began to realise Exeter barely ever lost on the same weekend as a team social. In the 2014/15 season the Chiefs had endured a mid-season slump in the league but, with a social arranged for the next Saturday, had duly beaten Newcastle at home. As long as it helped to tighten the bond within the squad, Baxter was happy to trust Thomas, and others, to keep his players on the right side of the line. 'He'd say, "I'm going to treat you like men here. I'm going to give you a piece of rope, just don't hang yourselves." He's encouraged us to build relationships because sometimes they can be the difference between winning and not.'

Thomas was also among the prime movers in establishing the so-called 'business lunch' which gave the players an excuse to meet up on their days off. It earned its name because of the suit that Thomas – who was doing work experience with the wealth management company Charles Stanley at the time – would always be wearing when he turned up. 'We'd meet every Thursday on our day off. It was always in Wagamama and then we'd go for a coffee. Or as we called it "Coffee time with Mark Foster" where you'd hear what Fozzie had been up to that week. Sometimes it was fiction but, ultimately, it didn't matter. It was completely non-compulsory but sometimes we'd have 25 players there.'

On returning from away trips certain senior players would head directly to the city's Mosaic nightclub, still dressed in Chiefs polo shirt and shorts, and head upstairs, safe in the knowledge that a bottle of vodka would be waiting for them. Small wonder that leaving the uproarious Exeter 'bubble' has been tough for many. 'It's so much part of your identity and your life because you love it so much,' confirms Horstmann. 'It's not gradual, it's a light-switch moment. One minute you might have just played in a final, the next you're done. It can be brutal.' Bentley felt similarly. For him the end of his playing days was 'almost like a bereavement' when it finally came. 'It's like a pack of wildebeest on the savannah. If you start falling off the back you've got to let the rest of them go. It's when pre-season starts that you really feel it.' Not everyone could be like Thomas and step aside at a time of his own choosing – at the age of 34 – to take up an academy coaching role.

The end of the 2014/15 season, though, was also a good time to look ahead. Having lost just once at Sandy Park since mid-September in all competitions, Chiefs had wound up in fifth place in the league, one point short of third position, having smashed Sale 44–16 in their final game. Horstmann, for one, could feel the squad's self-belief growing. 'We were saying, "Guys, we're easily good enough to be a top-four team. What are we worried about?"'

Part of the solution was clearly mental. 'We had a really long chat about how good we were against the big teams – we'd clean up against the top four – but were really letting ourselves down against the lower teams. At that point we weren't used to getting ourselves mentally prepared in the same way we would for a big side. That reset process is something most clubs don't do well. They'll get a big win on a Saturday and they'll still be talking about it the following Thursday. They don't reset quickly enough. It's easy to say but every single member of the squad has to shelve the weekend's game by the end of play Monday. If you don't your season just goes up and down.'

SIXTEEN

ROOTS AND WINGS

From the terrace of Jack Nowell's family home overlooking Newlyn harbour, a career as a rugby professional seems impossibly distant. It is only a short stroll down to the atmospheric old quay and the fishing boats and, with the Cornish sun adding an extra sparkle to a sapphire sea, Twickenham feels like a parallel universe. 'I know people have dreams but it never happens to someone from down here,' murmurs Nowell as he heads up the hill and past the 'Gone Fishing' sign on the gate. 'There was no way you'd ever think you'd be here one day and the next at Twickenham playing for England. There was no way that was going to happen to me.'

England have benefited from a few sons of Kernow down the years but most have been forwards: Stack Stevens, Phil Vickery, Trevor Woodman. Even the legendary Cornish outside-half Richard Sharp first played for England while at Oxford University. Hence the collective anticipation in Newlyn when Nowell made his first England appearance against France in 2014. 'Mum said all the chalkboards outside the pubs simply read: "England v France. Jack Nowell. Make sure you're here." My nan went out to walk the dogs and said there were floods and floods of people.'

It is a classic mistake to assume that English rugby's heart beats strongest in the Home Counties. Before the 2015 Rugby World Cup, special commemorative World Cup banknotes were even commissioned in Exeter with the winger's image on the front. When he pulls on the national jersey, Nowell is effectively representing not just Newlyn but its bigger neighbour Penzance, the whole of Cornwall and Devon and every deep-sea fisherman in the country.

There is just one question mark hanging in the tangy coastal air. If Chiefs had not been promoted to the Premiership in the nick of time, would Nowell and his childhood friend Luke Cowan-Dickie have climbed the rugby ladder as they have done? The former suspects the answer might be negative. 'Exeter getting promoted came at the perfect moment for me and Dickie. We realised that if we went to Truro College and put our heads down there could be a chance for us.'

Had it not happened he might instead have gone into the armed forces, become a gym instructor or perhaps taken a job on the Isles of Scilly like several of his mates. It is his strong belief – and the Kilkhampton-reared Vickery has long felt the same – that way too much raw sporting material in the far south-west goes untapped. 'Definitely. The amount of talented players I've seen playing down here is amazing. At almost every club there always seemed to be a guy who would be six foot at the age of 12. There was a guy at Penryn who always wore a blue scrum hat. He was awesome. And whenever we played against Bodmin, they had the "Bodmin Beast". We were only 14 but I swear he had a bigger beard than my old man. He'd make 50 metres with about five of us on his back. Every single local side has those players but you have to be lucky to get picked up from down here. When I was starting out my idea of what I was going to do in future was maybe to play for Penzance.'

The youngster who used to cling to his mother Louisa's leg and initially refused to play mini-rugby as a six-year-old at Penzance and Newlyn RFC has certainly come a long way. It helped when his father, Michael, offered him a pound each time he scored a try – until the deal was abruptly suspended when Jack scored 12 in one game. Even at that age, his good friend Cowan-Dickie would look across at him and shake his head. 'I thought he fancied himself a bit. He was one of those. He had all the gear: best boots, best everything. And his hair. He had a kind of swish-over bob thing. Then he touched the ball. I thought, "Bloody hell, he's all right."'

The pair have barely been separated since; even now the two of them and Yeandle live in adjoining houses in Broadclyst. As Cowan-Dickie says they have too much shared history to fall out now. 'We're Cornish and I've known him since we were toddlers. We both went to the same college and play at the same club. There's obviously a bond there: the sand is going to cement in at some point.' How would he describe his old mate? 'A top bloke, a class bloke. On and off the pitch he's a professional. He's played for England at stupid ages when he was young, he's played for the British & Irish Lions already. He's a family man now and his kids are going to have the best childhood you can have.'

Over the years Nowell has been forced to endure more than his fair share of injuries but the bond between him and his local community will never be broken. Not long ago he reinforced it by buying his favourite local pub, The Swordfish, where he spent many happy hours in his younger days. 'Back in the day I'd pretend I was helping land the fish, sort them and take them to market. Everything would start at 5 a.m. but we'd be finished by 11 a.m. or midday. They'd sell the fish, get the cash, go to the pub and split their earnings.

'I remember Mum and Dad going down there for parties when I was younger and the pub being absolutely rammed. It would be the centre of everything. But by the time I was old enough to start being involved it wasn't happening. Fishing is not as big as it used to be, more places opened and things kind of fizzled out. When it came up for sale I just said, "I'd love for it to be the old Swordfish." My brother's mates are 18 now and they've got a place where they can go and enjoy it how it used to be. It's been going very well.'

As are things, when fit, for Nowell the rugby player. From the tips of his sponsored boots to his tattooed limbs and ever-present headguard he is the epitome of everything the Chiefs have become: big, bold and box office. Two World Cups and the aforementioned Lions tour have established him as a buccaneering figure who consistently rises to the big occasion. If Johnny Depp had not already landed the role of Captain Jack Sparrow, the wholehearted winger would definitely have merited an audition for *Pirates of the Caribbean*.

At the very least there is no more reliable back in the English game when it comes to breaking a couple of tackles out wide. As an ambassador for his region he is better still, judging by the mileage some of Exeter's Cornish fans clock up to watch him play live. The club says that approximately 7 to 8 per cent of their supporters come from across the River Tamar and Nowell believes that figure could be a conservative estimate. 'When I sign stuff after the game the amount of people who come up and say, "I'm from Penzance, Truro or St Austell," is amazing. It's so good to have this kind of rugby down in the south-west. You get people from all over Somerset as well.'

Partly for that reason, he now feels an almost spiritual connection with his supporters at Sandy Park. 'One of my favourite parts of the game is the warm-up. The West Stand's still empty because they're still eating their food but the East Terrace is rammed. You can hear the crowd and the odd comment. It kind of gets me settled. It's also the time you get a feeling about what sort of game it's going to be. A lot depends on how we turn up in the first couple of minutes. We can lift the crowd with what we do and vice versa. If we get off to a good start and get the crowd behind us I'd hate to be a team having to play against that.'

The older he gets, too, the more he appreciates how Exeter's future is built on the old-school ethos of those who came before him. 'What we have now has come from the old days. We were a Championship team who worked hard at everything. We didn't change much when we were promoted: we didn't make many big signings, we didn't change our whole squad. A lot of it stems from how close we are as a team. It's harder when you're in, say, London. There are so many different areas, you live apart from your teammates. Here we live so close to each other we even spend our days off together.'

And when it comes to leaving every last drop of himself out there on the field, the collective example of his early mentors – Rennie, Steenson, Dollman, Jess, Shoemark, Thomas, Tui, Scaysbrook, Naqelevuki and Junior Poluleuligaga – still come to mind. Jess, as a fellow Cornish winger, looked after him when he started out and taught him what sheer desire looked like. 'Even when Jessy wasn't playing much he was still training as hard as anyone. He was a top-quality player but he was one of those guys who pulled us together off the field as well. The tighter you are off the field the better you play.' From Scaysbrook, he learned that commitment has no boundaries. 'Not many worked harder than he did. His body was giving up on him, you could tell, but he would still give absolutely everything. He was a tough old boy. That bled through everyone. No one was bigger than the team. If you were you'd be very quickly shot down until you felt about that big. Not in a bullying or a mean way but it was the culture that Rob and Ali wanted: everyone giving everything, in training as well as on and off the field. Our core foundation is the same: we're a team that will not give up anything. We could be 50 points down but we're still going to be making last-ditch tackles in the corner. The players who haven't quite made it in our team probably don't quite have that.'

Which is why Nowell takes none of it – the fame and, relatively speaking, the fortune – remotely for granted. His top-level experiences have merely taught him that nothing comes easy. 'Even now I've never really thought, "God, I've cracked this." It's just the way I am. I also think I've learned that from being here at the club. Initially, when I signed my first contract I thought, "I'll probably be here for three years and then see what happens." At the end of those three years I was playing for England. That's the way it's got to be for me for things to work. I'm never quite happy with where I am; I never feel I've made it. That's when you stop trying and stop wanting to be the best you can be.' It matters not where your journey starts, as Nowell now appreciates.

* * * * *

Even Nowell's odyssey could not compete with that of his teammate Alec Hepburn. Pick up a map of Australia and look for the most south-westerly corner of that vast, scorched continent. In the middle of nowhere between Esperance and Albany, you will find a small dot called Hopetoun. It is closer to Antarctica than Europe and, growing up, Hepburn and his friends could roam pretty much wherever they wanted: 'We'd have unlimited freedom. My mum would barely see us all week; she'd just see the fridge being emptied.'

The son of a £10 Pom who migrated to Australia in the 1950s, the laid-back Hepburn played Australian Rules, basketball and netball in his youth and was still unsure whether he wanted to pursue rugby when Rob Hunter, then coaching England U20s, first met him as an 18-year-old in a coffee shop in Henley: 'He was umming and ahhing about whether to be a powerlifter or play Aussie Rules. He was doing all sorts.'

The powerlifting was particularly educational. It taught him, among other things, that a man's strength is not merely derived from physical commitment. 'I saw a quote from a Chinese weightlifter a long time ago. He said it didn't take him 12 years of physical training to attain a world record, it took him 12 years to convince himself he could do it.' For a while he thought about following the weightlifting path. 'In a different lifetime it would have been interesting to see where it could have gone but it's a very lonely sport. There is a feeling of contentment when you achieve something – but when you achieve something with a team it's ecstasy. More things have to go right; you have to rely on and trust other people. That's why, in my opinion, the highs are much higher in team sport.'

He ended up playing rugby for England almost by accident, via Wasps academy, London Welsh and, after a short spell back in Australia, Exeter. Had he not been injured at an inopportune moment he might have stayed down under but, early in 2015, he washed up in Devon. Later that same year the Chiefs bolstered their front-row resources further by signing another former Wasps academy reject, Harry Williams. The tight head had been plugging away without fanfare for Nottingham and Jersey, having also spent a spell working for his bricklayer father in south London. Among other things he had also paid the bills by sweeping out a bakery during a six-month stint playing for North Shore Rugby Club in New Zealand.

Then there was Jonny Hill, the son of a Herefordshire-based livestock trader who might have ended up shearing sheep alongside his brother – 'He does 15,000 a year' – had he not been spotted during an open trial at Hartpury College.

The possessor of a pedigree sporting bloodline – his mother's twin is Paul Loughlin, who played 297 games for St Helens and represented Great Britain – the six-foot-seven-inch-tall Hill is yet another example of Exeter's ability to dig deeper than most and find nuggets others have overlooked. He, Williams and Hepburn have all subsequently been picked for England while Tomas Francis, recruited from Doncaster, was playing for Wales within a year of his Chiefs debut. It says much for the Exeter environment but their forwards coach Hunter is quick to deflect any credit. 'There's not a strategy other than common sense, which is one of Rob's greatest attributes. I can remember talking about a non-international player at another club and him saying, "If it looks like a pig, smells like a pig and it oinks like a pig, it's probably a pig." I quickly learned from him to trust your own instincts.'

Hill's recruitment is a particularly fascinating case study. With Mumm having departed after three years of sterling service, two of them as skipper, and two other Australian locks, Mitch Lees and Ollie Atkins, due to be joined the following year by another compatriot in the shape of Dave Dennis, Hunter wanted to look closer to home for a young lock forward to lend Geoff Parling some assistance. 'I went to Rob and said, "Right, we need some tall English people. This kid is worth a look. He's massive and he looks like he's got a bit about him." The complication was that Hill had badly broken his foot and been sidelined for 17 months but, with Exeter offering to rehab him, Gloucester were happy for him to leave. The Chiefs quickly discovered that, as well as being a source of racing tips, the gangly Hill was much smarter than he let on. As Hunter put it: 'The thing I like most about Jonny is that he lollops around in the week, then you stick a first-team jersey on him and he suddenly looks like a giant. There's a very sharp rugby brain in there too.'

The net result was a pack who, physically, were not intimidated by anyone. Previously in Europe the Chiefs had ticked the boxes marked gallant and valiant without, ultimately, making it beyond the pool stages. In the aftermath of the 2015 World Cup and with England's new coach Eddie Jones watching in the stands, they were not only good enough to contain the full might of Clermont Auvergne but defeated the giant Michelin men 31–14. The scoreline was given an extra gloss by two catch-and-drive scores for the ever-lurking Waldrom, who had contributed three tries against Wasps less than a week earlier. It was no coincidence, either, that a pre-Christmas social had been arranged for the night of the Clermont fixture. As everyone had told each other repeatedly before kick-off, Chiefs never lost before a social. The game still ranks among Carl Rimmer's happiest rugby memories. 'That night we were unbeatable. There was just a feeling in the air it was going to happen. We had lost heavily to Clermont on two previous occasions and finally we sent those boys packing. On the pitch before the game began we felt like Conor McGregor walking out. I remember Mitch Lees going over under the posts and all of us piling on top of him. They're memories you can't get rid of.'

It was all the sweeter given the nasty fracture and dislocation of his right ankle suffered by Henry Slade at Wasps the previous weekend. The evening celebrations, with Waldrom dressed in his turkey costume, were almost as punishing, so much so that the No. 8 was still feeling the effects days later. 'I remember it all fondly but I didn't recover until the Friday. I enjoyed it but it taught me a lesson. When you're a little bit older you can't keep doing it over and over.'

Jones, though, was in no rush to fill up his first England Six Nations squad with Chiefs, much to Waldrom's dismay. 'I was a bit shocked when Eddie named his squad. I even went on social media which I normally wouldn't do. You can't be one of the best teams in England and only have three people in there. We were playing some unbelievable rugby but sometimes it doesn't

199

get recognised, which is a bit annoying. Mummsy felt the same. But it's Eddie Jones's opinion. If he doesn't like the way Exeter are playing, you're not going to make it.'

In Waldrom's view, the Exeter player most unfairly overlooked has frequently been Dave Ewers, the hulking back-rower with whom he struck up a particularly close bond. 'For some reason we just clicked and formed a great partnership. I wish we'd had a bit more time together. For those first two years it was like playing with my brother. We understood each other and knew what each other were doing. He was just a beast. We always had a good time off the field as well. He also has a sweet tooth and lived about 20 houses away. When Tomas Francis arrived as well, we ended up being very tight.'

With a little bit more luck Exeter's big forwards could even have had a European semi-final appearance to celebrate in 2016. Having somehow risen from joint bottom of their pool on the final weekend to make the last eight for the first time, courtesy of a late flurry of tries against Ospreys and a match-turning tactical howler by Clermont's Morgan Parra against Bordeaux, they were only narrowly denied when they coughed up the ball close to Wasps' line and watched their hosts surge away to score a game-clinching try at the other end.

It was still a day, nevertheless, that convinced Hunter the Chiefs were heading in the right direction. 'I was sitting there before that game thinking, "This is so exciting, it's insane." I thought my heart was going to explode in my chest. We lost 25–24 to a kick at the end having been 24–11 ahead but I remember thinking, "We're not far away here."'

* * * * *

Domestically, at least, another sizeable opportunity still twinkled. For the first time Exeter had finished in the top four of the Premiership; better still they had a home semi-final having finished second in the table, six points behind Saracens but having scored 11 more tries in their 22 games than their London rivals. This time there was to be no painful sting in the tail from their last-four opponents Wasps as Exeter, six years on from their promotion, reached the Premiership final for the first time, courtesy of a 34–23 victory which included two penalty tries.

Cue a sudden explosion of interest from near and far. Fleet Street's finest suddenly wanted to know all about the supposed straw-chewing country boys from Devon and Rowe had a juicy stack of quotes ready and waiting. 'Victory this weekend isn't a dream,' he cautioned. 'We don't have dreams – sometimes you wake up from a dream to discover it's a nightmare. What we do have is ambition. Our ambition here at the club is to be the best in England and eventually the best in Europe but we're in no hurry. We're here for the long haul.' He also served up a few decent lines on the subject of his head coach. 'Break Rob in half and he's got Exeter Rugby Club written through him. He's from farming stock and they never waste money. If you give Rob £20 and send him to the shop, he'll come back and give you change. Other coaches will come back saying, "I need another £20."'

The papers, naturally, lapped it up. Cup-final weeks are twice as much fun when colourful underdogs are involved, although Baxter also had some serious points to make. 'We're not going to be a team that just goes there and enjoys walking round in the sun at Twickenham beforehand. We are going to turn up and, if we do, we can make it very interesting. The big thing we have always done here is believed. The only thing that would really frustrate me is if we don't show the best of our qualities and put up a bit of a fight.'

Everyone lost sight of two crucial things. The first was that Saracens had won the European Champions Cup a fortnight earlier; this was destined to be a seriously tough challenge.

Perhaps even more crucially, the whole occasion was far, far bigger than anything Exeter had previously experienced. Their other mistake was to underestimate the Twickenham traffic. They were already running late when the team bus hit a taxi on a roundabout near the stadium. It was not the moment to be hopping out and exchanging details with an irate cabbie; all the while the hubbub outside was increasing. The scenes were so extraordinary that Steenson looked around to see many of his teammates holding up their phones to capture the moment. 'People were banging the life out of the bus on the way in. Some of our players were videoing it. I'm sitting there thinking, "We're supposed to be playing a final here." I normally listen to music but even I removed my headphones to listen to the noise.' Before he had even stepped off the bus, Baxter knew his players had been wrong-footed. 'It was a shock to them. The banging on the bus, the noise. It's true what people say: you need to experience these things to get used to them.'

One or two had not quite shaken the semi-final euphoria out of their system either. By half-time Exeter were 23–6 down, the game effectively over. For Slade, who had done well to return ahead of schedule from his serious leg injury, and several of his teammates, clad in their alternative white kit, it was a sobering wake-up call: 'I think we maybe drew breath and thought, "Shit, we've had a really good season." I don't know if shocked is the right word but in the first half we weren't quite ready for it. We were sitting back and taking in the environment. Sarries had been there and done it a few times before. It took us until that second half to realise that, actually, we were good enough to win it. We should never have let them have such a lead.'

Jack Yeandle, on the bench initially, felt as if he were watching a completely different team from the one he knew. Even after going on and scoring a try his own composure deserted him. 'I got over from a maul in the corner and flung the ball into the crowd. I was far too pumped and forgot they needed the ball to kick it.' Chiefs did momentarily threaten a grandstand finish when Nowell dragged his side back to within three points with seven minutes left but a third Saracens try, scored by the man of the match, Alex Goode, dashed the winger's hopes of a comeback. 'Briefly we were thinking, "Could we do this?" But even after we lost we were happy. We'd still had a good season. In retrospect we were all pretty happy just to be there and enjoy the occasion.' At least Saracens' big-game ruthlessness had taught Exeter's players and management a salutary lesson.

SEVENTEEN

KNOCKING ON HEAVEN'S DOOR

For the opening three months of the 2016/17 season there was nothing to identify Exeter as an upwardly mobile champion team. They were rock bottom of the Premiership table after the first two weekends, lost their opening three European pool fixtures and won just two of their initial seven league fixtures, culminating in a frustrating home defeat to an injury-time try by Bath's Semesa Rokoduguni in late October. Remarkably they were not beaten in the regular season thereafter, a 34–20 victory at Gloucester in round 22 clinching a home semi-final and second place in the table behind Wasps, impressive 35–15 winners over Saracens on the same day. Unbeaten at Sandy Park since November, Exeter's ability to learn from the mistakes of the previous season would define their campaign.

Rob Baxter: We started the season really poorly. In October, on the Monday before we played Ulster away in Europe, I told the team there was something wrong. We'd just been stuffed 35–8 at home by Clermont. Were we acting and talking like a team that wanted to win the Premiership? Were we really working for it? Did we think teams would roll over because we finished second last year? We had a really open chat. I said that nothing I was seeing suggested we were working hard enough or really fighting for anything.

Matt Jess: He sat us all down and asked, 'What are we all here for?' You could tell he really meant it.

Rob Baxter: The lads also had a big team meeting on their own. They knew they were letting the season slip away from them. We lost narrowly in Ulster but I could see some genuine emotion starting to flow through us again.

Jack Nowell: We were almost expecting things to happen. It was just about us going out there, attacking and actually grabbing it.

Dave Dennis: There was a bit of a turning point. We sat down as a group and said, 'Look, what are we trying to achieve?' Geoff Parling was quite influential in that first year. He called the shots around the line-out and was an older head, a bit more mature.

Carl Rimmer: A line was drawn in the sand. It was a case of 'Are we going to be Cinderellas who do our best and have a great time or are we going to have a great time and use that as motivation to get us somewhere?' Initially some of the older stagers weren't quite sure. We were thinking, 'We're doing fine, we're on an upward curve, we just need a bit of time.' Looking back, that was the moment when it became rugby first, fun second. Then we discovered something else. As the rugby got better so did the fun.

Kai Horstmann: There are loads of 'down points' in rugby. Injuries, contract talks, not getting selected. They can all be big mental challenges. But, ultimately, you're playing a game you fell in love with as a young child and driving towards the same goal with people you genuinely care about. You've also got a boss who wants you to be able to say, when you leave the game, that you got every last ounce out of yourself.

Rob Baxter: Our unbeaten run was all down to the emotion of the players. It was a monumental effort.

Kai Horstmann: The semi-final against Saracens was huge. We'd taken a 13–6 lead thanks to a Jack Nowell try three minutes after half-time. We were still leading 13–11 when I came off after about 60 minutes. Then, with five minutes left, Mike Ellery went over the top of Henry Slade to score and give them the lead. Even I was thinking, 'What have we done here?'

Rob Baxter: How did Saracens get back into it? We played so well.

Carl Rimmer: With hardly any time left I dropped the ball – or it got stripped – 65–70 metres from the try-line of the best defensive team in the league. I was thinking, 'That's just lost us the game. Or, at the very least, put the final nail in it.'

Kai Horstmann: Did Carl knock it on?

Carl Rimmer: The ref deemed it as stripped and gave a scrum to us. As soon as he said that I said to the boys, 'We're walking through this one, lads.' Not only did I have to redeem myself but it was the only way for us to win.

Rob Hunter: I've got a recording of that 90 seconds without any visuals. You can hear Wayne Barnes talking and our lads talking on the ref mic. What they're saying is exactly what we're going to do. Your hairs still stand up.

Carl Rimmer: The mistake they made was to leave their props on for 80 minutes. Mako and Koch were just goners at that point. When you watch it back you can see the difference between our pack and theirs. They look like eight tired bodies trying to cling on to a lead; they just folded into the scrum. We bolted on like a tank being built. From that moment you just know we're going forward.

Rob Hunter: When we were awarded the penalty you could hear Steeno saying to Sladey, 'Just make sure.' Sladey pulls off a great kick to the corner. A 1-in-50 kick maybe.

Henry Slade: To gauge the wind direction I always look at the little flags at the top of the posts. Don't tell anyone else. They're metal so they're the true indicator. You look at all the other flags and they're all going in different bloody directions. I didn't actually realise how far back it was until I watched the tape. I just said to myself, 'Fuck it, I'll go as big as I can. If I land it on the 22 there's no chance we're going to drive it from there.' I went to kick it as far as I could. It probably would have ended up 10 metres out but the wind took it to about five metres out. I remember Alex Goode standing underneath it and shuffling as if he was about to catch it. Luckily it carried.

Luke Cowan-Dickie: It was about time he helped out his forwards. Normally from halfway they kick it to the 10-metre line but every now and again they do us a favour.

Carl Rimmer: It was almost like there was an anchor attached to the ball. The further it sailed the more the team got pulled along with it.

Mark McCall (Saracens director of rugby): That was one of the great kicks of all time – if he puts that somewhere else I'm probably here talking about one of the great wins.

Kai Horstmann: It was the best thing Henry did all year – by some way. It was an unbelievable bit of skill. The absolute nuts on him. That's why he is who he is. He was just like: 'Right, this is having it.' Then the doughnut tried it again in the final and kicked it dead.

Carl Rimmer: It honestly felt like one of those sports stories with 'There Goes My Hero' by the Foo Fighters playing in the background when we were walking up to that line-out. It was as if there was a magnet pulling all eight of us towards the line. It was like we never broke stride. We went scrum, line-out, down, over.

Kai Horstmann: You could see the lads growing an inch or two taller as we huddled around Geoff Parling and talked as we walked. There was no way this wasn't going over. When you go to a line-out you tend to have three or four options but you'll have two main ones. Geoff says to Dave Dennis, 'I think I'm going to take this one on because George Kruis hasn't been on me most of the game.' Denno was thinking, 'Happy days, it's not going to me.' Then Geoff called it to Dave. Luckily, he caught it.

Rob Hunter: We win the ball and you can hear each stage of it. That was a better 90 seconds than winning the final. Everything that happened did so because the players knew exactly what they were doing.

Kai Horstmann: Look at how good Tomas Francis and Harry Williams are at the front of that maul. People often forget that.

Sam Simmonds bangs it in but look at how strong the front of the maul is. If you've got Franny lifting Dave Dennis, with Dave Ewers at the front, you're not moving them. They work so hard so people can have a walk-in. In fairness to Simmo he still had a bit to do. Some athlete he is. I just remember going absolutely crazy.

Carl Rimmer: The place erupted. I remember Rob trying to calm us down afterwards. He was completely right to do so. It was the semi, not the final.

Ian Whitten: I've never felt euphoria like it on a rugby field than when we scored that try. But then we were in the changing rooms going, 'Oh fuck. What if we don't do it next week now?'

Carl Rimmer: On the way home I stopped for a beer and a Chinese in Pinhoe with my dad. When we went into the pub there were a dozen people slapping me on the back and offering to buy me a beer. I had to say, 'No. Dad, we're getting our Chinese and we're going home.'

Ian Whitten: The only thing we were thinking, once we beat Saracens, was, 'We've got to do it now. We'll never have a better chance.' I know Wasps finished top of the league that year but you didn't play against them and think, 'They're better than Saracens.'

Carl Rimmer: We skipped in on Monday morning. I couldn't wait to get to training, have a recovery swim and chat with the boys. I had two split eyes but every knock I'd had all year was suddenly gone. I was running around like a 21-year-old. By Wednesday I already wanted to get on the bus. I'd never been to a Premiership final, apart from being one of the pissed-up non-playing squad members the year before.

Ian Whitten: It was a really weird week leading up to it. The ex-Leicester boys – Tank, Geoff and Julian Salvi – had a bigger influence than they probably ever got credit for. Especially Geoff. He did a great job that week of getting everybody calmed down and ready to play the final. It really helped having those really experienced heads who had done it before. They were winners, those boys, and knew how to do it.

Kai Horstmann: We were just so confident. Training was good, the intensity was good. No one had to try and correct anyone or say a great deal. It just seemed there was all this bubbling energy that was going towards the right place.

Jack Nowell: I remember going in thinking, 'We're never going to lose this. This is our game.' Playing against Wasps always suits us. They like to play the ball around, as do we. After the previous year, the boys also knew what it was like to play in front of 80,000 people.

Kai Horstmann: They'd brought in a mobile cryotherapy chamber to help us prepare. Rob asked me if I'd booked my session yet. 'Absolutely not,' I said. 'I've never done it in my life before. There's no way I'm starting this week.' He looked at me and said, 'I like that.'

Carl Rimmer: Travelling up on the Friday was lovely. We organised a bit of a quiz and had a bit of fun.

Gareth Steenson: After the way we beat Saracens it felt right. Everything was spot on. The lads weren't videoing everything this time, and no one was taking their headphones off. It was a case of 'You're having this.'

Mark Stevens (press officer): We didn't crash the bus this time either. We stayed at a different hotel around the back of Heston Services. It was a much easier route in and everything was planned with military precision. Everyone knew what to expect.

Carl Rimmer: I hadn't had any caffeine but I just felt on top of the world. As we approached the stadium I remember Jack Yeandle turning to me and saying, 'This bit's amazing.' Then you turn the corner and there's just a sea of people ahead of you. I had my headphones on but I turned my music off so I could allow the whole thing to sink in.

Dave Dennis: Twickenham's a huge place. It felt like there were 20–30,000 Exeter Chiefs fans, 20–30,000 Wasps fans and all the neutrals going for us. There were Chiefs flags everywhere. It was such an amazing day.

Henry Slade: It was just so hot.

Carl Rimmer: I'm not a superstitious bloke but ever since I played at Coventry I always like to hop up and float around in the aisle when we're two or three minutes from the ground. It became a thing and people would start looking around to check where I was. I remember Nowellsy standing up and I told him, 'Hey, I didn't see you doing this at London Irish away.' It turned out he'd only stood up to get his bag. It meant I was first off the bus. Outside people were going berserk. I remember thinking, 'I don't want this to change how I'm feeling.' But how can you not drink in something like that or not want to revel in it?

Kai Horstmann: One of the major reasons we won the title was because we had the best pack in the league. They were so good and so dominant and Tank is just so hard to stop from five metres out. It's his unusual body shape. I'd see him walking to the showers and think, 'This guy freaks me out. What would he look like if he wasn't a pro rugby player?'

Rob Hunter: We'd told everyone, Nowellsy included, to go flat out from the start and not hold anything back.

Jack Nowell: I knew I was going to get the ball, but I didn't know I was going to score. For it to open up like that, so early in the game, was ideal. Whose idea was it? Ali's very smart at that sort of stuff.

Kai Horstmann: We'd worked on it in the week. We thought we could stretch them there. There's real satisfaction when you practise something and it works an absolute treat.

Luke Cowan-Dickie: I gave him the scoring pass and I think I was the first one in to congratulate him. I'll never forget that moment: just seeing how ecstatic he was. That set the tone for me personally. If I think about the final that's the moment that clicks for me.

Rob Baxter: The worst thing about playing Wasps around that time was that their threat was everywhere. You could just never draw breath. Every time you felt you had control, something would always happen. It was the same this time.

Henry Slade: We had a good lead but then we let it slip a bit.

Jack Yeandle: We started so well but they got that all-important score just before half-time to get their tails up. You could see it really lifted them and put a bit of weight on our shoulders. I came on after 50 minutes but me and Dickie ended up playing about the same amount of time.

Kai Horstmann: We should never have allowed it to go to extra time. We got a few things slightly wrong but it added to the excitement.

Gareth Steenson: If you watch the game back, it was the five minutes before and after half-time when we almost blew the whole thing. We were in complete control but, fair play, Wasps defended outstandingly well. According to the final stats they made 299 tackles to our 114. I've never seen any other team defend like they did that day. Any other time we play them we tend to score four tries and be quite confident about doing so. When we play Wasps we always talk about keeping the ball against them. We talk about that against most teams, to be fair. As it turned out, our two tries were both from set pieces, one off a scrum and the other off a line-out. Off phase-play their defence was unreal.

Phil Dollman: The older I get, the longer I ran my try in from. In reality it was probably about 10 metres. Ollie Devoto gave me a lovely offload and I managed to scramble over the line. But the feeling of it, the noise, the people cheering, your name going up on the big board at Twickenham. It's something I'll never forget.

Ben Moon: Dolly's a class act. Put him out on the pitch and he's as good as anyone.

Carl Rimmer: Even when Elliot Daly went over for his try we were still thinking, 'We'll be all right.' Then they kicked another penalty. Oh shit. This isn't the right script. It's supposed to be going our way.

Don Armand: It was typical Wasps of that era. They got two tries from nowhere. The last time we played we drew 35–35.

Jack Yeandle: Some of the carry stats in that game were extraordinary. Thomas Waldrom made about 900. There were some big performances from a lot of people. I remember Geoff Parling being really big that day. He showed his leadership qualities and dug in deep. I also like to think a bit of farming stubbornness comes out in my rugby. I'm not flash, I'm just pretty stubborn.

Carl Rimmer: I'd love to say I was skipping around on the pitch but the heat was something else. Within minutes of coming on I was buggered.

Thomas Waldrom: I was just knackered. Absolutely shattered. It was only my second game back after breaking my hand. To be out for six weeks and then play 100 minutes, having managed only 60 in the semi-final, was very exhausting. I was so tired but you don't think about that. You just push yourself as much as you can and think of the reward afterwards.

Don Armand: We only got into extra time because Nathan Hughes went over a ball in the last minute of normal time within kickable range. That decision could have gone the other way and we'd have lost the final.

Rob Baxter: That Nathan Hughes penalty late on . . . I don't watch the game back that much. You've got to park things if you want to move on.

Gareth Steenson: That was the difficult one. Everyone always talks about the winning kick but if I missed this we were done. And it's one you shouldn't miss.

Rob Baxter: I was thinking, 'I don't know how Tom Waldrom is still running.' He made 37 carries and was still doing it in extra time. I was looking at him going, 'Really? How is this guy still doing this?' There was some really special stuff going on.

Thomas Waldrom: It was an unbelievable team effort. There's a whole bunch of us from different backgrounds with different personalities but we all got on really well. There was a great balance on and off the field.

Henry Slade: The fight we showed to get it to extra time was massive. We were just hammering at the door all extra time. The boys put in some massive numbers.

Don Armand: I'd never played in a game with extra time. It was so hot I got blood blisters on my feet; it was like running on knives.

Ben Moon: It was very hot but as soon as it went to extra time we all knew we were going to win. We always back our fitness.

Carl Rimmer: If you drop the ball or get turned over at that stage . . . bloody hell. Especially after my experience the previous week. But Tom Waldrom and Geoff Parling were genuinely amazing. They kept calling for the ball, even though they'd been on for the entire game. I was just more than happy simply to back them up. The crucial scrum? We knew we had to drive straight through the middle of them. It felt like we reset that scrum 20 to 30 times. Every time we were just looking at each other. I'm not in charge but I just like to shout. People were probably bored of listening to me. 'Do it right.' 'Stay square. Stay square!' 'C'mon boys. This is it. This is literally it.'

Gareth Steenson: I thought to myself, 'One of two things is going to happen here. Either we're going to get a penalty and

I'm going to have to kick it, or Wasps are going to get a penalty and we're going to be defending again.' But I was also thinking, 'There are still two minutes left. I might get another go in some shape or form. A drop goal maybe? A penalty shoot-out?' I was pretty confident. I'd kicked well in the warm-up and I felt good.

Geoff Parling: I've played with a lot of 10s and, without any doubt, Steeno's one of the best at driving home what a team wants.

Carl Rimmer: The scrum before the penalty we got the shunt. I know we did. But it got reset for some reason and the next one went down. We're on the floor. We heard the whistle but I've been involved in plenty of scrums where the ref suddenly throws one the other way for no reason. All six of us had our heads buried on the floor going, 'Which way has that gone?' I pulled my head out and saw it had gone the right way. It was just euphoria then.

Gareth Steenson: It was a penalty to us. I don't think there was any real doubt. You never quite know but I knew we were on top in the scrums. To be fair to Wasps they could have manipulated it after they'd lost a couple of props and gone to uncontested scrums, rather than bringing Marty Moore back on at tight head. They could easily have said, 'He can't play there.' I've met Dai Young a couple of times since. I like Dai and that just showed the calibre of them. They didn't take a shortcut.

Carl Rimmer: I didn't even think about Steeno's kick. I just trotted back before the realisation struck he still had to kick it.

Kai Horstmann: I was celebrating as soon as we won the penalty. I was so confident in Steeno's ability and I know how mentally strong and tough he is. You know it's going through. I wasn't even questioning it. He's so good at those moments.

Henry Slade: Yeah, we knew. He's been unbelievably reliable off the tee for a long time so we had every confidence in him.

Don Armand: It was in a relatively easy position. Or it would have been in a normal game. There was massive pressure but Steeno nailed it. He was never going to miss.

Gareth Steenson: It's weird. You can feel it's your big moment. I'm usually thinking about picking out a letter on a billboard but at Twickenham you have to look higher. The posts are absolutely irrelevant to me. Whenever I kick – even when it's past the posts – I try to watch and see if it hits the letter I've been aiming at. And I genuinely did think about my dad. I remember asking him, 'If you can help me with this one it would be good.'

Carl Rimmer: I knew it was over as soon as he struck it. Then it was just a case of trying to find a clock that would tell us how long was left.

Gareth Steenson: Both my calves went as I kicked it. On the TV the commentator said, 'He's got a wry smile on his face.' That wasn't a wry smile, it was a grimace.

Ian Whitten: Way back when we beat Bath in the LV= Cup semi-final, I tore my calf celebrating and we lost the final. When Steeno kicked the penalty in extra time I jumped in the air and both my calves went again.

Gareth Steenson: We'd talked in advance about what we were going to do in the final couple of minutes. I remember people saying, 'We can't go side to side because we'll get pinged.' I was saying, 'We have to play wide.' We tried to run it but ended up in front of our posts. I was thinking, 'We've got to win this ruck.'

If we'd lost it or conceded a penalty, they'd have kicked it and we'd have been back to square one.

Henry Slade: The last thing I remember is standing back in the pocket getting ready to kick the ball out. Then bloody Michele Campagnaro picked it up from the ruck and tried to kick it out himself. There were people climbing all over him and I was thinking, 'Shit, this is going to get charged down, they're going to score.' My heart was in my mouth but, finally, he kicked it out. I went and gave him a big hug and slapped him.

Rob Baxter: That final is probably the best argument for a strictly managed and controlled salary cap. What was it at the end? We were separated by just three points even after extra time.

Jack Nowell: It was the highlight of my career, to win it with my mates.

Henry Slade: It was the most amazing feeling.

Rob Baxter: The guy who really impressed me that day was Dai Young. I remember going over and shaking his hand. As elated as I was feeling myself, I knew it was as tough for him. There's nothing you can say. You just shake your head and say, 'Sorry, one of us had to come through.' They'd been on an incredible journey as well. That's what finals should be like.

Alec Hepburn: I was blind drunk because I was injured. It was hard to watch because there were such bittersweet feelings. I was very happy for a lot of friends but you're just not as much a part of it if you're injured. I think I harboured that for a while. I don't think I really let it go until I played my first game for England. I felt like I'd missed out.

Mark Stevens: Premiership Rugby wanted me to make players available for the media but none of them wanted to leave the changing room. They just wanted to be with their mates celebrating.

Kai Horstmann: The trophy was on the bus with us the whole journey. It got slightly tribal. A film crew from BT Sport wanted to stay on until Reading. Then they suddenly said, 'We can't film any of this.' Sarra Elgan was saying, 'Sorry, I'm getting off.'

Mark Stevens: It was nuts going back home. BT were doing a feature called 'The Rise of the Chiefs' and started filming, only for naked backsides to start appearing in the background. We hadn't even got to the end of the Whitton Road.

Jack Yeandle: The bus trip back was absolutely brilliant.

Dave Dennis: There were a few rituals that were an eye-opener to a new guy.

Luke Cowan-Dickie: We were singing songs I ain't even heard of, old boys singing songs from back in the day, probably before I was born. It's always been in the culture. When you have a couple of beers you chat about things. We still swear by it.

Kai Horstmann: The old grizzly crew were at the back, all the old-timers. A couple of youngsters sometimes used to try and sneak up. Nowellsy when he wanted a drink. Rob also came back and had a drink. Often he's at the front doing his analysis and coding but at moments like that you've got to have a drink with the lads. One of the hardest things going from playing to coaching is to pull yourself away from that. It's hard for him because that's a part of the game he loves.

Rob Baxter: You always wonder what it's going to be like. I remember sitting in the front of the bus . . . it felt similar to the trip back from Bristol in 2010. I had a few drinks with the boys but it was more about having something to savour. I remember thinking, 'This is incredible. We might never have a day like this again.'

Jack Yeandle: Coming off the bus I was with Carl Rimmer. Somehow he'd found a pair of cheap sunglasses and wore them the whole trip back. He walked off the bus topless, with his T-shirt around his head, holding the trophy. Everyone's expecting Jack Nowell or Steeno to walk off the bus first – instead they got Rimmer. Upstairs in the main bar was so rammed. Someone's got a video of me on stage, doing these ridiculous chants and songs. There's also a really good picture of me celebrating with my mates from uni who'd come up. We didn't realise the camera was there.

Rob Baxter: Sometimes you forget your wife and children have also had a long, stressful day. It was chaos up in the bar and when I looked over at my wife her face was white. She'd had an emotional day. She said she was okay but I said, 'Shall we just head home?' We got a taxi back, sat in the garden, put the patio heater on, put some music on and got out a couple of big Cuban cigars I had in store for a special occasion. We had a few drinks, stayed up late and just talked.

Jack Nowell: I went out all night, got in at 4.30 a.m. and had a taxi booked for 5 a.m. to go back to London to go on tour with the Lions. It doesn't happen very often, does it? These things are very special and I took every single second I could with the boys on the way home. I missed the bus parade and the days after but by that stage half of them wouldn't have known if I was there or not.

Ian Whitten: I don't really remember much. Shaun Malton passed out at midday on the Sunday and went home, absolutely done. I'd love to win it again. I think I would remember more about it this time. I lost three days of my life.

Mark Stevens: Everyone celebrated through the night and then they all had to meet at Steeno's house at 8 a.m. the next morning for our end-of-year social. It was a Robin Hood fancy-dress theme. Then we went to the Half Moon in Clyst St Mary for breakfast before walking back to the club and carrying on the social in the Wigwam Bar.

Gareth Steenson: I'd sat on the pitch with the Championship trophy so I was thinking, 'Wouldn't it be great to get a picture on the halfway line again?' It just seemed to make sense.

Mark Stevens: Steeno went out on to the pitch naked and had a picture taken with the cup covering his crown jewels, which he then posted on social media. Everyone was liking it until Tony Rowe's wife saw it and asked how they'd got the trophy, which had been locked in Tony's office. Someone had found the key and nabbed it. I think Tony came down later in the day and rescued it.

Gareth Steenson: I did have my clothes on when I was in town. It was a bank holiday weekend. It felt like one big celebration.

Jack Yeandle: The Sunday was a very good social event. The trophy parade on the Monday was absolute hell. It should have been one of the best days of my life but it was nearly one of the worst. I was so hung-over. I didn't move an inch on the bus. BBC *Spotlight* filmed me: 'Jack, how does it feel?' But I had no words. I felt absolutely awful.

Dave Dennis: The open-top ride on the Monday was really special. To go down the high street and see all the people . . . Exeter's not a huge place but everyone here seems to support us, whether they're rugby fans or not. There was so much love and support that year – and it's carried on, which is cool.

Phil Dollman: The few days after were terrible. I'd been picked to go on tour with Wales but I'd damaged my knee and was awaiting a scan. There was a camp organised in north Wales but it was a bank holiday weekend and it was easier to get scanned down in Exeter. Everyone else was into their celebrations but I was talking to physios and coaches and hoping for a good outcome. It was never to be. I would have been chuffed to bits to have had that opportunity but there's worse-off people than me.

Rob Baxter: I looked in the players' faces at the bus parade on the Monday and I didn't know how some of them were still alive. What they must have done to themselves on the Sunday. Let's just say they didn't need a lot of topping up on the Monday. When the parade was over I decided it would be nice to take the trophy home with me. I packed it up in its box, wheeled it through the crowds and, when my wife arrived to pick me up, stuck it in the boot of the car. It lived on our sofa for 24 hours: we took photos of us having a cup of tea with the trophy, breakfast with the trophy, all the corny fun things you can do. The next day my son was due to come round for a barbecue with his mates. When he walked in the first thing he saw was the trophy, sitting in the middle of the table in the garden, glinting in the sun, with a couple of bottles of champagne around it. For me that was a really enjoyable moment. Those kinds of memories are unbelievable. You can't buy those.

AVIVA PREMIERSHIP FINAL
Twickenham, 27 May 2017
Wasps 20 Exeter Chiefs 23
(After Extra Time; Score At 80 Minutes 20–20)

Wasps: W Le Roux; C Wade, E Daly, J Gopperth, J Bassett; D Cipriani, D Robson (J Simpson, 57); M Mullan (S McIntyre, 57), T Taylor (A Johnson, 64), P Swainston (M Moore, 27), J Launchbury (capt), M Symons (K Myall, 57), J Haskell, T Young (G Thompson, 64), N Hughes.
Tries: Gopperth, Daly. Cons: Gopperth 2. Pens: Gopperth 2.

Exeter Chiefs: P Dollman (H Slade, 46); J Nowell, I Whitten, O Devoto (M Campagnaro, 76), O Woodburn; G Steenson (capt), S Townsend (W Chudley, 49); B Moon (C Rimmer, 50), L Cowan-Dickie (J Yeandle, 50), H Williams (T Francis, 50), D Dennis (S Simmonds, 60), G Parling, K Horstmann (M Lees, 52), D Armand, T Waldrom.
Tries: Nowell, Dollman. Cons: Steenson 2. Pens: Steenson 3.

Referee: JP Doyle. Att: 79,657.

EIGHTEEN

THE INNER GAME

Once the hangovers had finally worn off – and Rob Baxter had collected an honorary doctorate from the University of Exeter – it was clear an even bigger challenge lay ahead. Sneaking a solitary title in extra time was all well and good but proper champions kicked on. If the Chiefs had ambitions to be serial winners, they could not sit around dwelling on last season's exploits. The previous year Baxter had stuck a blank picture frame up in the home changing room, to be filled only by the Exeter team that won the Premiership. A fresh source of motivation would now be required.

There was also a sizeable target pinned to their chests. Just two clubs – Leicester and Saracens – had won back-to-back league titles in the previous decade. Instead of being the hunters, they were now very much the hunted. Few had mentioned it at the time but, in the semi-final, they had been fortunate to catch Saracens just a week after the north London side had won their second successive European title, defeating Clermont 28–17 in the final in Edinburgh. Would Sarries have yielded in Devon in different circumstances?

Baxter, either way, was determined to show the 2016/17 outcome was no fluke. Ahead of the Chiefs' opening game of the 2017/18 season away at Gloucester, he challenged his side to raise their sights higher. 'I want us to go up there, throw some punches, get ourselves into the game and see what playing in the Premiership is like when you are currently the top team in England,' stressed Baxter. 'We are not going to be a team scared of losing a game just because we were champions last year.'

Perhaps not, but there was no sidestepping a 28–21 opening-night defeat at Kingsholm, nor home and away losses to Leinster in December which effectively scuppered another European campaign. The good news was that, in Sam Simmonds, Exeter had unearthed another local diamond. The previous year the red-haired back-rower from Teignmouth had been on loan with Cornish Pirates and had made just two Premiership starts for Chiefs. Just over 12 months later, in November, he was making his England Test debut against Argentina.

Simmonds' club captain Jack Yeandle certainly did not foresee such a steep rise when he was giving morning lifts up to training from Teignmouth to a scrawny academy kid who barely opened his mouth. 'Stone-cold silence, bless him. Nerves, I think it was.' No one, Yeandle included, imagined the skinny youth from a small coastal town becoming England's starting No. 8 within five years. 'Eddie Jones wants him to put muscle on top of muscle now but there was only skin and bones then.'

The teenager, whose father David and uncle Rob are in the crab- and lobster-fishing business, was 90kg when he first joined Exeter and still occasionally playing in the centre. These days he tips the scales at over 100kg: few blast past defenders more consistently and his try-per-game stats are even more impressive than Waldrom's. Baxter believes it is a mistake to perceive Simmonds as a square peg who does not neatly fit the round England hole that needs filling in Billy Vunipola's absence.

'Trying to compare them head to head is virtually impossible. If you want to pick Sam, you pick him for what he's good for. If you want to pick him because he is playing well for Exeter but don't give him a defined role in the team, you won't get the true value from him. If England want to pick him – and he's easily good enough – they have to give him a role where he is on the ball.'

Simmonds also remains a small-town Devon lad at heart. The first time he ventured into central London with his Exeter teammate Henry Slade, things did not go very well: 'We took the Tube but we didn't have a clue where we were going. We got off a couple of times and jumped back on what we thought was the right train, only to discover it wasn't. I guess I like the simpleness of Devon.'

* * * * *

Others in the Exeter dressing room are keener to explore pastures new. The Sydney University and Wallaby forward Dave Dennis had spent 10 years with the Waratahs and, for all the charms of the northern beaches, wanted a new challenge. Having had a semi-rural upbringing on acreage west of Sydney, back in the days when he played for Penrith Emus, he sensed plenty of similarities between Devon and Australia. 'I walked in here and knew maybe three people. Within a month I felt I'd known everyone for years.

'Inside the first two weeks I'm sitting in the gym with Kai Horstmann. Kai's old-school. He doesn't give a shit. Mark Twiggs is running the gym session and I'd been doing everything I'd been told. After a while I hear Twiggsy shout, "Boys, make sure you get your neck done at the end of the session." To which Kai replied, "Eat shit, Twiggsy!" Everybody is pissing themselves laughing yet Twiggsy just walks off as if nothing has happened.'

The dark-haired Dennis had faced the All Blacks' haka and won 18 caps for Australia but he had never seen anything quite like this. Where he came from, there was significantly more reverence for club staff. 'I was thinking, "Are you sure?" I would never think to say that to my strength-and-conditioning coach in Australia. It would never have happened. Aussies are quite jovial and take the piss but some things are different. Here no one cares. If you wear something to training that someone doesn't like they'll tell you. If you take your shirt off and you're carrying a bit of extra weight from the off season they'll say, "Denno, you look shithouse, mate."

'It can be quite confrontational but it breaks down any bullshit and barriers. Ever since those early days I've known I can be myself. That's a really healthy and powerful thing. You can become comfortable with who you are and that's very important. Some guys who are a bit bigger and carrying a bit of weight cop it every second day but that's their role in the team. The English are quite good at banter. We're a bit more boisterous, sarcastic and louder but the English are probably a bit more subtle and to the point. I kind of like that dry sense of "This is how it is." No one's safe; maybe Rob, that's all.'

He also found other aspects of the culture refreshing. Despite being a proud Waratah, the collective air of tension around Australian rugby had begun to get to him. 'It's no secret the game is struggling a bit in Australia. Maybe it was the back of my career and I wanted to have more fun but the crowd, the staff, the supporters . . . everyone was a bit on edge. "We have to win this game, we have to win this game." Here, all the supporters are pretty honest, working people. They live and breathe the rugby and they're really loyal. I remember my first season: we won two of our first eight games and lost badly against Saracens. I was walking off the field and everyone was standing up clapping, saying, "Good effort, you put your body on the line." You just wouldn't get that in Australia.'

No surprise, perhaps, that Dennis's phone was starting to ping with messages from other players back home. 'Mate, if there's anything going in Exeter just let me know.' The fun the Chiefs were having was starting to be noticed around the world. Dave's dad, John, also felt right at home. Growing up on a dairy farm in New South Wales, he had lost his own father young and, having opted to move away, had taught for 40 years in Richmond High School on the edge of Sydney. Every week he would loyally drive into the city to watch his son play for the Waratahs; the first time he pitched up at Exeter it was love at first sight. 'This is his type of rugby. He sits in the stand, enjoys a few ales – he's an ale or a dark stout man – and then he sits in the pub.' It was a pretty special day for the whole family when Exeter, with Dennis starting in the second row, won the 2017 Premiership. 'The Waratahs won the Super Rugby title in 2014 but I was injured for the final. Not to be playing, having worked so hard over so many years, hurt me. So to be actually out on the field and share the moment of victory . . . I wouldn't say it was karma but it filled a bit of a void.'

It did not take long, either, for Chiefs fans to warm to the dancing feet of Santiago Cordero, the gloriously elusive Argentine winger who had turned up to add some Latin flair to the backline mix, or Nic White, the Wallaby scrum-half, who had arrived from Montpellier. Tom O'Flaherty, signed without fanfare from the Ospreys, also had electric pace, scored eye-catching tries and offered something slightly different to the former Bath duo, Olly Woodburn and Ollie Devoto.

Matt Kvesic, capped by England as far back as 2013, was another smart signing on a three-year deal from Gloucester. It took a while for Chiefs to fashion Kvesic into the multi-faceted back-rower they wanted but the flanker found it fascinating to see how Exeter went about their business. 'When I was at Gloucester and Exeter were pushing towards the top six, it was a case of "What are Exeter doing that we aren't?" Having been here I've seen there's no magic formula other than hard work. What they do really well are the basics.'

Once his Chiefs apprenticeship was finally complete – 'It was a frustrating period for me because I wanted to play but it was to help me develop as a player in the long term' – he also noticed something else. 'I played three seasons at Gloucester but I never had the same enjoyment I've had with Exeter.' Rather than focusing simply on being a breakdown specialist, he was encouraged to broaden his game and playing alongside the likes of Dave Ewers and Armand was rarely a chore. He also enjoyed playing behind a front five who were generally going forward and were increasingly famous for their ruthlessness close to the try-line. 'Gloucester when I was there even called their pick-and-go move "Chiefs". I presume they still do now.'

In his first season Exeter hoisted some more silverware, albeit the increasingly low-key Anglo-Welsh Cup, with a 28–11 victory over Bath at Kingsholm under the guidance of Ricky Pellow. It was a special day, even so, for the soon-to-retire Horstmann, who captained the team on his 100th appearance for the club, and Joe Simmonds, Sam's younger brother, who kicked 13 points to reinforce his promise at fly-half. It did not, however, alter the season's main focus: putting together an end-of-season run good enough to defend their Premiership crown.

* * * * *

They would have to do so without a couple of floored warriors. Every professional knows they have a shelf life but Carl Rimmer's departure from the game had been shockingly abrupt. In January, after going on as a replacement at Newcastle, a scrum had gone down. Following the game he had experienced a mild headache but thought nothing of it. 'You can get headaches from neck strains because it's all connected muscle.' On the Monday his mood was not greatly improved when Baxter told him he wouldn't be playing the following weekend. 'We always joke that Rob should have worked in politics. He can drop you or deliver some bad news and still manage to leave the room with a handshake and a thank you. I don't know how he did it.' The next training day was a normal one: a swim session and then out on to the pitch for a run around. 'I was standing on the touchline and then started just trotting forwards. I didn't even touch the ball. Everything went a bit hazy and I did what felt like an eternity of sidesteps. In reality it was probably only two or three before I just hit the deck. I lay there thinking, "Something's not right. I'll just lie here for a minute and wait until it's time to get up." But that moment never came. It was probably a minute before anyone noticed and the physio alerted someone. It was a scary-ish time.'

It was to become even more frightening. As the club doctor, Adam Reuben, was driving him to the nearby Royal Devon and Exeter Hospital, the prop's symptoms intensified. 'All hell broke loose. My head was killing me and the light was hurting my eyes. I pulled a hoodie over my head but then I started to feel nauseous and threw up a few times.' It transpired he had suffered a stroke, having nicked an artery in his neck during that supposedly innocuous scrum in Newcastle. Looking back, he now realises how lucky he was. 'I'd physically hate to have been my wife. I was asleep for 23 hours a day for three days. We've got two young kids. At the time there was no guarantee of anything. I had three horrible days and woke up on the fourth. She wasn't sure if her husband was going to come home.'

It was obvious the 30-year-old Rimmer's rugby days were over. Obvious, that is, to everyone but him. 'They talk about the 12 steps of denial or anger, don't they? I went to denial straight away.' It was a few months before he could see things in a more positive light. 'I honestly think the stroke was one of the best things that ever happened to me. Eventually my sell-by date was coming, possibly that year given the way Ben Moon and Alec

Hepburn are going now. The way I look at it now is that at least I didn't have to have any awkward conversations. I just stroked out and that was that.'

Going into business with Steenson and helping to run the popular Stand Off bar in Exeter's Longbrook Street has since provided him with a different kind of challenge but there have inevitably been twinges of regret. 'I was talking to my wife about it. I haven't missed the actual sport of rugby too much but you miss being around the people. Chiefs had a Saturday night game and I went to watch. Even the smell in the car park was an odd one. There's that foggy, damp smell to it. I used to love a night game; it was always one of my favourite things. This time it really sent me into a bad mood. I had to go home and apologise to everyone later. That was the one time I remember thinking, "God, I miss rugby." As opposed to "God, I miss living the dream."'

* * * * *

In the case of Matt Jess it was a more gradual descent. A ruptured ligament in his big toe had sidelined him for four months but his rehab was going well. His sprint times were as good as they had ever been and, with his 33rd birthday looming, he was hopeful of another contract. Instead, he was informed in early spring that his time was up. 'It hit me hard. Normally they are quite transparent with you but I didn't get told until the March, which didn't sit well with me. In your head you start to question yourself. Could it have happened in a better way? Could I have gone in in January and asked about what was going to happen next year?'

Increasingly he also began to worry about what his future away from Sandy Park would hold. 'I'll be honest: I didn't really understand mental health when I was in the game. But when you're suddenly not playing at the top level any more, you get an inkling. You can understand how someone can spiral out of control. It's amazing what a void it can leave when an obsession – in my case a love of rugby – is taken away.'

It took six to nine months to deal with his bruised emotions. 'I suppose it's a vicious circle. I was thinking to myself, "What do I do?" I wasn't coming to terms with it, I wasn't being honest with myself and I'd try and block it out. I wouldn't say it's bitterness, it's more of a disappointment. Sadness, I suppose. But when you actually start to look at it, rugby's a business. The quicker players realise that, the more you can think about what to do next.'

Jess, now on the coaching staff at Cornish Pirates, is also keen for other players to seek help more promptly than he did. 'You can be so insular and internalise everything. But I've now realised it's important to be open and speak about it. There are players out there in their late thirties and loving life. But when you do finally have to give up, it's tough. It can also have an effect on your family. Then it becomes a matter of controlling that. It's never going to be easy but when I went to get help and did some counselling and started to speak to people, all the good things started to come flooding back. The memories, the trips, the beers with your mates. That's why it's important to talk about it. When dark thoughts start to crowd in, just speak to somebody.

'That's what I try and tell people now. If you can find something that gives you that same benefit, that will keep challenging you and keep you going, that'll keep your mental health where it needs to be. High-performance sport does have its consequences, particularly after it is gone. When you reflect afterwards you realise how many stresses and strains are involved. When you are in the thick of it they don't always register.' Sometimes it can be enough simply to play in a veterans match or, as Jess has done, organise a charity touch rugby festival on Exmouth beach and invite along some of his ex-teammates. 'Everyone's in the same boat: we've probably had exactly the same thoughts but we don't have to talk about them. We just know.'

The blunt reality, though, is that players of all ages can struggle to cope. As Horstmann points out, being a professional rugby player is not a normal, everyday existence. 'You get fully institutionalised; it becomes part of you. Even my wife, Caroline, doesn't quite get it. She thinks I'm completely bonkers. But they haven't experienced it.'

Ladled on top is the pressure to perform: clubs such as Exeter carry big squads and not everyone can play every week. Even during a normal training week when the team is winning, Jess believes many players are instinctively glancing over their shoulders. 'People see the games but they don't always look at what players are doing Monday to Friday. What if you haven't had a good game? What if your coach turns around and specifically says that? Are you going to be dropped? Is there going to be an email tonight? Is my name going to be on it? Self-doubt can play on your mind. The game's not happening until Saturday but already there's pressure on a Monday. At that point, who do you speak to? Someone who's also playing in your position? Your coach? Possibly not.'

This recurring stress can become corrosive. 'Some personalities are laid-back to the point of horizontal and don't really care if they're playing or not. Most people, though, are chomping at the bit. You go home and offload to your wife or girlfriend. Then the email comes through and, after all that, you're playing again. Boom. You're the happiest guy in the world again.' Next week, though, the news might be less good. 'You'd get the phone call. You'd know as soon as you see Rob's name flash up. If everything was hunky-dory, he wouldn't be phoning you. Sometimes I know when I've had a poor one or not had much of an impact. But occasionally he might just say someone else deserves an opportunity. It's not personal but it does affect you.'

* * * * *

Hence the reason Saturdays assume such huge significance for every player. Get it wrong and the consequences can be significant. Hence the butterflies that need soothing each week. Every club contains players with unusual routines and pre-game quirks but Exeter is particularly well stocked. Jonny Hill, among other things, dislikes sitting in the dressing room before away games: 'I prefer to go and sit in the stands, listen to some music and text one or two people. Changing rooms are not a nice environment. Everyone's full of caffeine and they're farting everywhere. I don't really want that in my life.'

Rather than resorting to motivational iPod speeches, Alec Hepburn also goes through his own unique pre-match schedule. The ritual starts the night before when, along with Harry Williams and a rotating cast of like-minded colleagues, he spends the evening cooking, drinking cups of tea and talking about everything under the sun. 'There's a lot of fun on Friday nights. Laughing our heads off, a big meal followed by a cup of tea. It's never the same people every week, it's not regimented but it helps that in Exeter you're within a few miles of each other. You can't overestimate the value of living in close proximity because it means you spend more time together. Even if you wanted to avoid people you couldn't. Walking down the high street you'll always see someone.'

Nor is Hepburn one for lying idly around in bed on a match-day morning. Getting up early means he can eat an extra meal – omelette on toast with five or six eggs by 9 a.m. followed by a little fish or chicken at 11.30 a.m. – and feel more alert. 'It keeps me sharper. I feel better from waking up earlier and having more hours awake. I also want to get plenty of food into me early so I'm not running around with it still in my stomach. The earlier I eat I also feel I'm less affected by excitement and nerves.'

To round everything off, he will then head to the bathroom and, regardless of the time of year, have a cold shower. 'I always have a cold shower on match day. I don't have to do it but I find it wakes up my whole system.' In his younger days, having changed and jumped into his car, he would then listen to some heavy rock. These days it is more likely to be 'You Oughta Know' by Alanis Morissette. 'I prefer to listen to something slightly calmer and more emotive that gives me a different sort of motivation and encourages a more emotional response. Ultimately, you've got to be emotionally ready to hurt yourself.' An early arrival at the stadium also allows sufficient time to grab a flat white from a stall at the ground 'and have a bit of a laugh and a chat before the gravity of the situation starts to kick in'. By kick-off, he hopes he will be as ready as he can possibly be.

High up in the stands, meanwhile, Tony Rowe will be similarly on edge. 'I get very nervous. I'm usually here three hours before and an hour beforehand I get a bit tense. I'm walking around, twitching a bit.' At least salvation is usually only 80 minutes away. Increasingly it takes a good side to turn over the Chiefs at home. By the spring of 2018, it was also clear Exeter would again be serious play-off contenders. From late February onwards they reeled off seven successive league victories, finishing top of the regular-season league for the first time. Not only that, they were eight points clear of second-placed Saracens and a massive 22 points ahead of fourth-placed Newcastle.

Before the semi-final against the Falcons, Exeter's record prompted Hepher to wonder aloud if recruiting big-name southern hemisphere coaches was actually more of a risk than backing some of the home-grown coaches operating in Britain and Ireland. 'History shows that English or home-based coaches have really dominated in the Premiership. Our nous for the game shouldn't be underestimated. People don't always appreciate the quality coaching going on in the Premiership. The style of rugby that our sides are playing would be competitive against any club side in the world. It would be very interesting if a group of British coaches went to the southern hemisphere. I'd back ourselves to win competitions there and I'm sure Mark McCall, Dai Young and Dean Richards would be the same.'

On this occasion Exeter's 36–5 semi-final win over the Falcons at Sandy Park was almost ludicrously one-sided. The home side enjoyed an astonishing 92 per cent possession in the first half, although Newcastle deserved much credit for their defensive resolve in the face of the relentless bombardment they had to endure. With Saracens brushing aside Wasps 57–33 it set up the Twickenham finale almost everyone had expected.

Would this be the day Chiefs buried any doubt about the identity of the country's best team? The answer was a disappointing 'No'. Saracens were slick and sharp-edged while Exeter performed well below expectations. Sarries' 27–10 win yielded their fourth Premiership title in seven seasons; as their rivals sprayed their champagne and posed for yet more ecstatic photographs with a major trophy, Exeter's players were all too aware they had badly underperformed. 'We were never in it,' confirmed Nowell. 'Sometimes you've just got to take your hat off to the other team. A lot of the boys were crying in the changing room afterwards. We'd finished first in the league and we thought we were going to beat them. That was the most upsetting thing. We just didn't turn up. Full credit to Saracens but I was as disappointed as I've ever been.'

Slade, his fellow England international, felt similarly. 'There was a completely different post-game feeling to the first one we lost. There was just absolute disappointment. We were gutted and told ourselves we never wanted to have that feeling again. It still hurts. In a way it showed how far we've come as a team. We now expect way more of ourselves, which I think we should do.' The inescapable conclusion, nevertheless, was that the era of Mako Vunipola, Maro Itoje, Owen Farrell, Jamie George et al. still had several more years to run.

NINETEEN

MEN IN BLACK

The prevailing view among the greybeards and bald eagles of the Twickenham press box and TV gantry was that Exeter would need to reinvent themselves slightly over the summer. Their preferred game plan worked a treat against middling Premiership sides, less so against stronger, more dynamic opponents or quality European sides. Joe Simmonds had endured an uncomfortable day at Twickenham and a number of popular individuals – Waldrom, Horstmann, Rimmer, the hard-edged Julian Salvi, Will Chudley and the talented but oft-omitted Italian centre Michele Campagnaro – had either retired or moved on.

Even the forwards' coach, Rob Hunter, found himself wincing at times during the first half of the 2018 final. 'I remember putting my pencil down and thinking, "We haven't come here to win this. We've come here hoping that maybe they'll underperform." I don't think we did have a Plan B.' Exeter were reliably strong and fit but they could not endlessly rely on Steenson or Dollman, both edging towards veteran status, to create holes or Whitten and the straight-running Sam Hill to reinvent themselves as all-singing, all-dancing midfield creators. It was not a massive surprise when it was announced in the autumn that the Scotland and Lions full-back Stuart Hogg would be joining the club after the following year's Rugby World Cup in Japan. The Chiefs needed a sharper cutting edge for those days when their close-range driving game was not quite enough.

There were already those who reckoned they were squeezing the joy out of the sport, that their keep-ball rugby was effective but ultimately made for repetitive viewing. Few criticise snooker or tennis players for their unerring accuracy when it matters but, as serial champions like Steve Davis and Pete Sampras had discovered, winning consistently is not enough for some. The coaches' view was that, in the end, it didn't matter what other people said or even whether England's head coach Eddie Jones picked certain individuals. If they could improve what they already did well, continued to work hard and were tactically smarter on occasions, they would be fine. Hunter, for one, felt the implied criticism of his players' skills was misplaced. 'I think it's a bit harsh and unfair. We've got some guys who are way better players than people think. We don't play the way we do because it's low risk. We do it because it just makes sense. If you understand why we're doing things, you'd probably go, "That's quite skilful, actually."'

The lesser-known Exeter forwards who had graduated to the international arena all tended to do so without missing a beat. Along with Cowan-Dickie, Williams, Hepburn, Francis, Sam Simmonds and Sam Skinner, Ben Moon was another perfect example. The 29-year-old was at a kids' birthday party with no signal on his mobile when England, suddenly short of fit and available loose-head props, called him up at short notice ahead of the autumn internationals. 'There was a bouncy castle and I was having a great time. But when I finally walked out my phone was going mad. My wife was at a friend's baby shower and she had no signal either, so I couldn't get hold of her.' There was also the small matter of having to drive from Devon to the Surrey stockbroker belt. 'It was half-two on a Sunday and some of the lads were already at the camp. It was a mad rush to find my boots and other bits and pieces and I was panicking. They told me not to worry but then I got caught in traffic on the M5. I was sitting there thinking, "Don't be late." My satnav was on my phone but my phone battery was dying. I was thinking, "Oh, no, this is all going to go terribly wrong."'

Happily he made it and, when the big day dawned, enjoyed an excellent game against South Africa. Jones subsequently dubbed him 'The Coalminer' for his uncomplaining, solid-as-a-rock attitude and he went on to win eight caps in total. To some extent he felt fortunate to have had any sort of chance – 'To be called up in the first place and get those eight caps was more than I thought would ever happen' – but his daughter, Mabel, has not always been so keen. 'Whenever I've put the England stuff on she'd say, "No, Daddy, take it off. I don't want you to go." It's heartbreaking. She associates the kit with me being away.'

In Exeter, though, they could not have been more thrilled. For Baxter, in particular, the belated Moon landing encapsulated pretty much everything rugby should be about. 'Compare it to some recent examples of guys flying in from another country, suddenly ending up with one cap and then disappearing back to their clubs. I know which story I'd rather follow and the one that emotionally means a lot to me and that's the Ben Moon story.'

Could something similar have happened to a few more Chiefs? Moon, in common with many of his teammates, is absolutely convinced Dave Ewers should have worn the red rose – 'I think he should have been capped a long time ago; he's not the sort of bloke you'd want to be putting too many shots on' – and would also have loved Phil Dollman to have had a Wales cap. 'He was very unlucky to miss out on that Welsh squad in 2017 because of injury. Dolly's a class act and still is now. Put him on the pitch and he's as good as anyone.'

On the plus side there had been a precious cap for the 20-year-old Jack Maunder for England in Argentina in 2017. Maunder learned of his tour selection while lying on the physio's table at Exeter, having torn a calf against Harlequins. Having regained fitness in the nick of time, a subsequent groin strain then threatened to ruin any chance of getting any game time behind Danny Care. Sitting in the living room of his family's farmhouse, he retains vivid memories of his brief Test bow in San Juan. 'I didn't think I was going to get on but, with two minutes to go, it happens. There's a line-out and we call my least favourite pass in the world where you miss 10 and hit 12 straight away. It's a long pass for my little arms. Then, all of a sudden, Denny Solomona's through and I'm behind him thinking, "Oh my God, he's going to pass to me, I'm going to score the winning try on my debut." Luckily, he just ran off and scored himself.' England won 38–34 and in common with his Blundell's school friend Dom Bess, who went on to play Test cricket, Maunder remains hungry for more. Both he and his younger brother, Sam, have already had the honour of skippering England U20s, while Williams, Ollie Devoto, Sam Simmonds, Hepburn and Jonny Hill have also, to a greater or lesser degree, caught Jones's selectorial eye. With the Yorkshire-reared Wales international Francis, Wales's Alex Cuthbert, Tonga's Elvis Taione and the exiled Ulsterman Whitten also possessing international experience, an increasing amount of big-game know-how is now on tap.

* * * * *

Exeter certainly began the 2018/19 season as if they had a point to prove. On the first day of September they thrashed an admittedly lacklustre Leicester side 40–6 and then rattled up

42 and 35 points respectively against Wasps and Sale Sharks. Difficult weather and the odd unforced error combined to blow them off course again in Europe but domestically they had been beaten only once in the league when Saracens, unbeaten in 22 games in all competitions, travelled down to Devon on the last Saturday before Christmas. The final scoreline was properly eye-catching: Exeter 31 Saracens 13. The Londoners lost their talismanic captain Brad Barritt with concussion early on and, gradually, Exeter's pack took control. Moon, Williams and the big Australian lock Mitch Lees all rumbled off the bench to turn the screw in the final quarter, during which the Chiefs banged in 21 of their points. Just a league game, sure, but no win over Saracens ever felt routine. 'It gives me real confidence that if we do what we do with real energy we're a good side,' murmured Baxter. Hepher, too, had not forgotten a game back in the club's early Premiership days at Allianz Park when Exeter were getting thumped. As far as their players and management were concerned, a line had been crossed that day. 'They dressed some big fat bloke up in a woman's outfit and started singing "Nessun Dorma". The "joke" being that it was already all over. That one sat with us . . . it was always a bit of a driver in the back of our minds. We thought it was slightly strange they had humility written on the top of their stand.'

There was also the recurring question of how, exactly, Saracens had managed to assemble such an extraordinarily high-calibre squad under the existing salary cap regulations. In early March 2019 an intriguing piece of investigative journalism appeared in the *Daily Mail*, revealing that the club's owner Nigel Wray had entered into business and property arrangements with several of the club's leading players. These deals were the subject of increasing scrutiny from Premiership Rugby's salary cap manager and calls were mounting for a full investigation.

Initially Exeter's players decided they would be better off

concentrating on issues they could control. Saracens' players might be higher profile and – by the sound of it – better rewarded, but they were not infallible. Maybe, though, Exeter's on-field response was not entirely coincidental. There was a growing authority to the way they were finishing off games, not least when Leicester were humiliated 52–20 at Welford Road in early April. It was the kind of result that would once have been unthinkable. The visitors even had a bonus point tied up after just 31 minutes, sensational offloads from Armand and Olly Woodburn sending Slade over for a sweeping try that no one in his right mind could possibly describe as boring.

Except, that is, for the former Bath and England fly-half Stuart Barnes after the Chiefs took Northampton apart 42–12 in the semi-final. Writing in *The Times* on the Monday morning, Barnes instantly made himself the least popular person west of Taunton Deane Services, arguing that Exeter relied excessively on their pack for close-range tries, that their multi-phase philosophy was 'efficient but ugly' and compared watching the Chiefs to American football without a quarterback or any wide receivers. 'Exeter?' wrote Barnes. 'They are a magnificent club. They are magnificently managed, magnificently supported. They are magnificent. But, God, they can be boring. A year ago I nailed my colours to the Saracens mast ahead of the final. I'm doing so again. The game needs the Saracens mindset to prevail once more.'

Baxter and his players scarcely needed any more motivation but, intellectual argument or not, here it was served up on a platter. 'If all you want to focus on is the periods of play when we are five metres from the opposition line, then fine,' retorted the director of rugby, icily. 'But there are 95 other metres on a rugby pitch. If you want to talk about what you see when we are at one end of the field, make sure you add to it how we get there and the decisions we make to get there. Open your eyes and actually see. If you really want to decide how we play look outside that five metres.'

And if Exeter had mastered the art of keeping possession rather than kicking it skywards and rushing up to clatter the ball-catcher, which of the two methods required greater dexterity and asked tougher, if not necessarily intellectual, questions of the opposition? The Chiefs had scored 89 tries in their 22 league games and, for the second successive year, had finished eight points clear of everyone else in the regular season. As Baxter pointed out in the build-up to the club's fourth straight Premiership final at Twickenham, his side were also becoming more assured when it came to coping with the biggest occasions. Hunter's message to his players was to stick to their guns. 'You've got to go out and win the game because they're going to score some points. You've got to play proper rugby against them.' Hepher even felt relaxed enough to pop out on the morning of the match and go in search of a wedding anniversary present for his wife. 'I felt pretty confident we'd be in a good place to do it. We'd been increasing our performance, the lads were in good nick.'

On another gloriously clear day at Twickenham, it took Exeter barely 28 seconds to underline that fact. Saracens misjudged the kick-off, the Chiefs pack reclaimed the ball and a sniping White had dummied over for the first try before anyone's pasty had cooled. It was to be the first of 10 tries on a tense, see-sawing afternoon which, at one point, seemed likely to produce a south-west winner. Exeter's defensive line speed was more urgent and it was Sarries who were being harried into errors. At half-time it was 22–16. Then, with 57 minutes gone, pandemonium. The classy Slade, having previously released a galloping Sam Skinner down the right touchline, regathered the lock's outstanding one-handed offload and stretched over to put Exeter 27–16 ahead. Surely the Devonshire cream would rise to the top this time?

Everyone reckoned without Saracens' never-say-die attitude and the fates that shape every ball game. Farrell went short with the restart and, crucially, Liam Williams rose above Dave Dennis to deny the Chiefs possession. The ball found the hands of Maro Itoje who quite clearly passed the ball forward to his onrushing prop Vincent Koch. Had the whistle sounded and a scrum been awarded to Chiefs – with an 11-point advantage and the chance to reset themselves – might the outcome have been different? No one will ever know. A couple of phases later and Farrell's brilliant cross kick connected with a soaring Williams who rose above a wrong-footed Joe Simmonds in the right corner to gather and score. Farrell, suddenly at his tilt-headed, side-eyed best, converted unerringly from close to the touchline to make it a four-point ball game.

When White had to limp off not long afterwards, it catapulted Jack Maunder into the fray at a critical moment. The scrum-half's first box kick, with the adrenaline pumping, flew fractionally long and Sarries launched an immediate counter-attack. Before Chiefs knew it, Richard Wigglesworth was through a hole. With the defence caught too narrow, enough room was created on the outside for Sean Maitland to beat Slade and Nowell to the left corner. Even worse was about to follow. The previously outstanding Nowell, trying to help out Sam Simmonds after the latter had been hammered backwards in the tackle by Alex Lozowski, got his leg trapped and twisted horribly, damaging his knee and ankle ligaments. Saracens' players queued up to shake the winger's hand as he limped off, exuding both sympathy and relief. With Chiefs' backline now significantly reshuffled, Jamie George added a further try for Sarries and Sam Hill's consolation effort for Exeter came too late to matter. It finished 37–34 to Saracens, their seventh successive victory in a Premiership or European final.

It was a desperately tough result to take from Exeter's perspective. With Matt Kvesic taking ages to complete his post-match drug test, it was also well past 8 p.m. by the time the players departed the stadium. To pass the time a few of them made a quick trip over the road to Tesco to buy some beers and stood in the car park, mulling over the game. The wafer-thin margins between success and failure had seldom felt so painful, not least for Hepher. 'That cross kick for Liam Williams and the catch . . . some things you can't do too much about. But that forward pass changes everything.' His skipper Yeandle felt similarly blind-sided. 'I was one of the last people to get changed. It just hurt so much. I know what we'd put into it all season. We adapted our tactics in the second half and got a fair bit of joy but that one stung.' Steenson could only lament Exeter's momentary loss of concentration. 'When we got two scores up, everyone stopped to take a breath. They scored within two minutes and the whole momentum of the match flipped on its head. It was a real "Oh no" moment and it's hard to get back from that. It felt like a wave rolling over the top of you.'

Rowe did his best to drown his sorrows with a couple of gins after the game but there was still a nagging sense of frustration he simply could not erase. 'I watched it again the next day and replayed the latter stages three times. It's no good winning the game in the first 10 minutes, you've got to win it in the last 10 minutes. Saracens know how to do that. They are a formidable team but we should have done them, particularly if that forward pass had been picked up.'

For Nowell there was the added pain of his injury potentially wrecking his World Cup aspirations in Japan. Lying stricken on the turf, the ramifications for his England career, however, were not at the forefront of his mind. 'A lot of people have asked if I was thinking about the World Cup. I honestly wasn't. It was all about not wanting to miss the remainder of game. There weren't a lot of tears afterwards, there was just frustration and anger. That game should have been ours. I know their guys well. You know when they're on their game. Maybe they were off it slightly but we were playing very, very well. You can feel when you're on top of a team and they had gone a bit quiet. Then Sladey scores in the corner and the place goes mental. I thought, "Yeah, this is definitely the year for us." But they're a team – like us – that never gives up. They've got players who can bring them back into games and they showed their class.'

* * * * *

Nothing lasts forever, not least in professional sport. Less than 72 hours after England had been hammered 32–12 by South Africa in the World Cup final in Tokyo in early November, a different kind of typhoon ripped through the UK newspapers. Premiership Rugby, following months of deliberation, announced that Saracens had been found guilty of breaching the salary cap regulations, fined them an unprecedented £5.36 million and initially docked them 35 league points. They stopped short of stripping Sarries of their titles but, with large sections of the game in uproar, the points deduction was ultimately increased by a further 70 points to guarantee their relegation to the Championship.

Few tears were shed in the West Country and Baxter, in particular, was less than sympathetic. Having spent hours himself poring over spreadsheets to try and work out how to build a competitive Premiership squad beneath the cap ceiling, he was unimpressed by the argument that Saracens were simply guilty of innocent naivety or muddled accounting. 'Everyone kind of thought there was something wrong for a number of years. But that's different to it being blatantly exposed. I don't care what anybody says, it's not been exposed as a little bit of an accident. Even the little bit they found, percentage-wise, makes an incredible difference within your squad. You're never really needing to lose a player because you can spread the money around and keep everyone happy. People look at it and say, "That's only four or five players." It's not. Not at all. It means you can keep your players on a wage level where it's not worth them moving to another club.

'I'm not saying Saracens don't do a lot of things well. They're well coached and they get the importance of building a good team environment and having a good culture. But on top of that they get to do it with 30 better players than any other squad can put together. That's the bit that has bugged me more than anything else. When I actually found out how deliberately it had been done and for how long . . . even then there was no apology, not even a hint of one.'

From the players' perspective there was also a nagging sense of professional and personal loss: of potential earnings, bonuses and international recognition. Had Saracens adhered to the letter and spirit of the rules and not had such a stellar squad, would they have won all those trophies and harvested all those caps? Armand, among the Chiefs players regularly overlooked for international honours, also flagged up a significant human dimension. 'We'd been sticking to the salary cap. That means you're not getting as much money as you know some of their guys are getting. If you go to Sarries and you've got a co-investment arrangement and your post-career is sorted, there is much less stress. You can just focus on your rugby and your fun trips away. It makes it a lot easier to focus on rugby day in, day out.'

When Armand looked around the Exeter dressing room, he was also reminded of those players who had left the club prematurely because the club, in order to stay under the cap, could not afford to keep everyone. 'We wouldn't necessarily have won those three finals we lost but if we had won a couple of them it would have benefited individuals who have subsequently left. They would have had a much better CV and their career earning potential would have been much better, as has happened when a

Saracens player has left to join a French side. There are also a lot of Exeter guys who should have played for England and haven't. I could name a few. Even those guys who have been in and out have lost out, not just on career-changing money but career-changing reputations. Those frustrations get brushed under the carpet publicly – from an individual perspective there's a lot that people don't see.'

On top of that, as Armand points out, there was something else hidden from the public gaze: the disappointment felt by the backroom staff. 'There are so many dynamics that aren't recognised. The people upstairs who work really hard in the ticket office, the community guys. We're representing them all. No one ever feels sorry for them but they're also affected. The more successful we are, the more successful the whole stadium is, the better their jobs are. It has a big knock-on effect.' On top of all that, for Armand, was the simplest, most primal disappointment of all. 'You'll never be able to replace a Sunday all-day piss-up with your old mates in celebration of a final victory. The memories you make last forever. It's the things you can't count that irritate me more than the money.'

Rowe, on his squad's behalf, was similarly upset and angry that Saracens had unfairly tilted the playing field. For a while, he declined to rule out legal action and even called for the authorities to go further. 'Saracens should have their titles taken away. Their names should be taken off the Premiership trophy for the seasons they won it while being in breach of the cap.' If anything, having absorbed the full details of Lord Myners' exhaustive report into Saracens' salary cap indiscretions, his views have subsequently hardened. 'It's proven – and the report's there for everyone to read – that for the last three years they've been winning trophies they've cheated. We're not saying we should have the trophies but they should not have their name on the trophy because they won those titles by cheating. We don't want the trophy but they shouldn't have it. I've known some of our lads since they were 15. At the end of last season's final they were broken and in tears. They got beaten fair and square, yes, but by a superior team that we couldn't afford by staying within the salary cap. I'm massively disappointed for the lads.'

Rowe also argued that Nigel Wray should not necessarily have to shoulder all the blame for a situation that led Lord Myners to conclude it was 'overwhelmingly clear . . . that trust has been damaged' across the English club game. 'Other people must have known what was going on. Okay, they may have been told by Nigel and his advisors that the salaries and contracts of each player were above board but I think they were kidding themselves. I think they still feel they've done nothing wrong. They're not regretful at all. I've been involved in sport since my early twenties. How can someone congratulate themselves or slap each other on the back knowing you've fiddled the system to get there?'

As for those wondering if the Chiefs, the solitary Premiership club to have made a profit in the preceding financial year, were entirely above board themselves, Rowe had a crisp response ready. 'Of course I'm bloody certain we're within the salary cap,' he told the *i* newspaper. 'I wouldn't be bloody saying all this about Saracens if I wasn't certain we play by the rules.' The only real consolation was that Exeter wouldn't need to worry about their rivals for the next two seasons but the Chiefs' coaches were swift to warn their players not to assume the title was now a gimme. 'It was the elephant in the room,' admitted Hunter. 'We said, "Right, let's make sure this is not a distraction. There's still another 10 teams who all want to beat you."' It was time to start looking forwards, not back.

TWENTY

FIGHT FOR ALL

What nobody realised, as the clock struck midnight on New Year's Eve, was that the 2019/20 season would shortly be disrupted by an onrushing pandemic. By late March sport had become relatively unimportant as the entire country went into lockdown. With the streets of London suddenly as deserted as the quietest rural Devon lane, it was not the moment to start complaining about the potential ramifications for West Country sporting ambitions.

Nor did it matter much, in the wider scheme of things, that infection rates in the south-west were relatively low. That said, the Chiefs' frustration was natural enough. As well as sitting five points clear of Sale Sharks at the top of the table when the music stopped with nine rounds of the regular season still to play, they were just running into some serious form. In their last two home games prior to the shutdown they smashed Northampton 57–7 and Bath 57–20 and a home play-off semi-final was already looking a safe bet. They had also secured a lucrative home draw in the quarter-finals of the Heineken Champions Cup against much the same Northampton team they had just pummelled at Sandy Park. Injury issues were starting to ease, the pitches were just starting to firm up and the club's new women's team was eagerly awaiting its Premier 15s league debut in the autumn. Talk about less than ideal timing.

Covid-19 was just about the only thing for which the management hadn't budgeted. 'Fight For All' had been the squad's chosen mantra from the outset, with the club's first European away game in La Rochelle identified as a particular test of their ability to fight on two fronts simultaneously. Previously they had flattered to deceive in Europe; this time they travelled down to the French Atlantic coast determined to give it everything and were rewarded with a 33–14 bonus-point victory, with tries from White, O'Flaherty, Slade and Simmonds. 'It gave the lads a lot of confidence that we could do something,' confirmed Steenson. 'We just went and played our game. Our game's evolved but if we play our way we win most games.' The evening was also a convivial one and set the tone for everything that followed in Pool 2. Glasgow were seen off at home before Sale were beaten home and away, Stuart Hogg creating one try and scoring another in Salford to underline why Baxter had been so keen to bring him in.

It also felt like serendipity when, across the Atlantic, the Kansas City Chiefs won the Super Bowl for the first time since 1970, overturning a 20–17 deficit with six minutes to go to beat the San Francisco 49ers 31–20.

'Ooooh-Oooh-Oooh, Ooooh-Oooh-Oooh!'

Or maybe not. There would soon be fresh pressure, rippling across from the other side of the Atlantic, to ditch the tomahawks and associated branded imagery out of respect for Native American sensibilities. Despite the local origins of the Chiefs' moniker, some argued a Celtic chief might be a more appropriate and respectful look in a changing modern world. The players, either way, were actively seeking to reinvent themselves slightly. The aim, it was collectively agreed, was to try and hit their optimum level more consistently, rather than simply plug wholeheartedly away. On a pre-lockdown midweek morning in the cafe at Dart's Farm near Topsham, there was a steely edge to Steenson's voice. 'We want to be better than the team that won the 2017 final. We also want to win a Heineken Cup. We put a real big emphasis on it this year. We sat down, looked at the group and thought, "We've been in the Premiership final four years in a row; we really should be doing something in Europe." We're being talked about as one of the top teams in Europe but, results-wise, we haven't been.'

It was also, to some extent, about getting rid of the limiting beliefs – 'We've never conquered Europe before; we can't win the big finals' – that can subconsciously affect many players. Instead of 'Do What We Do', the mantra had shifted to 'Do The Right Thing'. The management had recognised that going through the same old motions ultimately risked the team not reaching its full potential. 'We had to come away from that because we felt it was a safety net,' explained Hunter.

Harder to spot, too, was any lingering trace of romance, the 'plucky Exeter' tag having been replaced by something significantly harder-nosed. Hepher, ever-present on the trek from the happy-go-lucky Championship days to the upper echelons of Europe, keeps telling Rob Hunter he missed the really fun years. 'I guess there was a less pressured element to those days: everything was a bonus. We didn't used to have much to lose. But you don't want to think like that too often because that means you're not expected to win. You want to be expected to win every week because that means you're the best.' For Hepher, this mental shift felt like an entirely logical progression. 'It's a problem-solving exercise for me. I'm never happy or comfortable. If something's not working, why is that? What can we do better? I won't just accept it.'

The signing of the Scotland lock Jonny Gray on a two-year contract commencing in the summer of 2020 was all part of that ambition. Baxter had been tracking Gray for a number of years, the Glasgow forward's tireless work rate an obvious attraction. Flashing wads of cash, though, has never been Exeter's preferred modus operandi. Making their own young players better, fostering a genuine love of their club and encouraging them to push on towards international honours have been equally crucial to the formula.

Their fly-half Joe Simmonds has been a good example; loan spells at Taunton and Plymouth and his sobering Twickenham final disappointment are long forgotten now. Instead Chiefs have a goal-kicker who rarely, if ever, misses and would have been a strong candidate to tour Japan with England on their aborted 2020 summer tour. Some, including Steenson, feel he would already have been called up had he been playing his rugby for a different club. 'It seems to me that in terms of international call-ups there's something desperately wrong,' says Steenson. 'Maybe the English selectors don't come down to the south-west. You're talking about someone who has been captaining one of the top teams in Europe and has only missed two or three kicks in the league all year. And he's still not in the squad. I find that a bit hard to believe.'

As and when it happens, Simmonds' rise will be at least partly down to sibling rivalry. As kids there was one infamous occasion when his older brother Sam, enraged by being hit in the face by a ball, chased Joe up the stairs at home and forced the latter to take refuge in the toilet. Not fancying his chances of escaping unharmed – 'I was about to jump out of the window, I was that scared' – he slipped a £5 note under the door to bribe Sam to go away. To some degree his career has been based on a constant refusal to let Sam enjoy all the limelight. 'I didn't want to be that little brother who didn't do anything. I always wanted to be a sportsman and having an older brother was massive. He's played for England and that pushes me on even more. If I concentrate on performing well for Exeter . . . well, hopefully one day that day will come.'

Collectively, too, there was also an emphasis on becoming even harder to beat. With Luke Cowan-Dickie, Jacques Vermeulen, Jannes Kirsten and Sam Skinner adding to the Chiefs' dynamic forward game, Exeter simply needed to tighten up slightly when they did not have the ball. 'We've put a big emphasis on certain areas of our game,' confirmed Steenson. 'Kick chase, putting more pressure on teams . . . they're just common-sense things we'd probably glossed over before.'

They also now had the nous to tailor their tactics to the conditions and game situation more effectively. A 26–15 away win on Valentine's Night at Gloucester was a perfect case in point, four second-half Steenson penalties heaping crucial scoreboard pressure on the Cherry and Whites. When Hogg ostentatiously cradled the ball as he crossed the try-line, having butchered a simple score for Scotland against Ireland earlier in the month, it was also a reminder that Chiefs' international contingent were relishing their club rugby too.

And on the rare occasions when the team underperformed, the coaches could now show the players precisely how and why. When the Chiefs were beaten, slightly controversially, 34–30 at Harlequins in late February, post-match analysis showed the players had been involved in only 17 high-intensity ball-in-play minutes, less than half their normal average. Against Saracens the same stat, remarkably, was 51 minutes. The scoreboard can say what it likes but heart monitors never lie. 'It's not about not making errors,' stresses Hunter. 'It's about energy and intensity.'

Or at least it was until the shutdown arrived. From the moment the snooze button was pressed on the latter stages of the Six Nations Championship in mid-March, it was obvious the effects of Covid-19 would not be swiftly overcome. A week's hiatus stretched into several months as club owners and league administrators tried to work out how and when the season might conceivably be restarted. 'It all seems rather petty talking about the Premiership when we're in the grip of something potentially as big as it is,' observed Rob Baxter, keenly aware of the suffering being endured by so many families nationwide.

As the weeks drifted by, however, Baxter began to wonder aloud if every club was busting a gut to get the league started promptly. 'It's something I'm a little disappointed about when I hear other coaches and some players talk about the subject. We seem to be finding all the reasons not to play. Don't get me wrong. I'm not going to try and brush over the tragedies that have happened or the awful things that have occurred during the outbreak but, as we all try and get back to some kind of normality, I think we have to look at the positives around rugby. If anything, we're creating a safer environment for players and staff than in everyday life. It's far, far safer than going to the supermarket, where you're touching things other people may have picked up and put back.'

Even in lockdown, furthermore, the private view within the Chiefs' dressing room was that the club's location gave them a slight advantage over some other clubs. If you were absolutely forced to stay at home and run around your local area to keep fit, it was not the worst of sacrifices to have to do so in the fresh air, open spaces and warm sunshine of Devon in the springtime.

* * * * *

For Tony Rowe, even so, it was a worrying period. For the first time in 22 years the club would not be in a position to announce a profit. By late May, with the squad's return to training delayed by yet another fortnight, Sandy Park's conference facilities shut since mid-March and 206 full-time employees to worry about, things felt seriously grim. 'I don't mind saying I was pretty depressed as I couldn't see any light at the end of the tunnel. I was fearing the worst.' Even for a well-established business – turnover in 2018/19 was £21.7 million with a pre-tax profit of £1.59 million, more than the club's entire turnover in 2006 – it was a concerning time. 'We have had to work incredibly hard to help preserve the business as best we can. Because of the virus there will be a big fat hole in the accounts. It's not easy, particularly when you have no income coming in. Even with players and staff furloughed, running the club still cost us £900,000 a month. If we hadn't furloughed everyone that figure would be £1.5 million a month. I won't lie, it's been incredibly tough for all of us.'

Rowe, though, likes a challenge. For years he has gone on motorcycling holidays to far-flung locations, ranging from Africa and South America to Russia, eastern Europe and Scandinavia where, at the age of 68, he headed off for a 5,000-mile round trip immediately following the 2017 Premiership final. 'My friend Robin and I were sitting in a square in Prague one lovely, sunny day watching the world go by. I said to him, "Look at that silly old bugger over there." To which he replied, "That silly old bugger over there is probably younger than you." We decided then that we wouldn't consider ourselves to be old until we were 85. Then we'll think about it.'

Unforeseen problems, though, can materialise out of nowhere. On New Year's Day morning in 2019 Rowe's wife, Sharon, looked out of the window of the family home in Woodbury Salterton and saw a mask-wearing intruder with a Samurai sword attempting to gain access through the patio windows. When Sharon banged on the window, the stranger backed off and subsequently fled across nearby fields. Tony decided to give chase in his car – 'We do foolish things, don't we?' – without thinking too much about his own safety. When he caught up with him on a country lane he was threatened with what he thought at the time was a metal pole but was probably the aforementioned sword. Eventually the case came to court where it emerged that a local man, Brad McGauley, high on drink and drugs, had also broken into two cars and started a number of fires at a house in the village. Sharon Rowe made a victim impact statement in which she said she was finding it difficult to sleep and that the couple's son, who was 17 at the time, no longer liked being left at home on his own. It later emerged the intruder was suffering from serious mental issues at the time. A suspended sentence was handed down, a decision described as 'a joke' by Rowe. 'I'm probably a bit Victorian in my thoughts but I don't get law enforcement today. There was video evidence of him running around the house with a sword in his hand trying to break in.'

A summer invasion of the Sandy Park car park by a group of travellers was another headache, with the new arrivals, who had just been evicted from Crealy Theme Park, informing club officials they would only move on if they were paid £1,500. When Rowe turned up to make clear the club would not be acceding to such demands, he was swiftly advised to move his Range Rover away from the entrance if he didn't want a toddler carrying a wheel brace to make a few 'accidental' dents in his vehicle. The incident ended up costing the club between £3,500 and £5,000, with a swiftly granted eviction order forcing their uninvited guests to move on 24 hours later. Running a leading rugby club is not all about sitting comfortably above the halfway line on match days and counting the £600,000 net revenue that an average Exeter home game now generates.

There was also the new on-site hotel development which, after a certain amount of to-ing and fro-ing, has received the planning go-ahead. The 250-room, nine-storey Marriott Courtyard hotel will also feature a restaurant and a rooftop cocktail bar, with the aim of being the 'biggest commercial hotel this side of Bristol' when it opens in 2021/22. As yet, Covid-19 has also not derailed plans to increase the stadium attendance to just over 18,000 by upgrading the East and South stands.

Rowe, though, does not invariably have a magic touch. The club were accused of being 'tone deaf' to the calls to ditch their Native American branding – their only concession was the withdrawal of their mascot Big Chief – and there was also local disquiet when employees of the failed local airline Flybe were turned away from the ground for the game against Bath after their complimentary tickets were declared invalid. It was described as 'a commercial decision' but the subsequent offer to affected individuals to watch a second-team fixture instead regained little PR ground. Rowe remains unrepentant. 'We probably lost £100,000 on Flybe going bust. We only had the phone call to say they'd gone tits up on the Thursday morning. We said to them, "Well, if that's the case everything is null and void because the company still owes us tens of thousands of pounds." We didn't know they'd issued tickets to some of their employees as prizes.' In Rowe's view, making unpopular calls is an occupational hazard. 'Running a business is not easy sometimes. It's a very lonely place and you have to make tough decisions. It's not a popularity contest. When everything's going well you get all the accolades thrown at you. But you've also got to be big enough to make commercial decisions that are going to upset people. The guys who don't make tough decisions in business are no longer in business.'

It is also not unknown for Rowe to make life awkward for television and telecoms operatives. He has, in particular, an eye for stray cables few others would even notice. 'They put cables everywhere; it's like spaghetti. More than once I've gone to the riggers and said, "You need to move that." If they say, "No," I say, "Okay, I'll just come along and cut it." It soon makes them move it.

'People know it's either black or white with me. There are no grey areas. If I'm unhappy you'll know about it. But then that's it. Done. End of story. Let's get on.' Not many can argue with his business logic. 'I say to people that it's not easy to make money but it's easy to lose money. Sometimes it's about what you can save. We're a members' club, we keep our overheads very tight and that's what makes the profit. It's not been easy getting the club where it is but, today, the club has assets worth £80–90 million.'

And as long as people work sufficiently hard and deliver the necessary results he is more than happy to delegate. In August 2019, Natasha Pavis was among four women directors elevated to the club's board, having worked her way up from bars manager in 2006. 'I'm a great believer that if you employ someone to do a job, leave them to get on with it. Just give them the right tools. If you look after people – be tough but fair. Don't ask them to do something that's beyond their ability and you'll have a good team. You're only as good as the people you put around you.'

Rowe's relationship with Baxter, similarly, is based on mutual respect. 'When I put Rob in charge I had a pretty shrewd idea he was going to turn out good because I'd worked with him for a number of years. And do you know what? He's turned out miles better than I thought he would. He listens to people. We don't have regular meetings. He has a job to do and so do I. But we do chat on an impromptu basis about recruitment and finances. Every now and again we have dinner and a couple of beers. Rob's a really good director of rugby and I like to consider I'm a really good chief exec.'

The pair have certainly done their bit to boost visitor numbers to the city and, along the way, created a more expectant new breed of Exeter supporter. Horstmann, employed in corporate sales at the club until August 2020, has noticed a significant shift. 'You'll hear someone moaning now that we haven't won by enough. You think, "Sorry?" In 2012 we'd have given anything simply to win a Premiership game. People forget very quickly how much it takes to win Premiership games, even when you're at home.'

Certain things, though, do not change. There is never any question, in Horstmann's experience, of Baxter quietly settling for second best. 'At the start of every season he details exactly what it takes to be an Exeter Chiefs player: the type of person he wants and what he expects from you. If you deliver that, the rewards are huge. But you have to deliver.

'Ultimately, the most important people at the club are the players. There are two ways you can react to that. You can be arrogant and a dick or you can take that responsibility on your shoulders and say, "What an amazing opportunity this is for me," and be a good, humble guy. Rob's very clear that if it's the former you're not going to be here very long. He does a huge amount of research in terms of how he recruits and spends hours finding the right people. He also understands how to motivate men. He knows all the players' strengths and weaknesses and, as a result, he knows when you're even slightly off.' The dickhead count is negligible. 'I've been in clubs where it only takes one poisonous guy to rip right through the squad. You might get guys who are prone to drifting but as long as the hub of the squad is on the right track they'll fall into place.'

Like any farmer with a plan to rotate certain crops in a particular field over a number of years, Baxter is also not easily distracted from long-term goals by the occasional setback. Yes, it was a shame to lose White, Kvesic and Sam Hill, who departed for Australia, Worcester and Sale respectively without enjoying the farewell lap of honour their endeavours clearly deserved. His veterans Dollman and Steenson, though, both received short-term contract extensions to allow them to postpone their retirements and complete the delayed 2019/20 campaign. Baxter, in Horstmann's experience, rarely jumps to hasty conclusions. 'He doesn't fob you off with glib answers. He'll say, "I'm not sure, I'll come back to you on that." He's very good at looking at the bigger picture and not getting too bogged down in isolation. He only ever looks at it internally – what can he, his coaches and the players do better to win. Everything else is pointless. He's a hugely impressive bloke. There's no doubt they struck absolute gold with him.'

TWENTY-ONE

OUT OF DARKNESS

When the domestic season eventually resumed in August some wondered if it was worth the hassle. Several players had moved clubs, the Covid-19 situation remained uncertain and supporters were still not allowed inside the stadiums. Might it have been simpler to draw a line under the whole damn thing and start afresh? Or simply proceed straight to the play-offs? Not if you were a chief executive desperate for television income or anyone with a connection to a club near the top of the suspended table.

Once Rob Baxter had finally welcomed his full squad back, he made his view instantly clear. Exeter, to his mind, had a priceless opportunity. Between 15 August and 24 October, the revised date for the 2019/20 Premiership final, the players could create lifelong memories. In the space of 10 weeks, he told them, there was a chance to create their own destiny and achieve something special. All they had to do was block out any negativity – the absence of supporters, the rumbling row over the Chiefs' native American branding, the pay cuts, the extra midweek fixtures shoehorned into the calendar – and keep their eyes on the prize.

Harry Williams, the big tight-head prop, was among those instantly re-energised. 'There don't need to be spectators there to put in an unbelievable performance as a team. The easy thing to do is to blame the absence of the crowd and all the rest of it. But ultimately it's still a game of rugby. You can still have the best game you've ever played without a crowd.'

Like many others, the 28-year-old Williams had kept himself busy during lockdown, even picking up a community award for an entertaining live 'Bake Off' in which supporters were invited to make an orange drizzle cake with him. Never before had he enjoyed such a prolonged break – 'It was the longest period since I was a boy that I haven't played a game of rugby' – and his body had appreciated it. 'I found it quite reinvigorating. When you play with knocks and bruises what you can do in training gets reduced. Here was a chance to focus completely on training. None of the gyms was open and everyone had sold out of gym kit so we had to do what we could with what we had. One of my mates owns a nutrition company and is big into his training. He told me I should buy a 100kg sandbag, which you could get from anywhere, and do stuff with that.'

The Rugby Football Union had also supplied him with some weights and a watt bike and Williams turned his back garden into a high-performance centre. With team-mates posting their own training scores, there was also a genuine – if unseen – competitive edge. 'Because there wasn't loads with which to fill your days you could really focus on that kind of stuff. Then, after a couple of months, we gradually started filtering back into the club and running round local parks. I was visiting parts of Exeter I'd never been to before to run up hills.'

Jonny Hill was much the same, pounding the local fields and working out furiously at home. One selection on England's bench – frustratingly he never took the field to earn a cap – in Cape Town in 2018 had made him even more determined to push himself further. 'I was already motivated before I even saw Rob Baxter. I'm only 26 but I want to maximise every bit of potential I have and achieve as much as I can. As a young player coming through it's really enjoyable. You come home and relax and think about other things. Now I'm always thinking about how I can improve. I'm a totally different player and character now to when England picked me. I'm two years older and have another 50-odd Premiership games in me. I still feel I haven't reached my ceiling yet.'

The arrival of a top player like Jonny Gray, with over 50 Test caps to his name, in the same position had also propelled him from his comfort zone. 'Jonny was a big signing and was clearly more than likely to get selected. I thought: "Right, I want to be the guy who gets selected alongside him." Over lockdown I had a lot of time to think about that and didn't really ease up at all. I never spoke to the coaches or asked "Why have you signed Jonny?" If I'm having to challenge myself simply to get into my club side every week it's going to bring out the best in me.'

A couple of socially distanced squad barbecues after Friday-night training – in the absence of their annual boozy bonding trip to Spain – also helped break down social barriers with the newer recruits. Williams is among those adamant that enjoying each other's company is integral to Exeter's on-field performance. 'If you want to get to know people, the best way is to have a beer with them. I can't think of anyone who would have an issue blending in socially here. When I arrived I didn't know anyone. It's part of the fabric of the club that you make sure people feel welcome when they come in. There's no real hierarchy. I think that is a really good thing.'

There was only one snag beyond their control. Across the rest of the league the cast-lists of several of their rivals had altered significantly. Bristol, in third place and seven points behind Exeter when the league was suspended, now had the services of

England's tight-head prop Kyle Sinckler and the world's most destructive three-quarter, Fiji's Semi Radradra. Sale Sharks, in second position, had snapped up Manu Tuilagi after the England centre fell out with Leicester. The Tigers had a new head coach, Steve Borthwick, and a radically overhauled squad. The Chiefs could not afford to start slowly or assume their best form would instantly return on demand.

Hence the genuine air of nervousness prior to their first game back, at home to Leicester, in mid-August. A couple of in-house training games had been suitably competitive but not quite the real thing. As Williams glanced around the dressing-room, he wondered if his garden fitness regime would cut it. 'There was definitely a bit of tension. That was how it felt to me. It felt like every team was unveiling a new version of themselves.' Could Exeter crank things up accordingly? 'We spoke about it. There's no reason you can't improve a little bit over that kind of break. And there's also everything still to play for. The team that deals with all the strangeness and the setbacks is going to be the team that does the best. There are a lot of excuses you could give but the champions will be the team that doesn't give in to that.'

On top of everything else, there was also the issue of how to acknowledge the Black Lives Matter campaign in the wake of the sickening murder of George Floyd by a white police officer in Minneapolis. As with so many squads, the Chiefs' dressing-room contained any number of different characters and religious beliefs. Not every individual felt comfortable being lectured on how exactly they should respond. In the event the squad agreed they would collectively face the electronic scoreboard at the north-west corner of Sandy Park and then either take a knee or remain standing.

Most disconcerting of all, though, was the sound of silence. Williams and his teammates soon discovered the absence of a crowd had a direct effect on the game. 'We found the momentum of a game could swing a lot easier. If you give away a couple of penalties and the ball gets kicked down the pitch you haven't got a crowd to pick you back up. You can't feed off the energy in the stands. There was just silence. It was bizarre because the crowd – and everything that goes with it – is such a big part of the stadium. In a weird way it was almost like we weren't playing at Sandy Park. You've got to generate your own vibe. That said, it did feel nice to play compared with the routine of training. Previously the focus had been longer term. It was good to hone your focus down to one particular target.'

Despite several other distractions – Jack Nowell missed the match with a tweaked hamstring and Henry Slade's partner Megan gave birth to the couple's first child, a daughter named Olive, on the Friday before the opening game – the outcome was mostly reassuring on a humid, damp afternoon. Three of their four tries were the product of familiar close-range power and Stuart Hogg's 39th-minute score showed the coaches had not spent the summer lying idly in a hammock. A beautiful 'double pump' pass from Joe Simmonds opened up precious midfield space for a flying Olly Woodburn and Hogg's diving finish in the right corner was due reward to complete a perfectly executed set move.

The award of 22 penalties against the Tigers, courtesy of the stricter breakdown interpretations intended – eventually – to make the game more free-flowing, also helped and Williams enjoyed the run-out regardless of the 26–13 winning scoreline. 'There is nothing that can replicate actually playing a game. It's such a different feeling. It's a contented feeling, a release.'

The emotions of the coaches were slightly different. Baxter felt as saddened by the empty stands as anyone but dwelling on matters beyond his control was a luxury he could not afford. 'Twenty minutes into the game, when we were six points down, I realised I'd forgotten just how much I hate this part of the job. But then you get through the game, breathe, relax, have a beer and get ready to go again.' To recoup all the league's broadcasting money, the clubs had signed up to the tightest of schedules, with Exeter required to play significant away games against Sale and Bristol – their two nearest rivals in the table – inside 96 hours. There was no way they could field the same team for both fixtures: it was going to require a collective squad effort.

On a mild, dry Friday night in Salford, against a Sharks side that had conceded a measly 21 tries in its previous 14 games, they could not have made a better start. This time it was Slade with a glorious inside ball who sent Woodburn clear through the middle to release the supporting Sam Simmonds for a brilliant team try inside two minutes. The Sharks, roused into action, came back hard to lead 17–10 at the interval, only for a purple patch of 22 successive points in 14 minutes to secure a hugely significant 32–22 bonus-point victory for the Chiefs. Luke Cowan-Dickie was again outstanding, scoring one try and creating another simply by taking quick taps and hurling himself at the wall of bodies ahead of him. Steve Diamond, Sale's director of rugby, offered a blunt verdict afterwards. 'We got executed,' he admitted. 'We couldn't hold their scrum and their power five metres out.'

Even so, when the team-sheets were confirmed for the Bristol game at Ashton Gate on the Tuesday evening, it was hard to foresee more of the same. Bristol had most of their big guns – Radradra, Sinckler and their ultimate warrior, Steven Luatua – at their disposal while the Chiefs' line-up showed 14 starting changes. The visitors had also been required to travel up on two separate buses and change in different rooms, with gale-force winds howling around the stadium. Storm Francis was sweeping across the country, causing those driving over the Clifton Suspension Bridge to grip the steering-wheel tightly and pray.

It was a minor miracle, then, when the supposed supporting cast delivered a scintillating first-half performance, launched by a wonderful solo try from Phil Dollman. Making a rare start back in midfield after years as a specialist full-back, a 13th-minute set move off a scrum saw the Welshman surge past Radradra, Luke Morahan, Nathan Hughes and Luatua to score a try worthy of any world-class centre, let alone a 35-year-old who had just signed up to become player-coach of Sidmouth RFC. Among the first to congratulate him was his old mate Steenson, keenly aware how hard it is to carve up in the Premiership in the twilight of your career.

The defensive energy of the red-headed, bearded South African Jannes Kirsten was also striking and a second try, smartly started and finished down the blindside by their recently-signed Scottish scrum-half Sam Hidalgo-Clyne, helped extend the Chiefs' lead to 15–0. A determined Bristol fightback, however, looked to have succeeded when Ioan Lloyd, helped by Woodburn going down injured as he covered across, scored a 70th-minute try to put the Bears back in front. By now Exeter had a raft of young replacements on the field but the collective spirit and resilience endured. Deep into the closing moments they ratcheted up the pressure close to the home line and the 23-year-old Cornishman Billy Keast drove over to clinch a famous 25–22 victory, stretching the Chiefs' lead at the top to 11 points.

No matter who was wearing the shirt, it seemed, Exeter simply would not lie down. And when their big guns were wheeled out, it required serious artillery to subdue them. Their next opponents, Worcester, brought down a shadow squad to Devon and duly paid the price, conceding nine tries in a 59–7 thrashing. Hill, Exeter's galloping giant of a lock forward, scored the first hat-trick by a second-rower in the Premiership since Simon Shaw in 2003, and Sam Simmonds also left with a match ball after snaffling three tries. Hill could scarcely believe it – 'It was surreal walking in at half-time. I remember thinking: "Christ I've already scored a hat-trick".' – and was also surprised by how keen Worcester's forwards were to hear the half-time whistle. 'They were all saying: "We want to go in." My third try took a bit of finishing but I was up against their loose-head prop who wanted to be in the dressing-room.'

It set the scene for another extraordinary contest at Northampton the following Friday. Buoyed by the Bristol precedent, Baxter once again put his faith in his lower-profile squad members against a pretty much full-strength Saints line-up. Inside the first 12 minutes Exeter were 14–0 up, courtesy of well-taken tries from a charging Sean Lonsdale and the tireless Kirsten, only for the hosts to take second-half control. It required a Steenson penalty to keep Chiefs in touch before a quick-stepping Tom O'Flaherty found a way over on the left with 11 minutes to go. A 22–19 win, the club's sixth away victory in succession, was a glorious bonus for all the coaches. 'You've got to be massively proud when a changed-up side stick at it in tough circumstances,' confirmed Baxter.

Even an uneven, somewhat plodding, midweek display at home to Gloucester yielded five tries and a 35–22 victory, effectively securing a home Premiership semi-final and allowing Baxter to send out an entirely changed 23 for the subsequent Sunday trip to Saracens. Five players – Alfie Petch, Facundo Cordero, Tom Wyatt, Joe Snow and Harvey Skinner – were selected for their maiden league starts with six more fresh-faced debutants on the bench. Baxter's main focus was on the following week's European Champions Cup quarter-final against Northampton but he made a point of laying down a pre-match challenge to his young wannabes. 'It's easy for someone to come into the first team for a debut when the team is purring and everything is clicking. What I want to see is when you have to stand up and be a man. Especially when things are getting tough, I want that guy to stand up and fight for the whole 80 minutes because that is the time to show the great qualities you possess.'

It did not quite work out that way, with Saracens's own second string winning 40–17, but Sale's home defeat to Bath meant the Chiefs, even without a losing bonus-point, would finish first in the league for a third year in a row and top the semi-final seedings. It meant they could now concentrate fully on the European knock-out stages and securing a potential first appearance in a Champions Cup final.

The main issue with the quarter-final was self-evident: no one was giving Northampton a prayer. The Saints had been in grim form since the resumption and had struggled against Exeter in recent times. Northampton also had only one fit, registered loose-head prop available in the form of the 19-year-old Manny Iyogun, a relatively recent convert from the back row. Baxter's mood darkened, even so, when he heard his opposite number, Chris Boyd, suggest that 'the attitude Exeter take' would determine whether scrums went uncontested. Was he honestly suggesting Exeter should go easy in a European quarter-final? 'I think some of it is mind games, if I am honest,' said Baxter, stressing Exeter had previously offered to support Northampton in their bid to register an extra player. 'It was a weird comment all round, made to influence. It is a quarter-final, not a pre-season friendly.'

As it turned out, Iyogun put in a heroic shift and Northampton proved a stiffer-than-expected test but, at full-time, the scoreboard still read 38–15. Jacques Vermeulen scored a brace of tries to claim the man-of-the-match award and Jack Maunder and Jack Nowell also contributed eye-catching scores to propel Exeter into their first Champions' Cup semi-final a week later on their same favourite stretch of turf.

Their next opponents, though, were much more formidable. Toulouse had won their first European Cup when Exeter were still in the fourth tier of English league rugby. The Manchester United of French club rugby could also field two of the world's best players in scrum-half Antoine Dupont and Cheslin Kolbe, the Springbok winger who had helped South Africa clinch the

2019 Rugby World Cup. This was perhaps the stiffest test the Chiefs would face all year, with the stakes stratospherically high.

No pressure, then. As he prepared for an aerial duel with the six foot ten inch Rory Arnold – popularly known in his native Australia as 'three-storey Rory' – Hill knew it was time to front up. 'We've waited for this for a long time. And the longer we've waited, the more important it's got. We've never played Toulouse before. It's a real chance to focus on ourselves and say: "You guys come and stop us".'

On a gloriously sunny afternoon the initial signs were not terribly auspicious. A couple of early line-out malfunctions played into Toulouse's hands and the Chiefs had plenty of defending to do. When Baxter was asked how he was feeling midway through the first half, live on camera, he was calmness personified. He and his coaches had specifically told the players the key to victory would be playing at a high tempo in the first half and then asking questions of Toulouse's fitness later in the game. 'Big games of rugby are like boxing matches,' Baxter muttered later. 'At some stage the guy who can't get his hands up any more gets knocked out.'

A wheezing Toulouse, whose pack included the 37-year-old Jerome Kaino and the 36-year-old Joe Tekori, were reeled in. Dave Ewers led the tackle count with 17, with the Chiefs' starting front five making a further 62 tackles between them. Harry Williams, with two touchdowns, and Sam Simmonds supplied three of their team's four tries to increase the number scored by Exeter's forwards in all competitions during the season to 67. The sheer joy etched on the faces of Joe Simmonds, his brother Sam and every other Chiefs player as they dashed in to celebrate the fly-half's beautifully taken 70th-minute try summed up the day better than a written match report ever could.

The first line of their customary old-school victory song – 'The Exeter boys are HAPPY. . .' – had rarely felt so apt. The only downside, yet again, was the absence of supporters. It was painfully easy to visualise the packed bars and celebratory pints, not to mention the long queues for tickets to the final, now set to be staged just up the M5 at Ashton Gate. Then again, imagine the front-room euphoria across Devon and Cornwall should their lavender hill mob – even if their bespoke European kit was officially lilac – go to Bristol and enjoy a night to match their play-off triumph in the same city a decade earlier.

Assuming, that is, the final could proceed as scheduled. While a shadow Exeter side went through the motions in their last two low-priority league games against London Irish and Wasps – both lost – it emerged that their Champions Cup final opponents Racing 92 were dealing with several cases of coronavirus. To complicate matters further, a cluster of 19 positive tests were also recorded at Sale, forcing the Sharks' final Premiership game against Worcester to be postponed and delaying confirmation of the domestic semi-final line-up.

By the Wednesday morning it had still not been confirmed whether Exeter would be facing Bath, Sale or even Bristol in the last four on the Saturday. Only after a further eight positives were recorded at Sale – six players and two staff members – did sanity belatedly prevail. Sale's rescheduled fixture was called off and a mightily relieved Bath were handed the fourth and last qualifying berth. Three Premiership semi-finalists, for the first time since the format was adopted in 2005/06, would be from the south-west, with none from London. With Covid-19 rates starting to rise sharply in Exeter, particularly among the city's university students, and Jack Nowell sidelined with a foot injury, it was an awkward week all round. There was a creeping tension as Baxter and Co entered the defining phase of their uniquely long, mentally-taxing campaign.

TWENTY-TWO

SATURDAY NIGHT FEVER

Nerves? They were barely evident as the rumbling Exeter machine cut down another potential challenger in the last fixture of the season at Sandy Park. Bath, on paper, had players capable of posing awkward questions but, aside from a sustained period of pressure either side of half-time after a yellow card for Jonny Hill had reduced his side to 14 men, they suffered a similar fate to Toulouse. Entering the final quarter of the semi-final, the visitors were gulping in air, physically spent and struggling to cope with the relentless Chiefs bombardment. Exeter's fifth and final try, created by a jinking Joe Simmonds and finished by an exultant Ollie Devoto against his former club, capped an impressive 35–6 victory and secured a fifth consecutive Premiership grand final appearance. There was one crucial difference: their familiar rivals Saracens were out of the equation. Victory against Racing 92 at Ashton Gate and Wasps at Twickenham on successive weekends and the Chiefs would be able to celebrate a precious European and domestic 'double'.

Rob Baxter: Our defence won us the Bath game. Yes, we ultimately scored a lot of points, but it was the desire to defend every inch of the pitch that was incredible. That desire, energy and drive wore Bath down quicker than our attack.

Henry Slade: Even before we played Bath we had exactly the right attitude. No one's going to give it to us, we've got to go and get it.

Gareth Steenson: The message afterwards was simple, 'We could still end up with nothing and be the most disappointed team in England.'

Henry Slade: If you worry too much about the past or what is going to potentially happen in the future, you miss out on what is right in front of you.

Ollie Devoto: When we've gone well in the past, we've kept it simple. We're built on working hard and keeping the ball on the field as much as possible. If you overcomplicate stuff it can lead to trouble.

Stuart Hooper (Bath director of rugby): We've watched Saracens for years in the Premiership. These guys do it in a very different way but they're a quality team. When they get in tight they're pretty lethal.

Rob Baxter: We are very good inside the 22. It's a super-strength of ours but we don't assume it'll just happen.

Sam Skinner: We've definitely come together as a forward pack. We know each other's strengths and we're all singing off the same hymn-sheet. Everyone's got a clear understanding of what's going on.

Stuart Hogg: I'm not expected to pull a rabbit out of a hat every game because there are plenty of other boys who can do that. I've got Henry Slade inside me and Jack Nowell outside of me. How can I not perform?

Gareth Steenson: Ten years on from the Championship play-off, it was funny to have our first Heineken Cup final in Bristol. It was nice to have that connection but there aren't many of us left.

Stuart Hogg: These are the games that made you pick up a rugby ball as a kid.

Ollie Devoto: Rob Baxter's not quite as hands-on coaching-wise as he was but we particularly benefit from him going into these big games. He plays a huge part in getting us right mentally.

Rob Baxter: We usually get tested for Covid-19 on a Tuesday morning and don't start hearing the results until 5.20 a.m. the following day. Virtually all the staff were sat by their phones from 5 a.m. It's always an interesting period of time.

Tony Rowe: It was a nightmare week. Everything went wrong. I went in for a minor operation on the Monday morning and was supposed to be in and out in a day. In the end I didn't come out of the operating theatre until 7.30 p.m. on the Friday night. When I came round, I was texting everybody saying, 'Make sure I get out of here in the morning.' Fortunately for us, the chief executive of the hospital is a massive Chiefs fan and the head doctor is the head doctor at the rugby club, so I did have a couple of people in high places. I got out of hospital at 9.30 a.m. on Saturday, went home to have a shower and then we all jumped on Doris and went up the motorway.

Gareth Steenson: The occasion felt pretty special. I didn't think I would still be around. I thought I would be sitting up with you guys watching from afar.

Carl Rimmer: Steeno's probably in the best shape of his life. I don't know if he's having a mid-life crisis but ever since he stuck a home gym in during lockdown he's trained the house down. I went round the day after the semi-final and he was doing weights. I never saw him lift one in the prime of his career.

Gareth Steenson: I was pretty chilled going into the game. I thought the boys had prepared really well. I felt we were in a good spot, with a good plan. I don't want to say it was written in the stars but it felt like it was our day. There was a really good feeling. A real calmness that we were going to get there.

Rob Baxter: We stayed in a hotel the night before. We always do, even in Bath and Bristol. There's no way of predicting what the M5 will be like. People also still don't realise how much physical preparation players go through even five or six hours before kick-off.

Carl Rimmer: I woke up on the Saturday morning and couldn't wait for the game. That's the first time that's happened to me since I've finished playing. I spoke to at least half-a-dozen ex-players who were all the same.

Chris Bentley: I was in The Stand Off [pub] dressed in the full Chiefs' European 2012 strip, complete with mouthguard.

Tony Rowe: The lunch we had up in Bristol was lovely. A little bit of à la carte. You had to hold your little finger out when you drank the tea. But it seemed like we spent an eternity waiting for kick-off. The nerves beforehand – and during – were incredible. I can't remember feeling more tense. I felt nervy and sick and just wanted the game to start.

Carl Rimmer: Usually in The Stand Off we'd be standing shoulder to shoulder on those days. We had BBC and ITV doing some filming outside but we had to keep everything within government guidelines. Forget the business side, it was such a shame.

Tony Rowe: It was really strange having no people in the stadium. We weren't even allowed to take our reserve players. There were probably only 20 of us trying to make the same noise as 20,000. A couple of the French guys turned up with those bloody air horns. All they did for the 80 minutes was mess around with them. You felt like going down there and sticking them up their backsides.

Teddy Iribaren (Racing scrum-half): I hurt myself the day before the final. I shouldn't have played. Even in my worst nightmare I could not have imagined such a performance.

Tony Rowe: We were 14–0 up inside 16 minutes but I didn't think Racing were done. I'd watched them the week before and there's a lot of pedigree in their side. I thought, 'They'll get the measure of us shortly.'

Joe Simmonds: We knew when we scored those two early tries that they would come back at us.

Rob Baxter: We just lost control in one or two areas, a little bit uncharacteristically. Especially when we went those two scores up, there was a period when a really good 10 minutes would have created real difficulty for Racing. We actually had our poor 10 minutes then.

Carl Rimmer: Most people thought it was done and dusted five minutes into the second half when Jack Nowell intercepted Finn Russell's attempted long pass and Henry Slade scored our fourth try. The score was 28–17 with 35 minutes left. But they just kept on coming.

Rob Baxter: The biggest challenge when you are facing a player like Finn Russell is getting the players to understand the need to deal with him as a team and not as individuals. On the whole we kept him pretty quiet. We dealt with his chips; none of them really came off and we plucked his wide pass. In some ways you could say we made him a weakness for Racing and that's something we should be pretty pleased with.

Sam Skinner: You feel more nervous when you're watching and can't influence the game. When you're involved you're just doing whatever you can to stop them scoring. In a weird way the yellow card for Tomas Francis freed us up a little bit. We were, 'Right, technically we're not favourites to win this now.' It brought out the best in us. We've always scrambled well and fought for our lives when we've had to. For Sammy Hidalgo-Clyne to get that turnover after 19 phases was epic. My tackle on Antonie Claassen? It was a case of chuck your body in front of him and hope for the best.

Carl Rimmer: Whichever way you look at it, it was classic Chiefs. I was thinking, 'If anyone can soak up this amount of pressure it's them.'

Rob Baxter: Nerves? I'm not sure anything will ever compare to the last 10 minutes of that game.

Tony Rowe: With 10 minutes to go I went downstairs with my son to the players' tunnel and missed the yellow card. I didn't realise we were only playing with 14 men until Gareth Steenson said something to me with two minutes to go. It was just heroic, wasn't it? If the guys ever had to dig deep they did then.

Jacky Lorenzetti (Racing president): Why not try a drop-goal when we were pounding away under the posts?

Henry Slade: It was twitchy-bum time at the end. The way we dug in and defended our line with 14 men was unbelievable. That was the message for the whole game, 'Just make sure we stay in it.'

Rob Baxter: It was pretty good, wasn't it? If we don't win that turnover, then the game would be so different.

Nigel Owens (referee): There was no ruck formed, it was a tackle. Hidalgo-Clyne was legal and the Racing player was penalised for holding on. I am convinced I got that decision right, 100 per cent.

Henry Slade: We got the penalty and there were only a couple of minutes to go. Obviously a lot can happen in two minutes but we have full confidence in our pack of forwards. They are unbelievable all the time. We had a bit of a decision to make at the end but we obviously got it right.

Rob Baxter: For Joe Simmonds to have the final say was pretty fitting because he had a fantastic Heineken Cup. He is starting to realise he can drive things and be a threat to the opposition himself. When he gets his hands on the ball and starts pulling defences around him, that's when he's at his very best. He's really starting to come of age and he doesn't miss kicks. Five points becomes seven most of the time. That creates scoreboard pressure which is difficult to deal with.

Joe Simmonds: The kick to the posts was definitely the right decision but there were a few different views. At first I was thinking of going to the corner and didn't take the clock into account much. Next time I'll take my time and think about things a bit more.

Gareth Steenson: Joe is still only 23 years of age. You have to think, 'Where could he be in a couple of years' time with this club?' He is a real catalyst for what we are doing now.

Joe Simmonds: I think the referee thought we were going to go for the corner. When we chose to go for the posts he asked for the time to be pulled back five seconds. Then, when I was setting up for the kick, the clock didn't come back on. I didn't want to change how I approached the kick or wait 10–15 seconds longer because I might have missed it. It was a relief when the final whistle went.

Tony Rowe: Nigel Owens looked pretty pissed off. He couldn't get a straight 'Yes' or 'No' answer from the TMO. But there was less than half a minute to go and Joe hadn't placed the ball on the tee, so he had a minute to kick it. The French interpretation, though, is bound to be different.

Henry Slade: The ref chat seemed to go on forever. Then he blew the whistle. I ran to Jonny Hill first. That sticks in my mind.

Rob Baxter: I'll tell you what I was thinking. 'Rob Kitson's just written a book about Exeter Chiefs and look what's happened: we've just won the Heineken Cup.' No, to be honest, I was sitting in the middle of the grandstand screaming, 'Why isn't the clock running?' We'd decided to take the kick at goal because there was less than a minute left. The clock should have gone to zero before Joe kicked. To be fair to the officials, they noted it and ended the game, which is the way it should have been.

Tony Rowe: I've never seen Rob beam so much. I said to him, 'Mate, we've done it. We're European champions. What are we going to do now?' He said, 'We're going to do it again, aren't we?'

Rob Baxter: I called my wife afterwards. Jo was pretty emotional and it made me a bit emotional. We've been together a long time and she has seen the highs and lows. It was a special couple of minutes. To start with, she was just screaming at me in emotional joy. Then we managed to have a few words and talked about the journey to get here.

Tony Rowe: It wasn't a thing of beauty. Rugby's not a beauty contest. But it was good, wasn't it? A full-spirited game. The big shame was we didn't have our supporters there.

Rob Baxter: The cruellest thing was that the families weren't there. That's why there were a lot of emotional people on the pitch, myself included. Five or six guys were in tears because they wanted to look over and hug their wife and kids. That's a big part of it. We've achieved something hopefully no other team will achieve – winning the Heineken Cup in an empty stadium. You'd like to hope that will never be done again.

Henry Slade: I remember back to being a kid watching this tournament and wanting to be in it one day. To have the chance to go and win it is such a special feeling. To do it with these boys makes it even better.

Rob Baxter: A couple of players said to me, 'Imagine if we'd played well, Rob.' But nobody in that team has been in a Heineken Cup final before so you can't expect perfection. Our attitude was amazing and that's what saw us through. Over the course of the season we have shown the character that matters. I know Jonny

Gray and Stuart Hogg have dropped in quite recently but on the whole this group of players have been together for five or six years. They've had a lot of heartache and have never backed away or not kept fighting. They're always looking to take the next step forward and I think they have taken a huge one. This is a vindication of a group of players who care about each other and want to achieve something.

Joe Simmonds: Jack Yeandle was telling me how to lift the trophy because he'd done it before. If I'm honest, it was really heavy. Luckily Jack was alongside to help me.

Gareth Steenson: In the changing room afterwards it was really quite special. It was nice to have a few hours together. It was emotional for lots of reasons.

Chris Bentley: I was speechless. That's only ever happened to me once before when I got stuck at a service station with Tony Yapp for six hours and ran out of things to say. Initially I was dumbfounded. Then I went berserk. I remember when we moved to Sandy Park in 2006 and Tony Rowe said we were going to be European champions. Even I thought, 'C'mon, mate.' No one can ever take away that the end of the M5 is now home to the gold-star European champion team.

Tony Rowe: After the game I received a message from Shaun Sawyer, the chief constable of Devon & Cornwall Police. The police said they wanted to see us safely back to Sandy Park as a tribute. We came down the motorway and, as we passed Cullompton, we were picked up by police cars with flashing blue lights who escorted us back to the ground.

Carl Rimmer: I was messaging blokes I don't think I messaged even when I was in the team. Later I received a few pictures of them still in the car park at 1.30 a.m. Either someone drove them around for four hours or they closed the blinds at the club and had a few there.

Tony Rowe: We went into the club and, obviously, we had a very serious debrief meeting and drank water. Ha! We had a few quiet drinks on our own. It was what the boys wanted. We couldn't go out on the town because of Covid and we couldn't do anything daft because of the Premiership final.

Rob Baxter: I stayed up for a bit with my wife. We had a few drinks, had a bit of a giggle and did a few silly things, as you do. We managed to sing along to a few songs we probably shouldn't have sung along to. Which songs? I can't say, it's too embarrassing.

Carl Rimmer: Steeno sent me a picture of a pint of Guinness in his garage at 10 a.m.

Gareth Steenson: I had a drink in my bar in the garage and then went and played golf with my kids. It wasn't necessarily what you'd expect after winning the Heineken Cup final. A few of the lads had a beer but you couldn't do an awful lot because we had to get ready for the Premiership final.

Jack Nowell: The celebrations were very, very tame. Probably only around 60 per cent.

Carl Rimmer: The beauty of Rob is that as long as everyone turns up ready to go on Monday, he's happy. It's also a final. The players could have put their last pint down at 6 a.m. on Monday morning and they'd still turn up ready to train. Your mind just takes over.

Rob Baxter: I was anticipating Sunday either being more raucous or chilled out but, actually, it became a normal Sunday. We were going into another big game and it's funny how quickly you get your feet back down on the ground. I said to the lads, 'Do you want me to start shouting at you that you're not training properly? I'm not going to tell you to work harder, and be tougher, because it would all seem a little bit false. But these are decisions you have to make. Do you want to turn up against Wasps and let them dictate the intensity of the game? How do you want to be feeling after the game? Do you want an 80 minutes that could define your career to slip by or are you going to stand and fight now?'

Joe Simmonds: As a squad we don't need to be told to get up for a final. Losing in finals had definitely been a driver for us.

Jack Nowell: There was a bit of chat around the boys that we didn't want to be called 'bottle jobs' in finals.

Rob Baxter: Initially we were being told it was more likely we'd be playing Bristol. It was great to have a message from [Wasps head coach] Lee Blackett saying their Covid testing had gone well. I've known Lee on and off for quite a long time. He was playing for Rotherham when I played my last game for Exeter. It was an emotional day. The boots came off and they never came back on, even for training.

Joe Simmonds: It was a similar week to when we played Bath. We only found out on Wednesday that we were going to play Wasps so training was mostly all about us.

Ollie Devoto: We've got a small group of us who go down and swim in the sea at Exmouth on our days off. We don't wear wetsuits. The sea has been getting colder, though, so the time we've spent in there has significantly decreased.

Gareth Steenson: We had a jersey presentation on the Wednesday which was emotional. You get to address the lads and the coaching staff which is obviously tough. I just said, 'Thanks for having me.' I'd got my head around the fact this was going to be my last week; I've also been lucky to have been part of a lot of great Exeter teams. I was more interested in making sure we had the right emotional levels for the Wasps game.

Joe Simmonds: We're a tight-knit group and Rob Baxter started all that. The players he brings in aren't just good players. They fit in and are willing to go deep for everyone.

Jack Nowell: I ruptured all the ligaments in my big toe in the last 10 minutes of the Toulouse game. I'm not going to lie, it was horrendous. After the European final I spent the whole week getting the swelling down. What I said to Rob, the physios and the doctors is that I'd never have forgiven myself if I didn't give these two games a go. I didn't train for the last two weeks.

Rob Baxter: His attitude towards getting on with things is always massive. He'll come back a better player again.

Jimmy Gopperth (Wasps centre): We had to be adaptable with everything that went on in the build-up. It was disappointing not to have a few boys available for the final but that wasn't the reason we lost; it was just down to one or two situations on the field that made the difference.

Joe Simmonds: It was a scrappy game in tough conditions. Wasps really came at us for 75 minutes.

Rob Baxter: I thought it was a fantastic performance from Wasps. They made it a final worth winning.

Stuart Hogg: It was absolutely horrible. Not a day for being a full-back, that's for sure.

Jack Nowell: The weather wasn't great for us. We wanted to throw the ball around a little bit.

Nick Mullins (BT Sport commentator): Henry Slade! Oh, that is brilliant. A try to light up a dark autumnal evening at Twickenham.

Lee Blackett (Wasps head coach): Whenever we got a foothold in the game we made a quick mistake which set us back. Our line-out certainly didn't work so well.

Jack Nowell: We had to dig extremely deep. Those were two very good packs going at each other. If it wasn't for our big boys in the forwards, I don't think we'd have won.

Rob Baxter: We'd controlled most of the second half but hadn't managed to make the game safe. That acrobatic catch and fantastic kick by Lima Sopoaga which led to the penalty that made it 13–13 entering the final quarter could have been a killer punch. Did I think it could have slipped away with five minutes to go? Of course I did.

Lee Blackett: The penalty kick to the corner late on with Exeter leading 16–13? I'll never question that decision. Once we make the decision it's all about our execution. We had our opportunity and didn't manage to take it.

Rob Baxter: We defended that first maul really well. I thought we were a little bit unlucky to get penalised considering how other mauls had been defended throughout the game. Then we did what we wanted to do defensively in the line-out. I'm not saying it was lucky but whatever Wasps were doing broke down and we came up with the ball.

Stuart Hogg: Our line-out was unbelievable and the maul got us going forward and ultimately won us the final penalty and the game. Us backs definitely owed the forwards a few beers.

Rob Baxter: You've got to give credit to the players when they're prepared to see games off like that. It's a fantastic quality to learn to have.

Lee Blackett: Exeter probably had more field position and, on reflection, probably deserved their win.

Henry Slade: It felt so good.

Jack Nowell: It would have been very easy for us to dwell on the previous week and just think another win would come.

Henry Slade: The pain of losing teaches you how to win. We've been through the mill but we're using those learnings well. We're at a really good age across the squad and we feel really confident whenever we take the field. We can push on from here.

Tony Rowe: Usually in a squad that's done what we've done, you have old heads. But our old heads are actually young men. That squad has another three or four years before you'd think they are old, and they are getting better. We've also got one of the best coaching groups in the northern hemisphere.

Gareth Steenson: I think the club should go from strength to strength. This is not the finishing post, it's just another catalyst. It's always been about evolving and getting better. Hopefully now we'll be able to attract more top-line players – and keep producing them as well. If we want to stay where we are, we can't just sit and pat ourselves on the back. We're the hunted now and everyone is going to be coming after us.

Carl Rimmer: Steeno will probably find it tough when it all finishes. He's a hero of the club, he's been the Music Man, he's done the naked buses, he's lived the dream in typical Gareth Steenson fashion. I remember thinking he'd timed his testimonial season right when we won the league that year and he kicked the final points.

Rob Baxter: We had both trophies in the changing rooms after the game. I think we needed them both there so we could celebrate the European victory as well. If we hadn't won against Wasps it would have taken the shine off a little bit. Instead it allowed us to stop, look back over a very good season and spend some time reflecting on how important the work these guys have done has been to the club.

Stuart Hogg: I've played 23 games for Exeter this year and I haven't felt as good in a long time.

Rob Baxter: We could have turned up in the Premiership in 2010 and said, 'We've achieved everything we wanted to achieve.' Now we've won these trophies, have we achieved everything? No. There's always something to move on to, isn't there?

Jack Nowell: I'm sure we'll have Sarries back here in a final in a couple of years' time. That's the one we want.

Tony Rowe: Eventually Rob's ambition may be to coach England. But, personally, I think it will be a long time before he leaves. Eddie Jones is here until the next World Cup and, irrespective of whether they ask Rob or not, I still think he will stay here for a while. I'd like him to stay for as long as he likes. Rob is a big family man and when you are doing the job of national coach you're never home. I don't think that would suit him. I know what he's like and I know his family. They're very close.

Rob Baxter: We've got to use the players' desire to experience these moments again. We've also got a group of young players who need to get some work done because they're not good enough at the moment. The only thing we've ever tried to achieve is to become a little bit better, month by month, year by year.

Tony Rowe: I'm always a great believer there's no reason to rush anything. You've got to have faith in yourself, put the pegs in the ground in terms of where you want to go to and surround yourself with good people. That's the key. You have to build slowly, have some solid foundations and then add bits to it as you go.

Carl Rimmer: There is a whole new multitude of Exeter fans now. Whether you want to call it the Manchester United effect or not, they're a really cool club to support. People going to a game might not know all the players but they love supporting a club that is winning loads. It feels like it's a massive club now.

Tony Rowe: We can achieve even more. I want Exeter to be the premier club in the world and the ingredients are here. I said [in 2017] we'd do Europe in five years. How about we do the world in the next five? It would be nice to have a world club game. We've got a lot more to prove.

HEINEKEN CHAMPIONS CUP FINAL
Ashton Gate, Bristol, 17 October 2020
Exeter Chiefs 31 Racing 92 27

Exeter Chiefs: S Hogg; J Nowell (I Whitten, 67-69), H Slade, I Whitten (O Devoto, 59), T O'Flaherty; J Simmonds (capt), J Maunder (S Hidalgo-Clyne, 65); A Hepburn (B Moon, 55), L Cowan-Dickie (J Yeandle, 55), H Williams (T Francis, 55), J Gray (S Skinner, 59), J Hill, D Ewers, J Vermeulen (J Kirsten, 55), S Simmonds.
Replacement (not used): G Steenson.
Tries: Cowan-Dickie, S Simmonds, H Williams, Slade. Cons: J Simmonds 4. Pen: J Simmonds.
Sin-bin: Francis 71.

Racing 92: S Zebo (K Beale, 65); L Dupichot, V Vakatawa (O Klemenczak, 76), H Chavancy (capt), J Imhoff; F Russell, T Iribaren (M Machenaud, 41); E Ben Arous (H Kolingar, 50), C Chat (T Baubigny, 50), G-H Colombe (A Oz, 50), B Le Roux (D Ryan, 67), D Bird, W Lauret, F Sanconnie, A Claassen (B Palu, 76).
Tries: Zebo 2, Imhoff, Chat. Cons: Russell, Machenaud. Pen: Machenaud.

Referee: N Owens (Wales).

GALLAGHER PREMIERSHIP FINAL
Twickenham, 24 October 2020
Exeter Chiefs 19 Wasps 13

Exeter Chiefs: S Hogg; J Nowell, H Slade, O Devoto, O Woodburn; J Simmonds (capt), J Maunder (S Hidalgo-Clyne, 61); A Hepburn (B Moon, 61), L Cowan-Dickie (J Yeandle, 61), H Williams (T Francis, 61), S Skinner, J Hill (J Gray, 55), D Ewers, J Kirsten, S Simmonds.
Replacements (not used): J Vermeulen, G Steenson, I Whitten.
Try: Slade. Con: J Simmonds. Pens: J Simmonds 4.

Wasps: M Minozzi (L Sopoaga, 56); Z Kibirige, J de Jongh (M Le Bourgeois, 74), J Gopperth, J Bassett; J Umaga, D Robson; T West (B Harris, 54), T Taylor (G Oghre, 51), J Toomaga-Allen (B Alo, 66), J Launchbury (capt), W Rowlands, J Willis, T Young, T Willis (J Gaskell, 46).
Replacements (not used): B Morris, B Vellacott.
Try: Umaga. Con: Gopperth. Pens: Gopperth 2.

Referee: C Maxwell-Keyes (England).

TWENTY-THREE

THE EXE FACTOR

It is early morning on Mexico's Yucatán Peninsula, just outside the popular resort of Cancún. Even workaholic directors of rugby occasionally need a holiday. With jet lag messing with his body clock, Rob Baxter cannot sleep. He gets up, sticks on a pair of trainers and a Chiefs top and heads over to the gym. As he enters he notices the member of staff on reception smiling at him. It is 6.30 a.m. but the man behind the desk clearly wants to talk.

'You support Exeter Chiefs?'

'No, I'm the coach.'

'You . . . Ro-ob Baxter?'

'Yeah.'

'Ha! Hello, coach! I play scrum-half for Cancún Hammerheads!'

Not technically a Mexican stand-off, then, but an illustration of the increasing global awareness of Exeter's exploits. For a rugby man like Baxter it summed up both the shared fellowship in the game – 'That's what rugby is about' – and how far the Chiefs' gospel has spread. When your club's badge is being recognised by total strangers thousands of miles from home, you must be doing something right.

Even further away, in New Zealand, a more familiar observer still follows Chiefs' results with a keen eye. It is also Thomas Waldrom's strong belief that Exeter's impressive trajectory will be maintained for a few years yet. 'I think it will keep going because of the people who are there, both in the office and the dressing room. When he's signing a player Rob gets the right fit every time. I think that's why people get a bit jealous of Exeter. People come and go but they've got the right systems in place to keep moving forward. Once you get a taste of success and you know what it takes to get there you've got the basic recipe. All you have to do then is tweak it to ensure you continue to get it right every time. When I was at Exeter we always learned from our mistakes. That was one of the great things about the team.'

With Jack Nowell, Henry Slade and Luke Cowan-Dickie still in their late twenties, there is every chance they will remain competitive for a while yet. No fewer than 30 players have been signed on revised long-term contracts while the academy production line continues to churn out talented products such as Richard Capstick, Rus Tuima and Sam Maunder. Baxter's recruitment also remains shrewd. In addition to Scotland's Gray, the squad has also been bolstered by the arrival of the back-rower Aaron Hinkley, the full-back Josh Hodge and the centre Corey Baldwin from Gloucester, Newcastle and Scarlets respectively. All three of them are exciting prospects who have represented their countries at U20 level, while the Australian-reared, English-qualified fly-half Jack Walsh and Argentine Facundo Cordero, younger brother of Santiago, also have crowd-pleasing ability. Also now awaiting his chance is the precocious Wales U18 lock, Christ Tshiunza, signed on a four-year academy contract which will allow him to combine his rugby with studying for a degree at the University of Exeter.

Baxter, whose own son Jack graduated with a first-class law degree from the same institution, appears in no hurry to step aside and settle for a quieter life. 'We feel we have a group here now who can achieve an awful lot together.'

Whenever he sees a Chiefs flag in the backroom of a country pub or glimpses an Exeter car sticker on a battered farm vehicle he is also reminded of the extended fan base that, for him, makes it all worthwhile. 'The thing I'll be most proud of is that you've got young lads in the middle of Cornwall or Devon, only eight or nine years old, who want to play for Exeter Chiefs and be the next Jack Nowell or Henry Slade. They've seen us win the Premiership, they've seen Exeter players play for England and the British & Irish Lions. They can see them on TV winning games at Sandy Park, they can come here on Super Saturday and feel part of it. If that's still the case when I finish . . . well, that's what will encapsulate it all for me. That would tell me that what we've got here is something people want to be part of.'

That little dagger of a sentence – 'When I finish' – contains the three words no Exeter fan wants to contemplate. The club's head of sports medicine, Professor Adrian Harris, told *The Rugby Paper* in May 2020 he could see the 49-year-old Baxter staying on at the club for another decade before progressing to the England job. Ask Baxter himself and he sounds in no particular rush. 'The day I'm sitting up there and I realise it doesn't really matter as much, I'll know I'm in the wrong place. That'll be the time to hand it over to the other guys because I know they'll still be feeling like that. As long as you're sitting here and you don't want anybody else to have your job you're in the right job. That might sound an odd way to look at it but that's how I feel. I'm very happy doing what I'm doing. And if I'm not doing it I don't mind saying I want Ali and Rob to be doing it. They're the guys who know what we're about and they're the guys who deserve to be heading it up.'

Okay. But what if the RFU decide that England, post-2023, could benefit from a home-grown head coach with an outstanding track record? If he did ever say 'Yes' it would have to be very much on his terms. 'The England one is a funny one. I'm probably the same as a lot of coaches. You think, "If I was doing this I'd do things differently." That's not the same as saying you want the job and everything else that goes with it. That's a completely different thing.

'I'm part of something good here. I'm also a massive believer that if you're part of something good, you should make sure you stop and appreciate it. I often say the same to the players. Stop, take a breath and appreciate it. The worst thing, when you're in a good environment, is taking it for granted. The minute you do that, you start kidding yourself there's something better and see things that just aren't there.' Baxter is also aware the club has more growth in it, on and off the field. 'The reality is that Tony's an ambitious guy. We're not planning on adding more seats as a vanity thing. We're not building a hotel to say, "We've got a hotel." It's there to make us a better rugby club business-wise. Being part of clubs like that is quite exciting in itself.'

In addition, there is the whole cargo ship of freight that comes with the England coaching job. Baxter is fully aware of the difference between steadily building a club team, week by week over many years, and achieving instant results at international level. The two jobs are not always interchangeable and the risk, as an international coach, of being spat out the other side is no fun either. 'If there's one thing you learn from watching Eddie Jones – whether you like his management style or you don't – it's that he's doing things the way he wants to do them. Ultimately that's the only way to be successful.

'I wouldn't want to do it thinking I still need to find another job afterwards. If you're doing the England job thinking, "Where's my next job going to be?" you're a bit of a fool. If you're going to do it, you do it on your own terms, in a way you're comfortable with. I don't think international coaching works in any other way. Not successfully anyway.' Baxter also knows that, in a fast-changing, uncertain world, there can be no absolute guarantee the Chiefs will keep soaring indefinitely. Two or three other English sides – Bristol, Bath and Sale Sharks – are clearly on the up and others – Wasps, Saracens, Leicester, Harlequins and Gloucester – are also regrouping.

The mind, even so, drifts back to the Baxter family farm in Exwick. It was John Baxter who, along with Bob Staddon and many others, helped to sow the seeds of Exeter's rise decades ago. Shiny modern-day trophies, positive win-loss ratios and juicy contracts are all very well but they will soon lose their lustre if the club falters once the Baxters and Rowe bow out. That does not sound particularly likely when you listen to Baxter senior's considered overview. 'We're still on this journey. We don't know where it's going to take us but as long as you do your best and stick together you can't do any more. There'll come a time when I'm not going to be there and Tony and Rob are not going to be there. But Exeter RFC is still going to be there. This journey is not going to end.'

There is even less danger, he insists, of the Chiefs abandoning their principles. 'Rob wants to see the coaches and players progress. He wants to do the right things for the right reasons and he likes to gather like-minded people. If you bring up a young player who goes on to play for England you've achieved something. You've not just got your chequebook out. When the chips are down in the last five minutes, it's not the size of the cheque that matters. It's what it means to you. When you're at Exeter it's not like watching England. It's not like watching two other clubs play. When your club's involved it's something more. It's indefinable.' There is a momentary pause, as he reflects on a lifelong passion. 'To me it goes beyond rugby. Rob keeps saying to me, "Just enjoy it, Dad. Enjoy it while you can." If we lose, we lose. It doesn't ruin my life. You've just got to have a clear vision. Keep doing the best you can and, if Lady Luck shines on you, make the most of it.'

Outside, through the windows behind him, the West Country shadows are lengthening. It is time to say goodbye and head out through the farmyard and into the lane which heads back towards the timeless River Exe. These days there is a similarly constant stream of local sporting pride, tumbling down from the moors and out to a distant sea.

APPENDIX I

A list of the 184 players who have represented Exeter's first team in a competitive fixture since they joined the Premiership in 2010 (NB Figures do not include friendlies; correct as at 1 November 2020)

NAME	APPS	START	REP	T	C	DG	PG	PTS
Simon Alcott	71	27	44	10	-	-	-	50
John Andress	56	46	10	3	-	-	-	15
Don Armand	158	130	28	33	-	-	-	165
Jack Arnott	7	4	3	1	-	-	1	8
Luke Arscott	96	87	9	11	-	-	-	55
Ollie Atkins	59	30	29	1	-	-	-	5
Corey Baldwin	4	3	1	-	-	-	-	99
Kevin Barrett	131	81	50	19	2	-	-	99
Greg Bateman	17	2	15	3	-	-	-	15
Richard Baxter	434	400	34	126	-	-	-	630
Chris Bentley	120	89	31	11	-	-	-	55
Justin Blanchet-Dufresne	3	2	1	-	-	-	-	-

NAME	APPS	START	REP	T	C	DG	PG	PTS
Sam Blanchet-Dufresne	1	0	1	-	-	-	-	-
Max Bodilly	37	20	17	7	-	-	-	35
Chrysander Botha	6	4	2	1	-	-	-	5
Alex Brown	59	17	42	-	-	-	-	-
Chris Budgen	101	52	49	20	-	-	-	100
Ryan Caldwell	11	5	6	-	-	-	-	-
Gonzalo Camacho	26	26	0	3	-	-	-	15
Michele Campagnaro	27	10	17	9	-	-	-	45
Richard Capstick	12	6	6	2	-	-	-	10
Will Carrick-Smith	11	6	5	2	-	-	-	10
Josh Caulfield	9	7	2	-	-	-	-	-
Will Chudley	120	74	46	15	-	-	-	75
Neil Clark	155	86	69	16	-	-	-	80
Joel Conlon	9	4	5	-	-	-	-	-
Kyle Cooper	2	0	2	-	-	-	-	-
Rob Coote	2	0	2	-	-	-	-	-
Santiago Cordero	33	32	1	10	-	-	-	50
Facundo Cordero	2	2	0	1	-	-	-	5
Luke Cowan-Dickie	136	90	46	30	-	-	-	150
Tom Cowan-Dickie	1	0	1	-	-	-	-	-
Garrick Cowley	11	2	9	-	-	-	-	-
Harrison Cully	1	0	1	-	-	-	-	-
Alex Cuthbert	24	21	3	2	-	-	-	10
Kieran Davies	2	0	2	-	-	-	-	-
Paul Davis	2	0	2	1	-	-	-	5
Ryan Davis	15	11	4	1	15	1	31	131
Dave Dennis	80	62	18	9	-	-	-	45
Ollie Devoto	79	63	16	14	-	-	-	70
Phil Dollman	244	224	20	26	2	-	1	137
Myles Dorrian	9	6	3	3	1	-	1	20
Ignacio Elosu	12	1	11	-	-	-	-	-
Dave Ewers	173	148	25	20	-	-	-	100
Lloyd Fairbrother	6	1	5	-	-	-	-	-
Mark Foster	59	53	6	20	-	-	-	100
Tomas Francis	113	65	48	-	-	-	-	-

NAME	APPS	START	REP	T	C	DG	PG	PTS
James Freeman	6	4	2	2	-	-	-	10
Dave Gannon	35	7	28	-	-	-	-	-
Eoghan Grace	1	0	1	-	-	-	-	-
Romana Graham	5	4	1	-	-	-	-	-
Jamie Gray	1	0	1	-	-	-	-	-
Jonny Gray	9	8	1	-	-	-	-	-
James Hanks	190	159	31	7	-	-	-	35
Onehunga Havili Kaufusi	3	0	3	-	-	-	-	-
Tom Hayes	135	123	12	6	-	-	-	30
Tom Hendrickson	38	22	16	7	-	-	-	35
Alec Hepburn	106	59	47	5	-	-	-	25
Sam Hidalgo-Clyne	11	2	9	1	-	-	-	5
Andrew Higgins	12	11	1	2	-	-	-	10
Jonny Hill	91	79	12	22	-	-	-	110
Sam Hill	151	104	47	11	-	-	-	55
Aaron Hinkley	1	1	2	-	-	-	-	-
Josh Hodge	3	0	3	-	-	-	-	-
Stuart Hogg	22	22	0	6	-	-	-	30
Ed Holmes	5	0	5	-	-	-	-	-
Greg Holmes	57	31	26	3	-	-	-	15
Will Hooley	14	2	12	-	7	-	3	23
Kai Horstmann	100	49	51	7	-	-	-	35
Adam Hughes	9	8	1	4	-	-	-	20
Jack Innard	20	11	9	3	-	-	-	15
Tom James	39	30	9	8	-	-	-	40
Matt Jess	189	172	17	59	-	-	-	295
Matt Johnson	1	0	1	-	-	-	-	-
Tom Johnson	201	147	54	29	-	-	-	145
Barrie Karea	2	1	1	1	-	-	-	5
Billy Keast	31	7	24	2	-	-	-	10
James Kenny	3	0	3	-	-	-	-	-
Peter Kimlin	3	1	2	-	-	-	-	-
Jannes Kirsten	30	16	14	4	-	-	-	20
Matt Kvesic	58	43	15	13	-	-	-	65
Pete Laverick	3	1	2	-	-	-	-	-

NAME	APPS	START	REP	T	C	DG	PG	PTS
Tom Lawday	22	10	12	6	-	-	-	30
Mitch Lees	113	85	28	8	-	-	-	40
Dave Lewis	79	40	39	8	-	-	-	40
James Lightfoot-Brown	1	0	1	-	-	-	-	-
Drew Locke	2	0	2	-	-	-	-	-
Sean Lonsdale	34	18	16	4	-	-	-	20
Moray Low	71	34	37	7	-	-	-	35
Byron McGuigan	18	8	10	4	-	-	-	20
Paul McKenzie	45	36	9	24	-	-	-	120
James McRae	2	1	1	-	-	-	-	-
Shaun Malton	22	8	14	6	-	-	-	30
Josh Matavesi	10	6	4	2	-	-	-	10
Jack Maunder	76	37	39	9	-	-	-	45
Sam Maunder	12	5	7	-	-	-	-	-
Laurence May	2	0	2	-	-	-	-	-
Sal M'Boge	2	1	1	-	-	-	-	-
Luke Mehson	1	0	1	-	-	-	-	-
Ignacio Mieres	53	33	20	4	42	1	96	395
Andy Miller	63	52	11	6	-	-	-	30
Craig Mitchell	37	17	20	1	-	-	-	5
Ben Moon	265	150	115	11	-	-	-	55
Sam Morley	5	0	5	-	-	-	-	-
Aly Muldowney	51	16	35	4	-	-	-	20
Dean Mumm	70	67	3	13	-	-	-	65
Ruaidhri Murphy	16	6	10	-	-	-	-	-
Nemani Nadolo	5	3	2	-	-	-	-	-
Sireli Naqelevuki	61	41	20	14	-	-	-	70
Max Norey	1	0	1	-	-	-	-	-
Will Norton	1	0	1	-	-	-	-	-
Jack Nowell	128	118	10	33	-	-	-	175
Tom O'Flaherty	46	43	3	16	-	-	-	80
Jack Oulton	1	0	1	-	-	-	-	-
Jack Owlett	6	1	5	-	-	-	-	-
Geoff Parling	50	40	10	1	-	-	-	5
Alan Paver	1	0	1	-	-	-	-	-

NAME	APPS	START	REP	T	C	DG	PG	PTS
Lewis Pearson	3	0	3	-	-	-	-	-
Alfie Petch	6	1	5	-	-	-	-	-
Patrick Phibbs	11	6	5	1	-	-	-	5
James Phillips	49	23	26	7	-	-	-	35
Enrique Pieretto	9	4	5	-	-	-	-	-
Junior Poluleuligaga	25	11	14	-	-	-	-	-
Jordon Poole	10	1	9	-	-	-	-	-
Mike Pope	1	0	1	-	-	-	-	-
Tom Price	5	3	2	2	-	-	-	10
Bryan Rennie	77	60	17	14	-	-	-	70
Carl Rimmer	131	45	86	6	-	-	-	30
Ben Rogers	2	0	2	-	-	-	-	-
Toby Salmon	16	4	12	4	-	-	-	20
Julian Salvi	53	44	9	3	-	-	-	15
James Scaysbrook	124	112	12	8	-	-	-	40
Patrick Schickerling	1	0	1	-	-	-	-	-
Nic Sestaret	83	73	10	15	-	-	-	75
Jerry Sexton	6	5	1	-	-	-	-	-
Jason Shoemark	75	70	5	4	-	-	-	20
James Short	71	50	21	32	-	-	-	160
Peter Short	7	7	0	-	-	-	-	-
Joe Simmonds	83	61	22	9	189	-	53	582
Sam Simmonds	77	59	18	47	-	-	-	235
Harvey Skinner	15	10	5	-	7	-	2	20
Sam Skinner	71	35	36	6	-	-	-	30
Chad Slade	118	71	47	16	-	-	-	80
Henry Slade	158	133	25	24	64	-	82	494
Joe Snow	10	1	9	-	-	-	-	-
Stan South	4	3	1	-	-	-	-	-
Danny Southworth	4	0	4	1	-	-	-	5
Jack Stanley	2	0	2	-	-	-	-	-
Gareth Steenson	312	232	80	15	551	7	476	2,626
Lewis Stevenson	66	54	12	5	1	-	-	27
Marcus Street	35	6	29	1	-	-	-	5
Harry Strong	5	1	4	1	-	-	-	5

NAME	APPS	START	REP	T	C	DG	PG	PTS
Herbie Stupple	11	3	8	2	-	-	-	10
Brett Sturgess	165	129	36	10	-	-	-	50
Ceri Sweeney	16	9	7	1	21	-	21	110
Elvis Taione	78	18	60	7	-	-	-	35
Josh Tatupu	19	12	7	4	-	-	-	20
Cory Teague	1	0	1	-	-	-	-	-
Haydn Thomas	214	154	60	46	-	-	-	230
Stu Townsend	58	23	35	7	-	-	-	35
Hoani Tui	121	93	28	6	-	-	-	30
Rus Tuima	1	1	0	-	-	-	-	-
Lachie Turner	47	42	5	10	-	-	-	50
Fetu'u Vainikolo	28	18	10	10	-	-	-	50
Wilhelm van der Sluys	12	6	6	-	-	-	-	-
Jacques Vermeulen	26	25	1	9	-	-	-	45
Jon Vickers	3	0	3	-	-	-	-	-
Watisoni Votu	3	3	0	2	-	-	-	10
Thomas Waldrom	101	86	15	51	-	-	-	255
Charlie Walker-Blair	1	0	1	-	-	-	-	-
Jack Walsh	2	0	2	-	-	-	-	55
Damian Welch	102	82	20	11	-	-	-	55
Ben White	105	68	37	17	-	-	-	85
Nic White	61	54	7	14	-	-	-	70
Chris Whitehead	76	37	39	2	-	-	-	10
Ian Whitten	221	179	42	27	-	-	-	135
Harry Williams	107	76	31	14	-	-	-	70
Will Witty	8	4	4	2	-	-	-	-
Olly Woodburn	110	104	6	39	-	-	-	195
Jake Woolmore	1	0	1	-	-	-	-	-
Charlie Wright	2	1	1	-	-	-	-	-
Tom Wyatt	7	5	2	1	-	-	-	5
Will Yarnell	1	0	1	-	-	-	-	-
Jack Yeandle	193	120	73	23	-	-	-	115

APPENDIX II

Exeter's regular season Premiership record since being promoted in 2010:

Year	Position	P	W	D	L	For	Ag	Points	TF	TA
2010/11	8th	22	10	0	12	428	460	43*	32	42
2011/12	5th	22	12	0	10	436	421	59	39	38
2012/13	6th	22	12	1	9	542	446	59	51	43
2013/14	8th	22	9	0	13	426	480	45	40	51
2014/15	5th	22	14	0	8	663	437	68	70	46
2015/16	2nd (-)	22	15	0	7	585	361	74	71	40
2016/17	2nd (+)	22	15	3	4	667	452	84	86	55
2017/18	1st (-)	22	17	0	5	618	354	85	79	42
2018/19	1st (-)	22	17	0	5	630	438	86	89	51
2019/20	1st (+)	22	15	0	7	630	443	74	83	56

Total Premiership record (incl. play-offs, correct as at 1 November 2020):
P 230 **W** 142 **D** 4 **L** 83 **For** 5,896 **Ag** 4,479 **TF** 671 **TA** 486

Overall win ratio: 62.17%

(+) = Champions
(-) = Runners-up
* = Two points deducted for fielding ineligible player

APPENDIX III

CLUB HONOURS

HEINEKEN CHAMPIONS CUP
- **Champions: (1) 2019/20**

ENGLISH PREMIERSHIP
- **Champions: (2) 2016/17, 2019/20**
- *Runners-Up: (3) 2015/16, 2017/18, 2018/19*

RFU CHAMPIONSHIP
- **Champions: (1) 2009/10**
- *Runners-Up: (3) 2004/05, 2007/08, 2008/09*

COURAGE LEAGUE NATIONAL DIVISION 3
- **Champions: (1) 1996/97**

COURAGE LEAGUE NATIONAL DIVISION 4
- **Champions: (1) 1995/96**

NB: Exeter are the only club to have topped all four league tiers of English rugby.

ADDITIONAL HONOURS

ANGLO-WELSH CUP
- **Champions: (2) 2013/14, 2017/18**
- *Runners-Up: (2) 2014/15, 2016/17*

EDF ENERGY TROPHY
- *Runners-Up: (4) 2001/02, 2002/03, 2006/07, 2007/08*

DEVON RFU SENIOR CUP (TIER 5)
- **Champions: (16) 1889/90, 1970/71, 1971/72, 1972/73, 1975/76, 1977/78, 1979/80, 1981/82, 1988/89, 1989/90, 1990/91, 1991/92, 1992/93, 1993/94, 1994/95, 1995/96**
- *Runners-Up: (5) 1888/89, 1904/05, 1976/77, 1980/81, 1985/86*

ACKNOWLEDGEMENTS

A book like this would be impossible without the co-operation and generosity of those at the heart of the story. I am hugely grateful to all those who have shared their Exeter memories, not least the Baxter family and Tony Rowe who were kind enough to embrace the project from the outset. I am similarly indebted to the club's president, Bob Staddon, and his fellow trustee John Lockyer for their support. Without their collective backing, it would have been a far less rewarding assignment.

Special thanks must also go to dozens of past and present players, coaches and backroom staff. The following were particularly helpful: Don Armand, Chris Bentley, Ian Bremner, Luke Cowan-Dickie, Dave Dennis, Ollie Devoto, Phil Dollman, Peter Drewett, Mark Foster, Jonny Gray, James Hanks, Alec Hepburn, Ali Hepher, Jonny Hill, Kai Horstmann, Rob Hunter, Matt Jess, Tom Johnson, Matt Kvesic, Dave MacLellan, the Maunder family, Ben Moon, Dean Mumm, Jack Nowell, Steve Parrett, Carl Rimmer, Henry Slade, Joe Simmonds, Sam Simmonds, Sam Skinner, Gareth Steenson, Mark Stevens, Brett

Sturgess, Haydn Thomas, Thomas Waldrom, Tony Walker, Ian Whitten, Harry Williams, Tony Yapp and Jack Yeandle.

It is also important to acknowledge the encouragement and expertise of Pete Burns at Polaris, the statistical wizardry of Stuart Farmer and Mark Williams and the sharp-eyed assistance of my good friends Stephen Bale and Robert Woodward. The photographic skills of Getty's Alex Davidson, Dan Mullan and Dave Rogers, the *Guardian*'s Tom Jenkins and Pinnacle's Phil Mingo also deserve particular recognition, while several publications and specialist rugby writers have provided invaluable reference material and assistance. These include Hugh Godwin of the *i* newspaper, Neale Harvey of *The Rugby Paper*, Alex Mead from *Rugby Journal*, Alan Pearey of *Rugby World*, Daniel Schofield of the *Telegraph*, Nigel Walrond – author of *Road to Glory: The Inside Story* – and Nick Warren of the *Express & Echo*. The late, great Frank Keating remains an inspiration; no one told rural sporting tales with more warmth. A handful of interviews in this book were originally conducted for the *Guardian*: huge thanks to Will Woodward, Stephen McMillan, Claire Tolley and everyone else on the sports desk who has resuscitated my copy over many years. I owe you all a pint of Otter.

Last but not least, *Exe Men* is dedicated to my wonderful family. To Fiona, Alex, Louisa and Greg: all I can say is that I love you and am now available to clear out the shed.

Robert Kitson
November 2020